THEATER IN THE AMERICAS

A Series from Southern Illinois University Press

ROBERT A. SCHANKE, *Series Editor*

Other Books in the Theater in the Americas Series

The Theatre of Sabina Berman: The Agony of Ecstasy and Other Plays
Translated by Adam Versényi
With an Essay by Jacqueline E. Bixler

Messiah of the New Technique: John Howard Lawson, Communism, and American Theatre, 1923–1937
Jonathan L. Chambers

Composing Ourselves: The Little Theatre Movement and the American Audience
Dorothy Chansky

Women in Turmoil: Six Plays by Mercedes de Acosta
Edited and with an Introduction by Robert A. Schanke

Unfinished Show Business: Broadway Musicals as Works-in-Process
Bruce Kirle

Staging America: Cornerstone and Community-Based Theater
Sonja Kuftinec

Words at Play: Creative Writing and Dramaturgy
Felicia Hardison Londré

Stage, Page, Scandals, and Vandals: William E. Burton and Nineteenth-Century American Theatre
David L. Rinear

"That Furious Lesbian": The Story of Mercedes de Acosta
Robert A. Schanke

Caffe Cino: The Birthplace of Off-Off-Broadway
Wendell C. Stone

Teaching Performance Studies
Edited by Nathan Stucky and Cynthia Wimmer
With a Foreword by Richard Schechner

Broadway's Bravest Woman: Selected Writings of Sophie Treadwell
Edited and with introductions by Jerry Dickey and Miriam López-Rodríguez

Our Land Is Made of Courage and Glory: Nationalist Performance of Nicaragua and Guatemala
E. J. Westlake

Angels in the American Theater

ANGELS IN THE AMERICAN THEATER

PATRONS, PATRONAGE, AND PHILANTHROPY

Edited and with an Introduction
by Robert A. Schanke

Southern Illinois University Press
Carbondale

Printed in the United States of America

10 09 08 07 4 3 2 1

Permission to use quotations from interviewees was granted by, among others, Jeanne Donovan Fisher and Charles L. Mee Jr. (copyright © 2005 Charles L. Mee) for chapter 5; Trish Pugh Jones, Director of Donor Relations, Actors Theatre of Louisville; Alexander Speer, Executive Director, Actors Theatre of Louisville; and Roanne H. Victor for chapter 12; and Gordon Davidson, Founding Artistic Director, Center Theatre Group; Bernard Gersten, Executive Producer, Lincoln Center Theater; Barry Grove, Executive Producer, Manhattan Theatre Club; Julia C. Levy, Executive Director, Roundabout Theatre Company; Virginia Louloudes; Jim Steinberg; Tony Taccone; and Seth Weingarten for chapter 14.

Library of Congress Cataloging-in-Publication Data
Angels in the American theater : patrons, patronage, and philanthropy / edited and with an Introduction by Robert A. Schanke.
p. cm.
Includes bibliographical references and index.
ISBN-13: 978-0-8093-2747-8 (pbk. : alk. paper)
ISBN-10: 0-8093-2747-3 (pbk. : alk. paper)
1. Performing arts sponsorship—United States. I. Schanke, Robert A., 1940–
PN1590.S7A54 2006
792.079'73—dc22
2006022202

Printed on recycled paper. ♻

The paper used in this publication meets the minimum requirements of American National Standard for Information Sciences—Permanence of Paper for Printed Library Materials, ANSI Z39.48-1992. ∞

— To Katy —
(Katherine Elizabeth Lyford)
my new granddaughter

"Sweetest little angel
Everybody knows
I don't know what to call her
But she's mighty like a rose."
—*From a family lullaby*

CONTENTS

ILLUSTRATIONS

ACKNOWLEDGMENTS

From first proposal to publication, working with Southern Illinois University Press has been a joy. Both Karl Kageff, editor in chief, and Kristine Priddy, assistant sponsoring editor, have been patient, gracious, and committed to this project. Wayne Larsen, project editor, has been meticulous, thorough, and extremely helpful.

I owe an enormous debt to the authors who contributed chapters for this volume. They were phenomenal in following the guidelines set for the chapters, meeting deadlines, making revisions, and enduring my frequent e-mail requests for information.

We are so grateful for the professionalism and expertise of the librarians and staff workers at several institutions who assisted in our research: the Billy Rose Theatre Collection of the New York Public Library; the Ford Foundation Archives; the Rockefeller Foundation; the University of Illinois Archives; the Rosenbach Museum and Library; the Lucille Lortel Foundation; the Historical Society of Palm Beach County; Weston (CT) Public Library; Sally Grant Branca, of the Curtis Institute of Music; Dave Semonin, of the Neighborhood Playhouse; the Weston (CT) Historical Society; the Harry Ransom Humanities Research Center; the Senate House Library of the University of London; Actors Theatre of Louisville (especially Alexander Speer, Christen McDonough Boone, Roanne H. Victor, Marilee Hebert Miller, and Kyle Shepherd); participants at the International Conference on Scenography held in Prague (June 2003); Mary Cache, of the Shubert Archive; Geffen Playhouse (especially artistic director Randall Arney; Jennifer Edwards, director of grants and communications; and Debra Pasquerette, education director); James Hoffmann, of the John D. and Catherine T. MacArthur Foundation; and, finally, Ellen Stewart, Mia Yoo, and Ozzie Rodriguez, of the La MaMa Archives.

Countless individuals aided in shaping this book. They include Megan Alban, Kevin Anderson, André Bishop, Sue Bruns, Robert Brustein, Scott T. Cummings, Donald W. Curl, Gordon Davidson, Peter Donnelly, Oskar Eustis, Jeanne Donovan Fisher, Mark Farrelly, Bernard Gersten, Grant Goodman, R. B. Graves, Barry Grove, Todd Haimes, Esther Katz, Carole A. Krumland, Julia C. Levy, Paul Stephen Lim, Virginia Louloudes, Kim Marra, Lynne Meadow, Charles Mee, Max Moss, Mark C. Pilkinton, Tom Postlewait, Kari Schertzinger, Jim Steinberg, Michael Steinberg, Monica Stufft, Tony Taccone, Maria Vasio, Paula Vogel, Seth Weingarten, Barry Witham, William D. Zabel, and Mary Zimmerman.

Finally, I wish to thank my life partner, Jack C. Barnhart, for his faithful and loving support while I sat so many hours glued to my computer. With red pen in hand, he reads and edits virtually everything I want to publish and prevents my writing from becoming bogged down with unnecessary jargon and academic theorizing. He should be listed as coauthor.

Angels in the American Theater

INTRODUCTION: "HE WHO PAYS THE PIPER CALLS THE TUNE"

Robert A. Schanke

We often hear that "money talks." Angels—theater investors and backers with money—have a tremendous impact on what happens on stage.[1] Indeed, they make it all possible. Since box-office income usually pays for only about half of a production's cost, other sources of income must become a vital part of the process. With the power and influence of their money, therefore, angels often determine not only what is performed but also what is produced, even what is conceived. Angels have played a monumental role in shaping and developing the American theater.

Ironically, research and writing on the history of arts philanthropy is meager and of fairly recent practice. Very few theater historians have researched and studied our theater patrons, and those that have done so, for the most part, have focused on the Federal Theatre of the 1930s or on the National Endowment for the Arts (NEA).[2] Because so much previous scholarship has focused on them, they will not be addressed in specific chapters in this volume.

Certainly, part of the difficulty in doing this research has been the desire of private individuals to want their largesse to remain anonymous. For instance, the presidents of the three state universities in Iowa have argued that revealing donor names would hurt their fund-raising. A spokesman for the University of Iowa explained that foundation officials "have heard from some big donors who said they just wouldn't do it if their personal information wasn't confidential. For some people, true charity is anonymous."[3] A good example of this dilemma is Johnny Carson, who gave $5.3 million to the University of Nebraska–Lincoln in November 2004 to support the renovation and expansion of the theater building. Unfortunately, neither he, when he was living, nor university officials would discuss the donation beyond the standard press release. In fact, even after Carson's death, university officials went so far as to prohibit permission to quote the letter wherein they had refused to disclose any information.[4] Several regional theaters, when informed of this study and asked to furnish names of their important angels, refused to cooperate, arguing that they did not want their wealthy donors harassed by other theater groups. Often, foundations and corporations, reluctant to open their files to the public, have discouraged scholarly writing. What was written was usually by staff people, house histories, and usually little more than compilations of annual reports with no scholarly analysis. The authors tended "to magnify success and overlook or omit failure."[5]

Arts philanthropy has a long history. Beginning about 501 B.C. in ancient Greece, *choregoi* were chosen from among the wealthy citizens, and it was their duty to finance stage productions. In the Middle Ages, towns or guilds subsidized productions. In Shakespeare's day, companies received financial aid from their sponsors. In fact, the 1572 "Acte for the punishment of Vacabondes" required each new company to be authorized and financially supported by one noble or two judicial dignitaries. Renaissance artists certainly had patrons—Leonardo da Vinci worked for nobility; Michelangelo for the Medici. Probably the first theater to receive funding on a regular and ongoing basis was the Comédie Française, a state theater subsidized by Louis XIV. German states began to subsidize theaters around 1770, and by the nineteenth century, every German state and most cities subsidized theaters.

The history of patronage in the United States, however, is quite different. Unlike Europe, our country lacked a monarchy as well as an aristocracy to support the arts. As historian Kathleen D. McCarthy explains, "In a country devoid of these traditional sources of patronage, cultural development logically fell to the local elites."[6] Since most people in the eighteenth and nineteenth centuries subscribed to the Protestant work ethic, they would have considered it preposterous to spend public money on theater. They maintained "that if an adult had time to enjoy himself, he had time to work harder."[7] But after the Civil War, when real estate speculators and entrepreneurs such as Rockefeller, Mellon, Carnegie, and Morgan became wealthy on the strength of new railroads, oil and steel trusts, banking, and mining, it was the beginning of the American idea of aristocracy.

During the years of the Gilded Age, one of the main pleasures derived from being rich was the ability to parade wealth and exhibit it for all to see. A conspicuously grand house was an important, visible symbol of success. As C. Wright Mills puts it in *The Power Elite*, it was "a staging area from which a family may increase its participation with and ultimately be included in the upper class." A good house, he wrote, strengthened "unspoken claims for recognition."[8] The wealthy, for the most part, however, were not interested in supporting the arts. "The vast majority of rich people continued to behave as they always had," Judith Sealander observes, "giving little or nothing away to anyone not a member of their families."[9] The heads of the houses of Astor and Vanderbilt "were noted for their indifference to charity."[10] And Andrew Carnegie reportedly insisted that "the theater is not the proper field for private gifts."[11]

Fortunately, some millionaires believed that if they turned to philanthropy, their families had a better chance of being accepted into upper-class society. For one thing, writes Teresa Odendahl, they would be "demonstrating the proper values by giving rather than displaying wealth."[12] The specific kinds of donations were important. Especially prestigious was making big donations to the high arts.

Tom Riley writes in *Philanthropy* magazine, "It used to be so easy. You made your fortune in coal mining or steel or widget manufacturing and when you wanted to show the world that you had 'arrived' you plopped down a couple of big bags of money in front of the symphony or the opera or the art museum. If you were really great they named a wing or two after you. . . . Pay for a Picasso here, underwrite a *Swan Lake* there, and voilà—you went from middlebrow to highbrow with a couple strokes of the pen."[13]

Practices changed in 1913, when Congress established a federal income tax and four years later allowed deductions for gifts to nonprofits. Millionaires began to contribute up to the maximum for which they could receive a deduction since they could substantially reduce the taxable portion of their income. Philanthropic contributions "now took a surge forward; for even the stingiest Scrooge preferred to endow something rather than see the government make off with his hard-earned money. . . . It was amazing how charitable the social climbers became." As a result of the new tax laws, "Wealthy people who could not see giving any help to human beings were sometimes better disposed toward supporting the arts."[14]

Because of the tax advantages, many wealthy Americans invested some of their fortunes in endowments to establish philanthropic foundations. The money they invested generated income for the foundation to use. Years later, the Tax Act of 1969 would require foundations to disperse annually at least 5 percent of their endowment earnings.

Through the generosity of individuals and their endowed foundations, "the creation of an institutional structure for the arts in this country remained for a long time," writes Paul Mattick Jr., "the work primarily of private citizens. . . . [P]rivate philanthropy has played an undeniably crucial role in the creation of artistic institutions in the United States."[15] Indeed, the country did not have a national gallery until a private individual, Andrew W. Mellon, gave $14 million in 1937 to build the National Gallery of Art. Estimates from a multiyear study show that 20 percent of all contributions to the arts come from private individuals and an additional 13 percent from their foundations.[16]

The federal government entered the picture as a major theater angel in 1935 when it allocated nearly $7 million to establish the Federal Theatre. The theater's purpose was twofold: to provide work for unemployed theater artists during the Great Depression and to make their work accessible to Americans around the country. One requirement was that 90 percent of the appropriation had to be spent on wages. Among the 12,700 people employed at its height were actors, writers, designers, musicians, dancers, stagehands, and front-of-house personnel. During its existence, more than a thousand theater productions took place in twenty-two different states. Sadly, the project came under attack by the House Un-American Activities Committee for having communist leanings and providing propaganda for President Roosevelt's New Deal. Some politicians objected to the idea of subsidized theater altogether and questioned whether it was an appropriate role for the government. Congress abolished the program in 1939.

About the same time that the Federal Theatre was established, a change in the laws allowed corporations to deduct up to 5 percent of their net income before taxes for contributions to charitable groups. The arts, however, were seldom considered legitimate areas of corporate funding. As Alvin H. Reiss explains, "the typical viewpoint of yesteryear was that culture neither needed nor warranted the support of big business. The arts were special and esoteric and reached a select audience who could afford to pay for their private pleasures."[17] Corporations that did support the arts seldom advertised their efforts "either for fear that other fund-seeking groups would descend on them en masse, or because they simply believed that support of the arts was not a significant enough activity to promote."[18]

Sentiments changed dramatically in the 1960s. In 1959, corporations donated only 3 percent of their contributions to the arts, but this increased to 11 percent by 1981. In terms of dollars, the increase went from about $22 million in 1965 to more than $500 million in the early 1980s.[19] A recent government study concluded that 7 percent of all contributions to the arts comes from corporations.[20] Certainly, catalysts for the change were the publications of the Rockefeller Panel Report, *The Performing Arts: Problems and Prospects* (1965), and the Twentieth Century Fund's report, *Performing Arts: The Economic Dilemma*, by William J. Baumol and William G. Bowen (1966). These studies described the expansion of the nonprofit professional performing arts in the United States, pronounced their benefits to society, and recommended more government and philanthropic support. The chapter in the Rockefeller Panel Report titled "Corporate Support for the Arts" proclaimed, "Support for the arts is a part of community responsibility, and a healthy cultural environment is clearly in the self-interest of the business community."[21] Two years later, David and John D. Rockefeller III provided the seed money of $100,000 to establish the Business Committee for the Arts, whose mission was to provide "businesses of all sizes with the services and resources necessary to develop and advance partnerships with the arts that benefit business, the arts and the community."[22]

The motivation behind corporate giving, however, differs from the motivations of individuals and foundations. "Corporations are about making money for their stockholders. They're not about being Maecenas to the arts in this country," cautioned the late Peter Zeisler, former director of Theatre Communications Group (TCG). "Furthermore, the only reason they have any interest in the arts, or at least the primary reason they have an interest in the arts, is one of visibility and public relations."[23]

A few months before he was assassinated, President Kennedy established an arts commission that ultimately led to the founding of the National Endowment for the Arts in 1965. Rather than supervising programs themselves as the government had with the Federal Theatre, the NEA established peer-review advisory panels that channeled funds to nonprofit organizations. It established incentive grants and matching grants with a principle of decentralization—part of the mission was making the arts accessible and available outside major cities. According to Senator Claiborne Pell, the idea of using the NEA "as a catalyst . . . [to] help spark nonfederal support . . . was the key to the entire proposal."[24] The initial appropriation in 1965 of nearly $3 million had grown to almost $159 million by 1981.

In the words of historian Arthur Schlesinger, the 1990s marked "a time of crisis in the state of the arts."[25] It began in May 1989, when Senator Jesse Helms condemned Andres Serrano's *Piss Christ* in an NEA-funded exhibition at the Southeastern Center for Contemporary Art in Winston-Salem, North Carolina. The next year, Dennis Barrie and the Contemporary Arts Center in Cincinnati were indicted for pandering obscenity after opening an exhibit of Robert Mapplethorpe's photographs, seven of which were considered depictions of sadomasochistic acts. Later that year, Karen Finley, Holly Hughes, Tim Miller, and John Fleck (labeled the NEA Four) were unanimously approved for grants totaling $23,000. Responding to complaints of nudity, vulgarity, tales of violence, sexual abuse, and racial hatred in their performances, David Gergen, a *U.S. News and World Report* editor, screamed, "They want to engage in wanton destruction of a nation's values, and they expect that same nation to pay their bills," and a *Washington Times* editorial labeled the NEA "a kind of federally funded porn palace."[26] One critic declared, "If you care for the quality of life in our American democracy, then you have to be for censorship."[27]

One result of the furor was congressional action that banned federal funds for art that "may be considered obscene, including but not limited to, depictions of sadomasochism, homoeroticism, the sexual exploitation of children, or individuals engaged in sex acts and which, when taken as a whole, do not have serious literary, artistic, political or scientific value."[28] All persons receiving grants were then required to sign an antiobscenity clause. By November 1990, more than thirty groups and individuals had refused to sign the pledge, including Joseph Papp, who opted to reject an NEA grant of $50,000 for Festival Latino. The situation became so heated that Theatre Communications Group, along with sixty-nine artists and individuals, assailed the NEA for aspiring to become an "art cop" and insisted, "The Constitution does not permit the government to manipulate a federal arts subsidy program into a vehicle for suppressing controversial speech." Although the antiobscenity pledge was ultimately scrapped, when Congress authorized the NEA in late 1990, it mandated that awards be made on the basis of "artistic excellence and artistic merit" and that they must uphold "general standards of decency and respect for diverse beliefs and values of the American public."[29] By 1996, as a result of the art wars, the NEA budget was slashed by almost 40 percent; this dramatic cutback lasted five years. The 2006 allocation was set at $124 million, approximately the same as it was in 1978. In a survey of 198 theaters, Theatre Communications Group concluded that contributions from the federal government to theaters in 2004 supported less than 1 percent of expenses.[30]

Even though its financial contribution is minimal, the NEA began to set the national tone for all arts philanthropy by courting the voter and defining art by its usefulness to society. As Robert Brustein complains, it causes "funders to measure value by outreach programs, children's projects, etc. It is making art into a social welfare agency. . . . Large and small private foundations now give their money not to general support as in the past but overwhelmingly to special programs conceived by the officers of the foundation." Programs that might lead to expanding marketing efforts, increasing community outreach, increasing audience diversity. Brustein calls this "coercive philanthropy." "Artists and institutions are obliged to follow the dictates of officious program directors or be exiled to an economic gulag." It has a "demoralizing effect on artists and artistic institutions. The entire cultural world is bending itself into pretzels to find the right shape for grants under the new criteria."[31]

The downturn in the stock market at the end of the twentieth century further affected arts philanthropy. On the state level, since appropriations are tied to tax revenues, arts budgets came under strong fiscal pressures. In 2003, state expenditures for the arts were at $354.5 million but fell to $273.7 million in 2004—a 23 percent decline. California cut its budget from $22 million to $2 million, and Michigan cut its budget in half. In the 1990s, the Alabama Shakespeare Festival received an average of $800,000 from the state. In 1999, it was cut to about $525,000 and to $125,000 in 2004. The artistic director predicted, "Next year it will be zero."[32] His prediction came true. Some states have talked about eliminating arts budgets altogether. Peter Zeisler laments, "The minute they [arts organizations] make waves, then they're going to make problems for the funders."[33]

As is true of corporate foundations, the corporations themselves "are under pressure to maintain a 'lean and mean' image and can ill afford to keep up costly, high-profile cultural projects while laying off thousands of people."[34] Marilyn Laurie, chair of the AT&T Foundation, states the position of corporations bluntly: "The pressure on companies is building to demonstrate their social responsibility by increasing contributions in support of other community needs. . . . When do we say yes? When a worthwhile request in some way is relevant to our business agenda and has the potential of enhancing our corporate reputation. . . . We want to build our brand. We want to enhance our market position. We are seeking to help build earnings."[35] Clearly, "The line between marketing and philanthropy has begun to blur."[36]

Corporate support was more difficult to come by in 2004, since corporate donors had begun looking for increased television coverage. "Unless there is a big media component to help them get visibility, it's a much harder sale," says Julie Diaz, vice president of development at the Philadelphia Orchestra Association (No. 182).[37] Still, another problem with corporate support is corporate mergers. A theater may enjoy a grant from a particular corporation one year but find itself rejected when that corporation merges with another or is bought out. John K. Urice, a specialist in arts management, doubts whether "foreign owned corporations care to subsidize the arts in the U.S."[38] In fact, corporate support of theater dropped 49 percent in the five years between 2000 and the end of 2004.[39]

Catherine S. McBreen, managing director of Spectrum Group, observes that "When the stock market began to crumble in 2000 as the Internet bubble collapsed, the wealthy substantially cut back their charitable giving."[40] After all the skirmishes of the 1990s, many donors could no longer see art as important. Especially after the tragedies of 9/11 in 2001 and Hurricanes Katrina and Rita in 2005, the United States seemed to have so many pressing needs. Add to those disasters the devastating earthquake in Pakistan and Afghanistan that killed eighty-seven thousand and left more than three million homeless. Even usually supportive patrons began to "struggle over whether arts are the highest good their charitable dollars can buy."[41] "Supporting the arts," suggests Urice, "might seem elitist if not insensitive in the world of the early twenty-first century."[42]

Because foundation giving is based on the income from endowments, when the foundation assets decline, so does the giving. The assets in foundations declined 10.5 percent between 2000 and 2002. In 2003, therefore, performing arts grant dollars from foundations decreased by nearly 10 percent.[43] Corporate foundations are equally vulnerable to reduced income. The amount of profits from their income is directly related to the giving potential of the corporation. When the corporation experiences lower profits, it has less money to contribute to its foundation and thus less money to donate to the arts. Although theaters are receiving more foundation gifts, the total of the gifts in dollars is not keeping up with inflation, forcing arts organizations "to apply for more grants in order to achieve the same contribution amounts."[44]

In a climate of dwindling endowments, Gara LaMarche, director of U.S. programs for the Open Society Institute and former associate director of Human Rights Watch, notes that during the bleak 2002 economy, few foundations "want[ed] to prop up an organization forever, or have it become dependent on their grants."[45] Ben Cameron, former director of Theatre Communications Group, attests to the frequency "and indeed the dominance in our world—of grant applications that begin, 'We do not fund general operating support, meetings, or conference, or groups outside our immediate geographic purview.'"[46] Average foundation support has declined every year since 2001 and now supports 2 percent less of theater expenses than it did in 2000. The average number of gifts per theater has remained steady at nineteen grants per theater, but the grants are considerably smaller.[47] According to a survey conducted by Theatre Communications Group, "Foundation largesse supported 1.4 percent fewer expenses in 2005 than in 2001."[48]

Because of the difficulties in gaining support from foundations and corporations, theaters are recognizing "the growing importance of individual donors as the backbone of the fundraising efforts." "We turned to individual donors," says Kent Thompson, formerly of the Alabama Shakespeare Festival, "and they have been our salvation."[49] Describing the theater angels in the nation's capital, for instance, Leslie Milk writes in *Washingtonian* magazine, "For every multimillion-dollar gift to construct a new theater, there are many $25,000 to $50,000 gifts to support one production or a piece of a production. One donor funded costumes for Shakespeare Theatre's production of *Cyrano* in 2004, contributing $36,000."[50] Theaters across the country reported a 68 percent increase in individual donations between 1998 and 2003. "Theatre boards are an important source of financial support," Milk stresses. "Members are expected to be sponsors. For example, Arena board members donate or raise $10,000 each season. Board members run the galas and benefits: They recruit the evening's underwriters and 'encourage' their friends to buy tickets. Boards can also be breeding grounds for angels." Fund-raisers agree that when soliciting a substantial gift from an individual, it helps if the donor knows someone at the theater.[51] Individuals give to individuals. Alvin Reiss writes, "While acquaintanceship alone seldom insures grants, it does provide an opening wedge."[52] The gifts from trustees and other individuals support almost 19 percent of theater expenses.[53]

Obviously, accepting gifts can create challenges. After donor Lurita Doan observed the final dress rehearsal of Michael Kahn's production of *Lorenzaccio* at the Shakespeare Theatre, she sent him two pages of comments. Kahn argues, "None of our donors has ever asked to be more than a supporter or friend." However, when Sidney Harman agreed to give $15 million for the same theater to expand its operation, there were strings tied to the gift—he insisted that the new theater be a downtown center for the performing arts.[54] When Daniel Sullivan was artistic director of the Seattle Repertory Theatre, he resisted foundation and corporation support, fearing their motivations and their desire for control.[55] After Senator Newt Gingrich attended a performance of Terrence McNally's *Lips Together, Teeth Apart* at the Theatre in the Square in Marietta, Georgia, in 1993, he convinced the Cobb County Board of Commissioners to withdraw its grant of $60,000 from the theater because of the play's discussion of AIDS and homosexuality. Edith H. Love, managing director of Portland Center Stage in Oregon, has boasted that it received $350,000 from the McDonald Financial Group in 2005 to sponsor its main-stage productions for two seasons, but she remarked that the theater felt the need to budget $46,000 of that money just for "major donor cultivation that we have not been able to afford previously." As she said, theaters "walk a real tightrope that you are not going to offend donors."[56]

With costs rising at the same time that foundation and corporation funding is declining, theaters today are faced with overwhelming challenges. "Theatres are scrambling to meet cash-flow pressures," writes Ben Pesner. "While many theatres are on stable financial footing, others continue to struggle."[57] From coast to coast, theaters have been forced to cut back on production costs, hire fewer guest artists, shrink cast sizes, and reduce rehearsal weeks and even the workweeks of production staffs. In spite of these measures, 46 percent of the theaters responding to the TCG annual survey reported ending 2004 with deficits.[58] Unfortunately, theaters cannot count on increased giving. Throughout American history, the support for arts philanthropy has been unpredictable, fluctuating with the state of the economy, the sociopolitical atmosphere, and changes in federal tax laws. Ironically, at the very time when American theaters need more financial support, the Congressional Joint Committee on Taxation proposed several changes in 2005 that would limit tax incentives for gifts to foundations, thereby reducing the amount of new gifts to foundations and decreasing the amount of money available for grants. Similarly, the push to lower personal income and estate taxes would hamper the establishment of new foundations and stunt the growth of existing ones. A decrease in taxes for wealthy individuals would certainly lessen their incentive for charitable giving. The theater needs more angels giving more money, not fewer giving less.

The new, never-before-published chapters in this volume, employing both a historical and a chronological format, examine two different types of angels: *individuals* and *institutions*. The chapters explore biographical and contextual information about the donors, how they became angels, their various motivations, the policies and restrictions they created, the kinds of productions and theaters they supported, the successes and failures they encountered along the way, and how funding sources have changed over the years and to what effect. While these chapters obviously do not include all patrons or profile all types of angels in the American theater, they do reflect a wide range of styles of philanthropy. But within these two categories, a variety of angels are examined. There have been wealthy individuals, such as Lucille Lortel and the Lewisohn sisters, who established their own theaters with their fortunes, as well as David Geffen, whose philanthropy has supported Broadway and Los Angeles theater.[59] Some patrons such as Alice De Lamar, Mary Bok, and Richard B. and Jeanne Donovan Fisher supported individual artists rather than theater companies. Otto Kahn supported both. The chapter on Peter Donnelly illuminates a different kind of angel. He was not wealthy, but even without halo and wings he was a guardian spirit who played a critical role in securing and distributing funds from various corporations for theater projects.

Further, while the generous patronage of wealthy citizens captures most of the media attention, the humble financial contributions of avid theatergoers are also vital to the shaping of our theater and are examined herein. These angels have been instrumental in developing both professional and amateur theater not only in New York and other major cities but also around the country in regional and university theaters. The importance of patronage should not be measured by wealth. Grant Goodman, an emeritus professor of Asian history, donates $10,000 every year to an award-winning playwriting program at the University of Kansas. New York's Castillo Theatre, maintaining that foundation and corporation grants would hamper its mission, relies on ten thousand people who generously donate a few dollars each year. These ordinary citizens, like the millionaires, play an important role in our theater. As the president of Wayne State University said in describing the donors that support its theater program, "These are people who appreciate beauty in art. They're the people who try and better the environment in which we live through beauty, through art, through the theatre."[60]

The philanthropy of institutions also demonstrates different kinds of projects. Although the Ford and Rockefeller foundations have a long history of supporting a variety of theater artists and companies around the country, the MacArthur Foundation is known in theater circles for awarding Ellen Stewart of Café La MaMa one of its "genius grants." Similarly, the Humana Foundation is credited for its backing of the Festival of New American Plays at the Actors Theatre of Louisville. And the Harold and Mimi Steinberg Charitable Trust has as its mission the support of new-play development. The recent contributions of Disney and Clear Channel have certainly left their mark across the country.

If there were no size limitations to this volume, so many more stories could be included—Cary Saurage and his establishing the endowed theater chair in honor of Billy J. Harbin at Louisiana State University; Hope Abelson, who supported the early development of several Chicago theaters as well as the Goodman Theatre; Marlin A. Miller's donation for the performing arts at Alfred University; the Chace family of Rhode Island, who has endowed the Trinity Repertory Theatre; the Goodyear Tire and Rubber Company support for the E. J. Thomas Performing Arts Hall at the University of Akron; the Target Foundation support of theater in Minneapolis; American Airlines' arrival on Broadway; Rita and Burton Goldberg's funding of the playwriting program at New York University's Tisch School of the Arts; The Understudies in Detroit, who support and champion the Hilberry Graduate Repertory Program; Martha Tatum's relationship with the theater at the University of Southern Mississippi; Richard Rauh and Philip Chosky's support of both professional and university theater in Pittsburgh; Marguerite Cullman, who was a major investor in Broadway theater in the 1930s, 1940s, and 1950s; T. Edward Hambleton's support of the New Phoenix Repertory Company in the 1970s; Lorraine and Valborg Sinkler's bequest to Appalachian State University; Clarice Smith, who provided more than $100 million for the new performing arts center at the University of Maryland; Frederick C. Miller's providing the support for the establishment of the Milwaukee Repertory Theatre; Altria Foundation's support of experimental theater and dance; Sidney Harman's sponsorship of the Shakespeare Theatre in Washington, D.C.; and Gilbert and Jaylee Meads's contributions to local theaters in Washington, D.C. Thankfully, the list goes on and on! Hopefully, the chapters in this volume will encourage more scholars to study the starring role that angels have played in making theater available to the American people.

But what of the future? "A great nation deserves great art," according to the National Endowment for the Arts in 1965. "Let us remember that the arts and humanities are a necessity, not a luxury, and every American deserves to have access to them," proclaimed President Bill Clinton thirty years later.[61] Challenging these noble quotations is the reality of the American theater, awash in predictions of cutbacks, scale-downs, compromise, and doom. Yet somehow over the years, theater in America continues to live and prosper. And on so many levels, angels make it so.

Notes

1. When, where, and how the word *angel* became a synonym for a patron or benefactor is unclear. An early reference is in Roy L. McCardell, *Conversations of a Chorus Girl* (New York: Street and Smith, 1903). In a chapter titled "In the Glamour of the Footlights," a fan tells a chorus girl that he is going to make her a star in a musical the next season. She responds, "it's nice to . . . know that you have a friend . . . who has money to arbitrate and who's anxious to be an angel. You know that he appreciates your art" (64).

2. For more information about the Federal Theatre, see Hallie Flanagan, *Arena: The Story of the Federal Theatre* (New York: Duell, Sloan, and Pearce, 1940); Rena Fraden, *Blueprints for a Black Federal Theatre: 1935–1939* (New York: Cambridge University Press, 1994); J. Mathews, *The Federal Theatre: 1935–1939* (Princeton, NJ: Princeton University Press, 1967); John O'Connor and Lorraine Brown, eds., *Free, Adult, Uncensored: The Living History of the Federal Theatre Project* (Washington, D.C.: New Republic Books, 1978); and Barry B. Witham, *The Federal Theatre Project: A Case Study* (New York: Cambridge University Press, 2003). For more information about the National Endowment for the Arts, see Jane Alexander, *Command Performance: An Actress in the Theater of Politics* (New York: Public Affairs, 2000); Donna M. Binkiewicz, *Federalizing the Muse: United States Arts Policy and the National Endowment for the Arts, 1965–1980* (Chapel Hill: University of North Carolina Press, 2004); John Frohnmayer, *Leaving Town Alive: Confessions of an Arts Warrior* (Boston: Houghton Mifflin, 1993); Fannie Taylor, *The Arts at a New Frontier: The National Endowment for the Arts* (New York: Plenum Press, 1984); and Joseph Wesley Zeigler, *Arts in Crisis: The National Endowment for the Arts Versus America* (Chicago: A Capella Books, 1994).

3. Erin Jordan, "Foundations Want Names Private," *Des Moines Register*, November 10, 2005.

4. Michael Rothmayer, who received his Ph.D. in theater from the University of Nebraska–Lincoln, planned to furnish a chapter on Johnny Carson for this collection, but he encountered too many stumbling blocks from the Carson estate and from university officials.

5. Richard Magat, "A Very Short History of Foundation Histories," *Foundation News and Commentary* 42, no. 5 (September–October 2001): 1.

6. Kathleen D. McCarthy, "Twentieth-Century Cultural Patronage," in *Alternative Futures: Challenging Designs for Arts Philanthropy*, ed. Andrew Patner, 2–3 (Washington, D.C.: Grantmakers in the Arts, 1994).

7. Judith Sealander, *Private Wealth and Public Life: Foundation Philanthropy and the Reshaping of American Social Policy from the Progressive Era to the New Deal* (Baltimore: Johns Hopkins University Press, 1997), 189–90.

8. Quoted in Mary Cable, *Top Drawer: American High Society from the Gilded Age to the Roaring Twenties* (New York: Atheneum, 1984), 89, 92.

9. Sealander, *Private Wealth*, 1.

10. Cable, *Top Drawer*, 163.

11. Ibid., 5.

12. Teresa Odendahl, *Charity Begins at Home: Generosity and Self-Interest among the Philanthropic Elite* (New York: Basic Books, 1990), 41–42.

13. Tom Riley, "Who's Afraid of Giving to the Arts?" *Philanthropy* (January–February 2000): n.p.

14. Cable, *Top Drawer*, 172–73.

15. Paul Mattick Jr., "Some Aspects of Art and Philanthropy in the United States," in Patner, *Alternative Futures*, 25.

16. National Endowment for the Arts, "How the United States Funds the Arts," http://www.arts.gov/pub/how.pdf, 13 (accessed October 17, 2005).

17. Alvin H. Reiss, *Culture and Company: A Critical Study of an Improbable Alliance* (New York: Twayne, 1972), 17.

18. Ibid., 69.

19. McCarthy, "Cultural Patronage," 16.

20. National Endowment for the Arts, "United States Funds the Arts," 13.

21. Quoted in Reiss, *Culture and Company*, 82

22. Business Committee for the Arts, "About BCA," http://www.bcainc.org/about.html (accessed October 10, 2005).

23. Quoted in W. M. Lowry, ed., *The Arts and Public Policy in the United States* (Englewood Cliffs, NJ: Prentice Hall, 1984), 133.

24. Quoted in McCarthy, "Cultural Patronage," 15.

25. Quoted in McCarthy, "Cultural Patronage," 21.

26. Quoted in Steven C. Dubin, *Arresting Images: Impolitic Art and Uncivil Actions* (New York: Routledge, 1992), 151; "She Walks in Chocolate," *Washington Times*, May 17, 1990.

27. Dubin, *Arresting Images*, 245.

28. "NEA Chronology," *Christian Science Monitor*, August 6, 1993.

29. Dubin, *Arresting Images*, 150–281.

30. TCG, "Theatre Facts 2004," http://www.tcg.org (accessed October 19, 2005).

31. Quoted in Arthur M. Melzer, Jerry Weinberger, and M. Richard Zinman, eds., *Democracy and the Arts* (Ithaca, NY: Cornell University Press, 1999), 20–23.

32. Quoted in Ben Pesner, "Theatre Facts 2003," *American Theatre* 21 (November 2004): 43–44.

33. Quoted in Lowry, *Arts and Public Policy*, 133.

34. Olin Robison, Robert Freeman, and Charles A. Riley II, eds., *The Arts in the World Economy: Public Policy and Private Philanthropy for a Global Cultural Community* (Hanover, NH: University Press of New England, 1994), xiv.

35. Marilyn Laurie, "Corporate Funding for the Arts" in Robison et al., *Arts in the World Economy*, 68–69.

36. Bill Catlin, "Sharing the Wealth: Corporate Giving," Minnesota Public Radio, September 20, 2000, http://news.minnesota.publicradio.org/features/200009/07_catlinb_philanthropy/catlin.shtml (accessed February 20, 2005).

37. Holly Hall, Leah Kerkman, and Cassie J. Moore, "Giving Bounces Back: Donations to the Biggest Charities Increased by 11.6% Last Year," *Chronicle of Philanthropy*, October 27, 2005, http://philanthropy.com (accessed October 28, 2005).

38. Quoted in David B. Pankratz and Valerie B. Morris, eds., *The Future of the Arts: Public Policy and Arts Research* (New York: Praeger, 1990), 252–53.

39. Ben Cameron, "Post-Election Realities—Issues in Theatre Organizations: Funding, Community, and Strategy for Renewal" (speech, National Theatre Conference, New York City, December 3, 2004).

40. "Wealthy Curtail Giving, Despite Better Market," *Des Moines Register*, August 29, 2005.

41. Riley, "Who's Afraid?" n.p.

42. Quoted in Pankratz and Morris, *Future of the Arts*, 252–53.

43. Foundation Center, "After Holding the Line for Two Years, Foundation Giving Declined in 2003," press release, April 5, 2004, http://fdncenter.org/media/news/pr_0404a.html (accessed February 20, 2005); Loren Renz and Steven Lawrence, "Foundation Grants to Arts and Culture, 2003: A One-year Snapshot," *Vital Signs: Snapshots of Arts Funding*, http://www.fdncenter.org/research/trends_analysis/index.html (accessed November 8, 2005).

44. Lorenz Renz, "The Foundation Center's 2002 Arts Funding Update," Foundation Center, http://www.fdncenter.org (accessed February 20, 2005).

45. Gara LaMarche, "The Virtues and Vices of Philanthropy Today and How Foundations Can Do Better," *The Philanthropy Roundtable* (January/February 2000), http://www.philanthropyroundtable.org/magazines/2000–01/lamarche.html (accessed February 20, 2005).

46. Ben Cameron, "Systems and Survival," *American Theatre* 22 (April 2005): 4.

47. TCG, "Theatre Facts 2004," http://www.tcg.org (accessed October 19, 2005).

48. Celia Wren, "At the Intersection of Optimism and Uncertainty: A Continued Recovery Harbors Some Worrisome Omens," www.tcg.org/publications/at/nov06/theatrefacts.cfm (accessed November 7, 2006).

49. TCG, "Theatre Facts 2004."

50. Leslie Milk, "Angels in the Wings," *Washingtonian* 40 (September 2005): 76.

51. Odendahl, *Charity Begins*, 37.

52. Reiss, *Culture and Company*, 27.

53. Milk, "Angels," 77; TCG, "Theatre Facts 2004."

54. Milk, "Angels," 76–77.

55. Daniel Sullivan (symposium, National Theatre Conference, New York City, December 4, 2004).

56. Edith H. Love (symposium, National Theatre Conference, New York City, December 2, 2005); Edith H. Love, e-mail letter to author, December 22, 2005.

57. Ben Pesner, "Through the Looking-Glass," *American Theatre* 22 (November 2005): 36.

58. Ibid.

59. Since Lucille Lortel and David Geffen began their theater philanthropy many years before they endowed their own charitable foundations, I chose to locate chapters about them in part 1, "Individual Angels."

60. Quoted in *Perchance to Dream, Perchance to Share: A 40th Anniversary Tribute to The Understudies of the Hilberry Theater*, DVD, produced by Aaron Harmon and Joel Silvers (Detroit: Wayne State University Department of Theatre and Communication, 2003).

61. Quoted in Cynthia P. Schneider, "American Art and Politics," (lecture, Groningen University, the Netherlands, February 20, 2001), http://www.usemb.nl/022001.htm (accessed December 29, 2005).

PART ONE

INDIVIDUAL ANGELS

1

MODERN COSMOPOLITAN: OTTO H. KAHN AND THE AMERICAN STAGE

Theresa M. Collins

A millionaire many times over and one of America's leading financiers, Otto H. Kahn (1867–1934) was no ordinary theater patron. He is impossible for theater people to overlook because, from the early twentieth century until the onset of the Great Depression, Kahn's wallet and wisdom seemed available for every art theater in New York, every major theatrical import from Europe, and the Metropolitan Opera. A complete roster of his patronage could be mistaken for an index to *Theatre Arts* magazine. The American premieres of Sergei Diaghilev's Ballets Russes, the Théâtre du Vieux-Colombier of Jacques Copeau, and Max Reinhardt's *Miracle* were all due to Kahn's sponsorship. He helped to put Stanislavsky's Moscow Theatre before American audiences, and he backed the Actors Theatre, the Civic Repertory, the Theatre Guild, and the New Playwrights Theatre, among other companies.[1]

For Kahn, the theater never stood outside life. The spectacle sprawled into lobbies, rehearsal studios, ritzy hotels, bohemian hangouts, and high-life nightclubs. It played out in Kahn's mansions, at his business offices, on his yachts, in his hotel suites. There always seemed to be a coterie of publishers, playwrights, producers, composers, and other talents prepared to try a pitch on him. Whether their careers were rising, stalling, fading, or shining, they looked to Kahn for money, advice, referrals, and recognition.

Alexander Woollcott once described a common sense among stage talents, "Whenever the zanies of the theatre gather together the conversation is bound sooner or later to reach the phrase: 'Now, If I were Otto Kahn—' and they're off."[2] In one way or another, Otto Kahn's support of operas, plays, films, ballets, and music—all arts with theatrical potential—defined a long era of opportunities for theatrical talent and initiatives. In 1932, as Lee Simonson looked back over the years, he acknowledged that Kahn was "the best friend the modern theatre has ever had in this country."[3] Less than a decade earlier, Kenneth Macgowan had made a nearly identical remark, when Kahn guaranteed the financial resources to resuscitate the Provincetown Players.[4] In as fine a tribute as any, Jack Poggi evaluated the robust theatrical activity of New York in the 1920s and concluded, "One wonders if the noncommercial theater could have existed in New York without Mr. Kahn."[5] In my own reading of Kahn's life, his patronage was all the more important because it secured a legacy of transatlantic modernism that prefigures globalism and still challenges us to think as much about cosmopolitanism as about nationalism and localism in modern histories.[6]

The son of a merchant banker, Kahn began his lifelong involvement with cultural initiatives in Mannheim, Germany, where he was born on February 21, 1867. A former palace town with rich musical traditions, Mannheim became an important harbor and industrial city during the nineteenth century, yet it managed to balance commercial prosperity with cultural prominence. Its National theater played a major role in Kahn's upbringing because his parents, aunts, and uncles were among its most studied, steady patrons.[7] Growing up smart and rich among cosmopolitan, theatergoing, and salon-hosting Jews, Kahn grasped the Wagnerian ideal of *Gesamtkunstwerk* and understood the German word of greatest importance to be *Bildung*—an ideal of fulfillment as citizens of cultural distinction.[8] In later years, when Kahn described himself as "a business man who has tried not to degenerate into a mere business machine," he attributed it to the "'all around *Bildung*'" of his schooling and home influences.[9] But what others appreciated as his "scholar's taste for good drama,

Otto H. Kahn, circa 1927.
From the private collection of Theresa M. Collins.

[and] patiently smiling contempt for bad"[10] was additionally attributable to five starstruck years that Kahn spent among London's sophisticates before he came to New York in 1893. Introduced into the circles of his newly aristocratic aunt, Elizabeth Lady Lewis (one of London's leading hostesses and friends of the theater), Otto Kahn was better than ten years ahead of the most advanced New Yorkers in breathing the social and artistic sensibilities of the newly modern "smart set."[11]

He did not burst upon New York's cultural scene immediately, in part because the social barriers to Germans and Jews were stiffer in New York than in London, but also because, except for its concert halls and opera houses, the stage world of New York in 1893 was pretty dull by comparison to what Kahn knew abroad. The lack of native talents and the effects of commercialization do not alone explain the shortcomings. The paucity of artistically interesting theater also reflected a set of weaknesses among New York's wealthiest, American-born patrons. At least that was the assumption that motivated Kahn and a small, wealthy cohort of like-minded art and theater enthusiasts in the early twentieth century, when they began to gain influence over New York's cultural direction.

Throughout his life, Kahn developed brilliant career prospects in tandem with brilliant social contacts. His status among Wall Street's financiers advanced after 1897, when he became a partner of Kuhn, Loeb and Company, the international investment bank that was second only to J. P. Morgan and Company at the time. In 1903, he became a stockholder and director of the newly formed Conried Metropolitan Opera Company, a profit-seeking performing company that leased the Metropolitan Opera House from the Metropolitan Opera and Real Estate Company, which represented the boxholders who owned the house. An active director from the start, Kahn eventually owned more than 80 percent of the performing company's shares. Cole Porter and Fannie Brice spoofed him in songs about operatic divas, and, when the fortunes of the Met and Kahn sank together during the Great Depression, his predicament surfaced in Broadway shows that made hay of the headlines.[12]

By the last years of his life, Kahn figured that his out-of-pocket contributions to the Metropolitan Opera amounted to as much as $3 million. It is impossible to determine exactly how he arrived at that figure, or to accurately assess the relative value of his operatic patronage, but the total might have amounted to $2.5 million more if during the 1920s Kahn had successfully convinced the Met's boxholders to accept his gift of land and plans for a new opera house. It is at least clear that the bulk of his direct underwriting came in the early and in the last years of his leadership at the Metropolitan Opera.[13]

Kahn expected to lose money during the start-up phase of an artistic enterprise, but he also cared about the bottom line and knew financial stability was essential to organizational continuity. His leadership at the Met set a tone. Following the company's reorganization in 1908, which retired the impresario, Heinrich Conried, Kahn tolerated only two more years of deficits under the new general manager, Guilio Gatti Casazza. Auditable accounts were introduced, and then a study of expenses was undertaken in 1909 by commercial theater producer, Charles B. Dillingham, acting as an outside consultant. Ultimately, a culture of fiscal oversight allowed the Met to balance its hefty budgets for twenty consecutive seasons after 1910.[14] A crucial leverage, though, was $1.2 million used to buy out rival impresario Oscar Hammerstein in 1910, which removed his popular (some would say better) Manhattan Opera from New York's cultural life.[15]

The story of the New Theatre unfolded and climaxed in the same time frame. Kahn's first major attempt to subsidize serious, noncommercial theater, the New Theatre was a millionaire's philanthropy that promised at once to equal the Metropolitan Opera in grandeur and the New York Public Library in democratic idealism. Boosted as a beacon of the theatrical uplift movement that was spreading in progressive America, it would "cultivate, develop, and elevate the public taste" for dramatic and musical arts, while presenting the best of English, Continental, and American drama and light opera, and would occasionally stake a claim as America's first national theater. It was also to be "run for the sake of art only and not in any way for the sake of profit."[16]

Aside from an illustrious list of founders and subscribers, which included contributions of $35,000 each from men such as Cornelius and William K. Vanderbilt, J. P. Morgan, and Harry Payne Whitney, the centerpiece of the New Theatre was a palatial Beaux-Arts house at Central Park West between Sixty-second and Sixty-third streets. With a price tag of at least $2 million for its mortgage, construction, and architects, it was "the costliest playhouse ever erected" in New York until that time.[17] With more than twenty-three hundred seats, it was also one of the costliest to operate, and the acoustics proved terrible, except as an example of the wrong way to build a theater.[18]

The New Theatre opened in November 1909, and when it closed after two seasons, it was $400,000 in the red.[19] Kahn later called it a "first-class, man-sized disillusionment."[20] Size and sound were only half of the problems. When Harley Granville Barker looked over plans for the "millionaire's theatre" in 1908, he famously indicated that the house would be too big for the kinds of plays "most characteristic of the modern dramatic movement."[21] Afterward, Norman Hapgood questioned the founders' qualifications to decide "what kind of theatre we need," when smaller, more intimate houses were in order.[22] Winthrop Ames, the New Theatre's artistic and administrative director, worried that the flaws of the house would inevitably reflect badly upon his management.[23]

Rival commercial managers were understandably apprehensive about competition from the idle rich who, as A. L. Erlanger phrased it, had "grown tired of ping pong and the horse show" and were taking up grand opera and theater as their latest diversion. At a meeting of the Association of Theatre Managers in January 1909, Erlanger said, "The first tune played in the New Theatre ought to be: I want to be an angel / And with the angels stand: / For a crown upon my forehead / I'll have a check book in my hand." On the same occasion, Marc Klaw milked the mood further by taunting, "it is not the first time the stage has been used as a jimmy to break into society." If not an allusion to the social ambitions of Otto Kahn, it was probably meant to offend Lee Shubert, whose appointment as business manager at the New Theatre had signaled its shift from an amateur to a professional business operation.[24]

In short time, the New Theatre left funding confidence in lasting shambles. As Percy Hammond wrote in 1911 for the *Chicago Daily Tribune*, "The founders learned that instead of the esthetic philanthropists they intended to be, they were merely unfortunate 'angels.' Their institution was denounced variously as 'art's gilded incubator' and 'art's spacious mausoleum.'"[25] With the effects still pronounced in 1920, Alexander Woollcott wrote, "The very vaguely comprehended disaster which overtook the New Theatre put a blight on the notion of endowing dramatic art in America—a blight which will take the passing of many years to wear off. Rich men wishing to do something handsome for the theatre have done so sheepishly, stealthily, lest they be laughed at."[26] Almost everyone, including Otto Kahn, turned away from "completely endowing a theatre in New York," as Sheldon Cheney was still observing in 1927. But Kahn, at least, and largely exceptionally, remained up for "the speculative game" that was (and still is) characteristic of theater economics. His involvement and reputation as a patron of dramatic arts grew larger in the wake of the New Theatre.[27]

In truth, many reasons kept millionaires away from extensive theatrical patronage, including the notion that theater was a desirable rather than an essential human need. Lawrence Langner of the Theatre Guild saw as big of a barrier in "the philistine attitude of the American public toward the arts," an attitude that he described as "generally prevalent except for a handful of people in the larger cities who were looked upon as cranks, eccentrics or 'sissies' by their fellow rugged individualists."[28] After 1918, Kahn would believe the greater deterrent to theatrical philanthropy was the punishing effect of federal personal income taxes,[29] but another regular impediment was the risk of moral censure, which crops up more readily with the theater than with hospitals, colleges, libraries, and similar charities. An additional dilemma in America was the absence of public funding, as compared with that in Europe, where governments and municipalities were better attuned to the "pubic utility" of subsidizing theaters and operas. American arts were largely "left to private initiative," and Kahn said, "It is very far from being appreciated as yet by our wealthy men that art can be as educational as universities[,] . . . as nourishing as soup kitchens, as healing as hospitals."[30]

The equivalency was harder to sell in the political and economic context of a world war. Kahn had already marshaled $100,000 (mostly his own money) to bring Max Reinhardt's *Miracle* to Madison Square Garden and to stoke Reinhardt's dream of getting a permanent theater in New York when the European conflict erupted in 1914 and derailed those plans, among others, including talk about arranging a visit to New York by Gordon Craig.[31] The war was also conveniently blamed for the demise of the popularly priced Century Opera Company, which Kahn and members of the City Club had opened at the Century Theatre (the former New Theatre).[32] But an extraordinary triumph for Kahn's legacy came in 1916, when, after more than five years of trying, he managed to deliver the American premiere and U.S. tour of Diaghilev's Ballets Russes. Produced under the auspices of the Metropolitan Opera's Musical Bureau, it cost him better than $250,000.[33]

Aside from its singular importance for the development of American modernism, the Ballets Russes helped accent Kahn's cosmopolitan ideals even in wartime. "I am thoroughly convinced that one of the most effective ways to bring nations nearer to each other," he wrote, "is to spread the knowledge of and understanding for each other's art."[34] His position ultimately proved incompatible with several realities after America entered the war in 1917, and Kahn succumbed to pressure from his fellow board members at the Metropolitan Opera, for example, when it banned the German language from its repertoire. Confiding to a friend, he wrote, "It is all right in theory to say that art has no country, but it really could not be expected even of so good-natured a public as the American that they would listen to Wagner in German and to German singers at this time."[35]

Artistic opportunities in New York, meanwhile, reached historic heights for America's allies, the French, and drew Kahn to support Jacques Copeau and Théâtre du Vieux-Colombier. Officially sponsored by Théâtre Français des États-Unis, of which Kahn was the chairman, Copeau's patrons for the 1917–18 season included former founders of the New Theatre, women's committees, and many subscribers from the opera crowd.[36] But it was Otto Kahn who ultimately bridged the gap between revenues and expenses, paying more than $25,000 for repairs on the Garrick Theatre and then guaranteeing funds for another year. In between seasons, Kahn also housed the company on his country estate in Morristown, New Jersey. While encamped there, Copeau's company trained in Dalcroze Eurhythmics, which, as noted in a feature article that followed in *Theatre Arts Magazine*, advanced the case for fusing dance and movement in the training of American actors.[37]

For nearly a decade, a succession of stagecraft imported from Europe had collectively, if not exclusively, helped jump-start American modernism in the collaborative arts and push New York onto the map with Paris and London as a leader of modern theater. Kahn's helping hand in the movement had also created certain impressions about his tastes and how to approach him for support. When attempting to groom Kahn's interest in the Provincetown Players, for instance, George Cram Cook emphasized the company's independent spirit and unique mission in "producing plays by American authors only," but he smartly noted Kahn's concurrent "interest in the French theater—whose leader, by the way, places an astonishingly high estimate of value upon the work of the Provincetown Players." Soon after, the Provincetown Players were receiving a monthly stipend of $45 from Kahn, to cover the rent of its Macdougal Street playhouse.[38]

A few months later, the Washington Square Players were reemerging as the Theatre Guild, and cofounder Lawrence Langner also laced his appeal to Kahn with validation from Copeau. Because Copeau had publicly praised the Washington Square Players, and visited their theater, school, and workshops a few times during 1917, the Theatre Guild could legitimately associate itself with his legacy. Because Kahn had contributed $6,250 to the Washington Square Players in 1917, the Guild could modestly expect further consideration from him. They also created a plan that looked not for operating funds or an endowment but instead requested good terms on the recently vacated Garrick Theatre, where Rollo Peters used "odds and ends of the scenery left behind by Copeau" for the first Theatre Guild productions.[39]

Kahn gave the Theatre Guild a specific safety net, permitting it to pay rent on the Garrick when it could make the rent, and the company regularly paid irregular amounts due on the lease. Over more than seven years, Kahn covered shortfalls amounting to $48,000. The Theatre Guild would chiefly finance itself through the audience-subscription model, and it never needed make-or-break handouts from Kahn, but there were at least three exemplary reasons for the company to value him: as a buffer in maintenance- and repair-related squabbles with the Shuberts, who owned the Garrick; as "a mark of approval" in the public eye; and as a booster for (as well as a buyer of) the bonds that underwrote construction of the Guild's own theater on Fifty-second Street. Along the way, Kahn also invested $40,000 in the company's preferred stocks, which the Guild bought back in the late 1920s.[40]

While the Guild grew and grew, its few early productions by American playwrights, like Elmer Rice's *The Adding Machine*, were quite overshadowed by European offerings—be it Shaw or Pirandello, Capek's *R.U.R.* or Molnar's *Liliom*. Otto Kahn meanwhile continued to provide opportunities for New Yorkers to see European as well as American stage arts, though he changed a key element in dispensing his support for productions from abroad. Acting in part upon the advice of Lee Shubert, Kahn wrote in 1921, "Experience has brought me to the reluctant conviction that to proceed with a theatrical invasion, without being backed by one of the important managerial instrumentalities here, means going against very heavy odds."[41] That attitude stood behind Kahn's backing of the commercial producer Morris Gest, in bringing *The Miracle*, Ballieff's *Chauve Soiris*, and the Moscow Art Theatre to New York and America—an invasion of such critical and commercial success that it helped freshly expose old feelings of American inadequacy.

In his preview of the 1922–23 season, for example, Oliver Sayler imagined a catalog in which the European works were printed in color and the American portion in black and white. Making exceptions for the blossoming ranks of American scenic designers, and, of course, the plays of Eugene O'Neill, the contrast between American and European offerings was starker—and more depressing—because both the Provincetown Players and the Neighborhood Playhouse would be dark for that season. Even so, it would be hard to figure how any native theater could steal the thunder from what was about to happen in New York.[42] By the end of the first quarter, Kenneth Macgowan was bowled over and wondering whether any comparable period in "the past three years—perhaps the past thirty" had been "more crammed with significance" for the American theater. Between "Stanislavsky's extraordinary company" and the Guild's production of *Six Characters in Search of an Author*, New York was presented with "material for reflection on every aspect of the theatre as a creative art." Wildly optimistic, Macgowan expected that "the trend of the American theatre towards repertory" would be hastened by the example of the Moscow Art Theatre. Adding to his thrill were reports of Kahn's rumored intention to build a theater for Morris Gest to host Reinhardt in New York.[43]

Like most of America's theatrical modernists, Macgowan could comfortably accept the need for visiting talents "to fertilize the American field." He could additionally appreciate the importance of a New York for the economic well-being of European companies, since postwar Europe was not enjoying America's postwar prosperity. However, when the "fashion . . . for the European" remained strong in the next season, a tired, unchanging dependency upon European masters took an upper hand, and Macgowan responded, "It is not good for a land to live on the stuffs of alien countries. . . . America has to make its own theatre and own plays."[44] Around the same time, former editor of *Seven Arts*, Waldo Frank, was writing, "Do we want great art? Easy: just import it,"[45] and elsewhere the frustration turned into criticism of the foreign-born Otto Kahn, for "encouraging the development of essentially foreign art in America." Kahn answered back at a dinner in honor of Reinhardt on January 24, 1924, then again in a speech before the New York Drama League on February 5, 1924, maintaining that the interplay of influences was necessary, as "Art manifestations of the leading peoples of the world have at all times reacted upon, and stimulated and influenced, one another." Then, as if to balance the equation, he renewed his commitment to "worthwhile, well conceived and promising American art undertakings or movements, as well as individual artists."[46]

In the days before Kahn's speech at the Drama League, he made an anonymous subscription of $1,000 to the Equity Players, which would become one of his regular benefactions as the Actors' Theatre.[47] A few days after the Drama League speech, Kenneth Macgowan sent him a plan to lease the Greenwich Village Theatre in conjunction with the Provincetown Playhouse and to "use two houses somewhat as Reinhardt used Deutsches [Theater] and Kammerspiele."[48] Thereafter, in any given year of the remaining decade, Kahn was the most important patron of the Provincetown as well as the Greenwich Village Theatre, and in 1926, he endorsed the merger of the latter with the Actors' Theater.[49] Also in 1926, Kahn invested $3,000 in John Howard Lawson's *Nirvana* (which ran briefly at the Greenwich Village Theatre), and between 1926 and 1928, he pumped $53,600 into the New Playwrights Theatre, led by Larson, John Dos Passos, Francis Faragoh, Mike Gold, and Em Jo Basshe. After the New Playwrights folded, Kahn advanced another $5,000 to Basshe for "Theatre 1929, A Corporation," and in 1930, he invested $2,500 in *Hoboken Blues,* a play by Gold.[50] Add Kahn's subscriptions to the Neighborhood Playhouse and his support for the Civic Repertory into the mix, and it is easy to see why he was considered the "first among financial helpers of independent theatres."[51] In another essay in this volume, Robert A. Schanke discusses more fully Kahn's support of Eva Le Gallienne's Civic Rep.

Much of Kahn's patronage was extended as loans because loans could be written off as losses for tax purposes. He also took profits as well as losses from investments in commercial shows, and he sometimes collected debts from talents who could afford to repay the loans, like Paul Robeson, Herman Mankiewicz, and Marc Connelly. But most of Kahn's advances to stage talents and investments in theatrical enterprises chalked up as losses. To suggest only a sampling of the money, he lost $65,000 backing Norman Bel Geddes as the director, scenic designer, and coproducer (with Richard Herndon) of *Arabesque* (1925); $3,000 on Paul Green's *The Field God* (1927); $43,450 on Elizabeth Marbury's production of *Say When* (1928); $12,500 on a promise "to establish a Negro theatre in New York," which resulted in Frank Wilson's play, *Meek Mose* (1928); and $10,000 on a Shubert revival of *Peter Ibbetson* (1931). In 1930, he pumped $24,635 into the coffers of producer Morris Gest and put $28,000 at the disposal of Rudolf Kommer, an associate of Gest and Reinhardt. Between 1926 and 1931, Kahn also forgave and discharged as much as $10,650 in advances to actress Eileen Huban; $2,500 to the Erni Belian Theatre; $1,500 to the Independent Theatre Clearing House; and $2,500 to playwright Patrick

Kearney, best known for his dramatization of *An American Tragedy*. Over the years, Kahn additionally forgave loans or advances in the amount of $500 to dancer Paul Swan, $200 to actress Asta Fleming, $502 to actress Bertha Kalich, and $3,000 to the Lenox Hill Players. There was also $700 to writer-director Virgil Geddes; $2,000 to designer Serge Soudeikine; $1,500 to the Yiddish Arts Theatre; and $900 to William D. Blake, to fund *The Pelican* and other plays at the Macdougal Street Playhouse (1929–30) after the Provincetown had closed.[52]

No universal tagline adequately described Kahn's support for the stage arts. Professional writers often compared him to the Medici of Renaissance Italy and Maecenas, the great patron of letters in ancient Rome. While the latter term had greater currency in the early twentieth century than it does in the early twenty-first century, it was hoped that patrons of more moderate means could earnestly identify themselves as Maecenases, yet Otto Kahn still stood out "as an exceptional and princely individual giver."[53] He tried to get people to think of him as an amateur, which was at once a self-effacing signal to theater professionals and an acknowledgment that aristocratic pretensions posed problems for American egalitarianism. Kahn also knew theater well enough to back away from the label of angel, and to wink at the sexual expectations of theatrical benefactors, when he once joked that "the impulses which actuate the 'angel' are generally looked upon as being not precisely angelic." Kahn's own flirtations and affairs with stage women were a sophisticated variety of the cash-Clarence or stage-door-Johnny type. The singers Grace Moore and Maria Jeritza both received career-related consideration in tandem with Kahn's extramarital affections, but he kept guardedly private about his intimate encounters, and the extent of Kahn's flirtations with many women is a mystery. Eyebrows will rise with mention of Louise Brooks, Lydia Lindgren, Elsie Ferguson, or Eleanor Fitzgerald. Otto Kahn was self-conscious, at least, that sexual games could tarnish critical judgment. "When it comes to the question of artistic worth-whileness," he was proud to say, "the tests are basically different than those prevailing at a 'beauty contest.'" He additionally knew that financiers were the bane of begging talents, that patrons' demands could choke creativity, and, most important, that the successful patron had to be in love with the theater.[54]

At time of his death, in 1934, an editorial in the *World Telegram* still suggested that "Broadway's slang phrase 'angel' might have been coined just for Otto H. Kahn." But its drama critic knew to make a distinction: "The street has a sleeve name for Angels—Suckers," but Otto Kahn "was never a sap on a sleigh ride."[55]

Notes

I wish to gratefully acknowledge the comments of participants at the International Conference on Scenography: "Patronage, Spectacle, and the Stage," Prague, June 18–22, 2003; the assistance of Maryann Chach, director of the Shubert Archive in New York; and the generosity of Esther Katz, Maria Vasio, Franca Zambonino, and Max Moss.

1. At the time of Kahn's death, the drama critic for the *New York Evening Journal* wrote, "it is doubtful if even he remembered all the shows he backed, all the authors he had helped, the painters, designers, and so on that he had sent abroad to work just because they asked him and because he liked doing it." John Anderson, "Kahn Generous Drama Patron," *New York Evening Journal*, March 30, 1934.

2. Alexander Woollcott, "Second Thoughts on First Nights," *New York Times*, April 25, 1920.

3. Lee Simonson to Kahn, November 13, 1932, Otto H. Kahn Papers, Department of Rare Books and Special Collections, Princeton University Library (hereafter, Kahn Papers).

4. Kenneth Macgowan to Kahn, September 7, 1924, and June 25, 1923, Kahn Papers.

5. Jack Poggi, *Theater in America: The Impact of Economic Forces, 1870–1967* (Ithaca: Cornell University Press, 1968), 140.

6. Theresa M. Collins, *Otto Kahn: Art, Money, and Modern Time* (Chapel Hill: University of North Carolina, 2002).

7. Burkhard Laugwitz, "Robert Kahn and Brahms," *The Musical Quarterly* 74 (1990): 595–611.

8. On the significance of *Bildung*, see Marion A. Kaplan, "Redefining Judaism in Imperial Germany: Practices, Mentalities, and Community," *Jewish Social Studies*, n.s., 9, no. 1 (Fall 2002): 1–33.

9. Kahn to Prof. Dr. von Schulze-Gaevernitz, January 3, 1921, Kahn Papers.

10. Gilbert W. Gabriel, "Kahn Known as Courtliest First Nighter," *New York American*, March 30, 1934.

11. While living in London, Kahn befriended the poet Richard Le Gallienne and made the acquaintance of William Heinemann, Ibsen's publisher in England, among others. Through Heinemann, Kahn was introduced briefly to Elizabeth Robins, London's leading lady of Ibsenian drama. For an introduction to the Lewis family and their circles, see "The Catalogue of the Papers of Elizabeth, Lady Lewis (1844–1931) and the Lewis family, 1849–1982," Department of Special

Collections and Western Manuscripts, Bodleian Library, Oxford University; and Richard Davenport-Hines, "Lewis, Sir George Henry, first baronet (1833–1911)," *Oxford Dictionary of National Biography*, Oxford University Press, 2004, http://www.oxforddnb.com/view/article/34514 (accessed January 9, 2006).

12. Cole Porter's "Opera Star" was for *Out of Luck*, a 1925 production of the Yale University Dramatic Association. Fanny Brice introduced "Is There Something the Matter with Otto Kahn" at New York's Palace Theater in 1927. *Hey Nonny Nonny* (1932), a summer show, had a number in which Kahn is encouraged to let burlesque impresario Billy Minsky rescue the Met; and the Moss Hart-Irving Berlin hit, *As Thousands Cheer* (1933–34) used "Kahn" to rhyme with "the opera must go on" in the song, "Metropolitan Opening." Being the Met's leading patron was so strong an element of his public identity, that, for a laugh, someone imagined that his given name, Otto Hermann ("O.H."), bore initials that really stood for opera house. For one instance of the joke, see "Love of Art an Asset," *Atlanta Constitution*, March 30, 1914.

13. Collins, *Otto Kahn*, 68–78, 212–21, 251–55.

14. Comparative Financial Statements and Board Minutes, Metropolitan Opera Archives, New York; "The Opera Directorship," *New York Times*, February 12, 1908, and "Opera Directors Call in Dillingham," *New York Times*, January 5, 1909.

15. John F. Cone, *Oscar Hammerstein's Manhattan Opera Company* (Norman: University of Oklahoma Press, 1966), 276; "Oscar Hammerstein Sails; Otto Kahn, on Same Ship, Says No Money Is Made on Opera," *New York Times*, January 11, 1912.

16. "New Theatre Incorporated," *New York Times*, May 18, 1906.

17. "Plans Filed for the New Theatre," *New York Times*, August 17, 1907; "Palace of Drama Shows Its Splendor," *New York Times*, November 7, 1909.

18. "New Theatre Has Bad Opera Acoustics," *New York Times*, November 4, 1909; Adolph Klauber, "The New Theatre and Its Beginning—The Question of Diction and Acoustics," *New York Times*, November 14, 1909; and "Plan Buildings Now for Good Acoustics," *New York Times*, February 14, 1915. For more recent mention, see Emily Thompson, *The Soundscape of Modernity: Architectural Acoustics and the Culture of Listening in America, 1900–1933* (Cambridge, MA: MIT Press, 2002).

19. "The New Theatre Lost $400,000 in Two Years," *New York Times*, March 3, 1911.

20. Otto H. Kahn, "The American Stage," in *Of Many Things: Being Reflections and Impressions on International Affairs, Domestic Topics and the Arts* (New York: Boni & Liveright, 1926), 89.

21. "Granville Barker Not to Stay Here," *New York Times*, April 4, 1908.

22. "Mr. Norman Hapgood on the New Theatre," *New York Times*, April 14, 1908.

23. George Foster Platt, "A History of the New Theatre of New York," ca. 1911, the Shubert Archive, New York.

24. "Theatre Men Gibe the Metropolitan," *New York Times*, January 16, 1909.

25. Percy Hammond, "Affairs of the Theater in News and Comment," *Chicago Daily Tribune,* December 24, 1911.

26. Alexander Woollcott, "Second Thoughts on First Nights," *New York Times*, April 25, 1920.

27. Sheldon Cheney, "At Last America Subsidizes the Theatre," *New York Times*, March 20, 1927. See also Emilie Hapgood to Kahn, c. February 1914, and Lee W. Haggin to Otto Kahn, April 26, 1916, Kahn Papers. Additionally, see Joyce Meeks Anderson, "Otto H. Kahn: An Analysis of his Theatrical Philanthropy in the New York City Area from 1909 to 1934" (Ph.D. diss., Kent State University, 1983), 63, 72, 84.

28. Lawrence Langner, *The Magic Curtain* (New York: E. P. Dutton, 1951), 90.

29. Kahn to James M. Beck, December 9, 1921, Kahn Papers.

30. Otto Kahn, "Art and the People," May 4, 1916, Kahn Papers. See also Kahn, "An Experiment in Popular Priced Opera," April 1915, Kahn Papers, and "Plan Theatre for Shakespeare Shows," *New York Times*, May 5, 1916. As he approached retirement, actor E. H. Sothern said, "In America I see a new day dawning of the Higher Drama. Otto Kahn is the prophet of this new day." "Sothern Speaks His Farewell to the Stage," *New York Times*, May 28, 1916.

31. Norman Hapgood to Kahn, June 8, 1914; Max Reinhardt to Kahn, January 21, 1913; Rudolf Tombo to Kahn, October 13, 1913; Edward Sheldon to Kahn, c. December 24, 1913; and "American Miracle Co." folders, Kahn Papers. See also "The Miracle for Madison Square Garden," *New York Times*, May 14, 1914; "Arrangements for the Miracle Here," *New York Times*, July 12, 1914; and Sheldon Cheney, "The Aesthetic Movement," in *The New Movement in Theatre* (New York: Mitchell Kennerley, 1914), 45–63.

32. Kahn said he had sunk more than $75,000 into the Century Opera, Kahn to Lois Ewell, December 12, 1914, Kahn Papers. See also Ronald Webster, "The Demise of the Century Opera Company," *Chicago Daily Tribune*, December 27, 1914.

33. Langner, *The Magic Curtain*, 90; Lynn Garafola, *Diaghilev's Ballets Russes* (Oxford: Oxford University Press, 1989), 180, 186–88, 196, and 202–9.

34. Kahn to George Bakhmetieff, October 2, 1916, Kahn Papers.

35. Kahn to Henry Russell, January 16, 1918, Kahn Papers.

36. "French Theatre Patrons," *New York Times*, July 21, 1971.

37. Maurice Kurtz, *Jacques Copeau: Biography of a Theater* (Carbondale: Southern Illinois University Press, 1999), 50–52, 59; and Elizabeth S. Allen, "Eurhythmics for the Theatre," *Theatre Arts Magazine* 3 (January 1919): 46. See

also Lee Shubert to J. J. Shubert, July 14, 1918, and J. J. Shubert to Otto Kahn, July 29, 1918, Shubert Archives, New York.

38. George Cram Cook to Kahn, September 25, 1918; Cook to O. Hacher, November 4, 1918; and Private Secretary to Fitzgerald, January 22, 1919, Kahn Papers.

39. Lawrence Langner to Kahn, January 7, 1919, Kahn Papers; Anderson, "Kahn: Analysis," 73–77; Norman H. Paul, "Jacques Copeau Looks at the American Stage, 1917–1919," *Educational Theatre Journal* 29 (March 1977): 62; and Walter Prichard Eaton, *The Theatre Guild: The First Ten Years* (New York: Brentano's, 1929), 34.

40. J. J. Shubert to Kahn, May 5, 1924; and Resolution, Theatre Guild Board of Managers, December 3, 1924, enclosed with Theresa Helburn to Kahn, December 4, 1924, Kahn Papers. See also Eaton, *Theatre Guild*, 32, and Kahn, "The Theatre Guild," in *Of Many Things*, 83–84.

41. Kahn to James M. Beck December 17, 1921, Kahn Papers.

42. Oliver Sayler, "The Year Ahead with Europe as Preceptor," *Theatre Arts Magazine* 6, no. 4 (October 1922): 267–75.

43. Kenneth Macgowan, "And Again Repertory," *Theatre Arts Magazine* 7, no. 2 (April 1923), 89, 92.

44. Kenneth Macgowan, "Imported and Domestic," *Theatre Arts Magazine* 7, no. 4 (October 1923), 266, 272.

45. Waldo Frank, *Salvos, An Informal Book About Books and Plays* (New York: Boni & Liveright, 1924), 51

46. "Kahn Proud of His Aid to Foreign Art," *NYT*, January 25, 1924; Kahn, "Art and America," in *Of Many Things*, 20–21;"Otto Kahn Guest of Drama League," *New York Times*, February 6, 1924. See also "Kahn Defends Opera Policy Here," *New York Times*, October 16, 1925.

47. Kahn to Frank Gillmore, January 30, 1924, and Gillmore to Kahn, February 4, 1924, Kahn Papers; Anderson, "Kahn: Analysis," 103–5; Kahn to David Wallace, December 30, 1925, Kahn Papers; and Robert A. Schanke, "Actor's Theatre," in *American Theatre Companies, 1888–1930*, ed. Weldon B. Durham (New York: Greenwood Press, 1987), 4–8.

48. Macgowan to Kahn, February 17, 1924, Kahn Papers.

49. Anderson, "Kahn: Analysis," 64–72; Helen Deutsch and Stella Hanau, *The Provincetown: A Story of the Theatre* (New York: Farrar & Rinehart, 1931), 104, 169, 173, 175; and Macgowan to Kahn, April 22, 1926, enclosed with Macgowan to Paul H. Turner, April 22, 1926, Kahn Papers.

50. H. S. Meinhardt to Kahn, "Bad Debts Written off the Books, 1926–1931," May 10, 1932, Kahn Papers.

51. Sheldon Cheney, "At Last America Subsidizes the Theatre," *New York Times*, March 20, 1927.

52. Collins, *Otto Kahn*, 3, 167–73, 177; "Bad Debts Written off the Books, 1926–1931," Kahn Papers; and Wells Root, "What's Doing in New York The-

aters," *Los Angeles Times*, May 23, 1926. In 1926, Kahn also wrote off a $4,500 advance to singer Grace Moore, with whom he was involved romantically.

53. Sheldon Cheney, "At Last America Subsidizes the Theatre," *New York Times*, March 20, 1927.

54. Otto Kahn, "The American Stage—Reflections of an Amateur," in *Of Many Things*, 87, and Collins, *Otto Kahn*, 10–11, 149–52.

55. "Otto H. Kahn," *New York World Telegram*, March 30, 1934, and Douglas Gilbert, "Broadway Mourns First Angel," *New York World Telegram*, March 30, 1934.

2

COPPER HEIRESSES TAKE THE STAGE: ALICE AND IRENE LEWISOHN

Melanie Blood

Alice and Irene Lewisohn occupy an unusual place in the history of American theater—they were at the forefront of artistic experimentation during the Little Theatre Movement, knowledgeable about the European avant-garde and several Asian performance styles, *and* they had the capital to fund their own experiments. The Lewisohn sisters built the Neighborhood Playhouse, served as administrative staff with Helen Arthur and Agnes Morgan, and participated integrally as artists during its amateur and professional years from 1915 to 1927. Other New York little theaters, such as the Provincetown Players and Washington Square Players/Theatre Guild, thrived during this time, but none matched the Neighborhood Playhouse's dedication to experimental styles or its ability to fund those experiments. Critic and historian Thomas Dickinson wrote in 1924, "Among institutions working for the new art of the theater in America the Neighborhood Playhouse occupies almost the favorite place for the researches of the historian. It is the only 'new' theater to have survived for ten years. And it has survived at the expense of no backward step, of no compromise with expediency."[1]

The Neighborhood Playhouse was never driven by purely literary values. Instead, like Edward Gordon Craig, the Lewisohn sisters and their collaborators specifically displaced the written word as the center of the theatrical production and carried out experiments in scenery, lighting, costuming, sound, music, dance, and acting styles. The theory driving such artistic explorations the Lewisohns termed "lyric drama." Irene Lewisohn wrote,

> Like the players of the Italian Comedy of Art; like the players in the theaters of the Orient where a performer is called actor, dancer, or singer quite indiscriminately and performs easily the functions of all, our company must be ready to dance, act, or sing; or rather act to music or without, with a sustained or staccato tone, move to measure or create a plastic climax through pure suggestion of mood. It is all one, after all. Back of each of these mediums lie the same principles of form, rhythm, and color, and deeper yet, an understanding of life and the power of interpreting it.[2]

While many recent historians have constructed a more streamlined historical narrative by downplaying stylistic experimentation in favor of a literary purpose, even at the expense of the complexity of this formative time in American theater history, contemporary critics like Dickinson viewed the Neighborhood Playhouse's commitment to theatrical experiment as exemplifying a critical function of American art theaters. The Neighborhood Playhouse's freedom to experiment, without compromise, certainly came from the Lewisohn sisters' financial, just as much as their aesthetic, commitment.

In the 1910s, American little theaters sought to redefine American theater on three fronts: its economic basis, the audience's taste in drama, and artistic vision. As early as 1917, Thomas Dickinson, whom Kenneth Macgowan called the little theater's "first philosopher and propagandist,"[3] wrote, "We have seen the great need of the theater in three respects, a better system of expense values; a more dependable and enlightened audience; an impulse coming from the artists rather than the investors."[4] This chapter examines the Lewisohns' artistic vision as enacted at the Neighborhood Playhouse and the economic issues that arose during their active years from 1915 to 1927, and it offers comparisons with both the Washington Square/Theatre Guild and Provincetown Players.

As unusual as the combination of experimental artist and financier is Alice and Irene Lewisohn's choosing careers in the arts at all, given their upbringing and their family's social status. For most wealthy nineteenth-century families, a daughter choosing the stage was scandalous. Alice was born in 1883 and Irene in 1892, the eighth and tenth children of Leonard and Rosalie Jacobs Lewisohn. Leonard came from Hamburg, Germany, in 1865 to represent his father's export business, and Rosalie was the daughter of a prominent banking family in New York. In the United States, Leonard and his brother Adolph formed Lewisohn Brothers, which made their fortune when they shifted from lead to copper production, then merged with the Rockefeller family company and United Metals in 1898, and finally branched out into banking.

Like many other wealthy families, the Lewisohns contributed to a number of charitable causes, including the Henry Street Settlement. Leonard Lewisohn introduced Alice to Lillian Wald, founder of the Henry Street Settlement, in 1901, a year after Rosalie's death and a year before his own. Alice was moved by her first view of poverty on her trip to the Lower East Side and was highly impressed by Wald and the settlement activities she viewed.[5] While attending the Women's Medical College, Lillian Wald volunteered to teach a weekly home-nursing class on the Lower East Side. There she encountered settlement house philosophy for the first time at the College Settlement. Settlements were an effort to change the structure of Victorian charities and respond to rapid industrialization, urban growth, and immigration. Settlement founders and residents were generally educated, middle class, and often female; they moved into poor neighborhoods out of the belief that personal contact across economic divides would benefit both settlement residents and the local population. Settlers traced poverty and its attendant social problems not to defects of character, like their Victorian predecessors, but to flaws in government and society. Settlers studied local problems and approached them both by advocating for social change and by training neighborhood residents. In 1893, Lillian Wald and fellow nurse Mary Brewster founded both the Visiting Nurses Association and the Henry Street Settlement. They were active advocates of labor reform, child labor laws, standards for sanitation and housing, and pacifism. The Lewisohn sisters' visits to Henry Street would also have exposed them to settlement classes in such areas as home health care, cooking, needlework, music, dance, civics, and various sports; to general social clubs for men, women, and children; and to the settlers' efforts to answer any request for help or advice brought by a neighborhood resident.

Both sisters began to volunteer as club leaders for girls at Henry Street; they were free to plan anything with the girls from trips and parties to teaching them specific skills. Alice describes visits to the girls' homes as particularly eye-opening, and the Lewisohns responded with help to needs of the children's whole families. By 1906, the sisters were doing substantial work in music and dance with the children, and they began an annual performance.[6] Alice and Irene came to view Wald as a mother figure. When Alice and Irene were orphaned in 1902, each received approximately $2 million in assets. Alice describes this as a burden for the two girls: "Like children in a mythical tale we were sent into the stormy world with a heavy bundle to seek our fortunes. Free in a sense, because that bundle contained nuggets of gold, yet they added considerably to its weight. . . . We were gripped by the burden of responsibility, an incredible weight for youth."[7]

Alice and Irene had attended progressive schools and had always studied the arts—Alice taking acting with Sarah Cowell LeMoyne and Irene pursuing Delsarte with Genevieve Stebbins, for example—but it was not until after their parents' deaths that either considered the stage as a profession. They continued their educations in the arts, through study in New York and later trips abroad to see the European avant-garde. Alice describes the choice as "not without conflict. For at one end of the spectrum of my values was a passion for acting and the desire for study, at the other end, a social conscience."[8] Alice's one appearance on the Broadway stage, in the 1906 revival of Browning's *Pippa Passes*, brought negative press, denouncing her as a dilettante, in spite of her use of a stage name. In 1907, their brother Oscar garnered much negative press upon his marriage to actress Edna May. Thus, it is not surprising that Alice and Irene Lewisohn created their own theater under the umbrella of the Henry Street Settlement, given that settlement work provided a venue for educated and upper-class women to explore their interests and use their talents within the socially acceptable realms of social work and philanthropy.

Whereas many of the Lewisohns' female collaborators, like Agnes Morgan and Helen Arthur, are clear examples of the New Woman, the

Lewisohns' class status and the prominence of their family led them to different work and life choices. In her memoir, Alice tantalizes with such confessions as "our personal values did not conform with the traditional world of family or of producing a family,"[9] but she fails to provide details, personal or contextual. Excellent examples of the New Woman, Helen Arthur and Agnes Morgan were both from middle-class families, college educated in fields traditionally dominated by men, respectively of law and theater, and found it difficult to break into those professions. In addition, they were lesbians who lived together from the early 1900s until Arthur's death in 1939. Everyone at the Neighborhood Playhouse was aware of their relationship, and the Lewisohn sisters even bought them a house.[10]

Alice and Irene's upper-class status led them to disagreements with Morgan and Arthur over many elements of the Neighborhood Playhouse's expansion. Whereas Morgan and Arthur embraced growth and professionalism, so as to aid each artist to earn a living, demonstrated in such choices as installing a professional acting company, transferring successful productions uptown, and running the annual *Grand Street Follies* through the summer, the Lewisohn sisters resisted such marks of professionalism in favor of experimental aims and a commitment to the Lower East Side community. Everyone but the Lewisohns was concerned with making enough money, whether through the Neighborhood Playhouse or through theater and a day job, to pay their bills. The clearest example of this economic disparity is perhaps the Lewisohns' decision to close the theater for the 1922–23 season, during which they traveled throughout the Near East, studying various Asian performance traditions and pondering the mission and goals of the Neighborhood Playhouse. Morgan, Arthur, and the rest of the paid company, on the other hand, were concerned with their own livelihoods and the potential loss of audience in the year's absence. The Lewisohns prevailed, but they paid the staff's salaries and kept the school open during the dark season. Occasional disagreements aside, all four women worked together as an administrative collective, in what Kenneth Macgowan called in 1929 "our one thoroughly feminist theatre"[11]—from the first full-length production of a play at Henry Street in 1912 until 1927, encompassing the full span of the American Little Theater Movement.

American little theaters, which opened in great number starting in 1912, were nonprofessional in direct response to the monopolistic business practices of the Theatrical Syndicate and the Shubert brothers. The only real challenge to the Syndicate's power came when the Shubert brothers joined Mrs. Fiske and David Belasco from 1903 to 1905 in an attempt to break the Syndicate's monopoly over theater in American cities. In 1907, they filed a criminal suit against the Syndicate "for criminal conspiracy in the restraint of trade."[12] The Shuberts went on to accelerate the trend toward businesses providing financial backing for productions in and out of New York. The response of most theater artists to the rising control of big business over the theater industry was similar to that of workers in other industries: unionize. The National Alliance of Theatrical Stage Employees was founded in 1910 and Actors' Equity and the Dramatists' Guild in 1912.

The three most important little theaters in New York City were all founded in 1915—the Provincetown Players, the Washington Square Players, and the Neighborhood Playhouse. All three were amateur from their inception, and all three struggled to shift from amateur to professional during the 1920s, during the same years that Equity and the Dramatists' Guild became closed shops. Jack Poggi, in his *Theater in America: The Impact of Economic Forces, 1870–1967*, offers the Provincetown Players and Washington Square Players as opposite models of financial development in the Little Theater Movement: whereas the former stayed relatively small and experimental until its dissolution in 1929, the latter became the Theatre Guild, moved uptown, and eventually was virtually indistinguishable from the Broadway houses it had set out to challenge.[13] The Neighborhood, according to Poggi, resembled the Provincetown's pattern but with the significant economic difference of the Lewisohns' endowment and theater ownership. Thomas Dickinson wrote in 1917 that a New York professional theater must make $7,000 per week or more to be profitable. During the same time period, a little theater could mount a production for less than $100, and the Neighborhood Playhouse, which spent more than most little theaters, mounted its most expensive show of the 1910s for $2,300.[14]

In the 1920s, all three New York little theaters changed their mode of production as a result of economic factors. Both the Provincetown and the Neighborhood hired professional actors beginning in 1920, the former on a show-by-show basis beginning with the hiring of Charles Gilpin for Eugene O'Neill's *The Emperor Jones*, and the latter forming a small professional company to take on the major roles of the season, beginning with a production of Galsworthy's *The Mob*. At the Provincetown, the company splintered twice over the rising costs of productions: in 1922, when the company took a year's hiatus, and again in 1925. The Neighborhood also took a year off to review its mission in 1922.

While both the Provincetown and Washington Square companies were avowedly experimental and chose to work in opposition to professional theatrical models, the Washington Square Players, according to cofounder Lawrence Langner, "fought the issue of the art theatre versus the commercial theatre."[15] Its goal was more clearly defined in terms of audience development than artistic experimentation: it sought to raise the audience's demand for better plays and higher-quality productions. By the third season, Washington Square leased the 700-seat Comedy from the Shuberts, whereas the Provincetown's newly renovated theater, transformed from a stable, seated 220, and the Neighborhood Playhouse, newly constructed by the Lewisohns in 1915, seated 399. After a brief period of disbanding during World War I, a nucleus of the Washington Square group reformed as the Theatre Guild, with a clear mission to compete with the commercial theater; actors were paid and received a share of profits. Their second production, St. John Ervine's *John Ferguson*, directed by and starring Augustin Duncan, brother to Isadora, ensured the Theatre Guild's success. This production, and many later ones, transferred to large Broadway houses after proving themselves in the Theatre Guild's smaller venue. In 1928, the Guild also began to tour its successful productions. The Theatre Guild was the only one of the three New York City little theaters to survive the stock market crash and ensuing Great Depression.

While members of both the Provincetown and the Washington Square Players donated money to their clubs and paid dues, these theaters' economic model was more like a social club than that of the Neighborhood Playhouse. The Lewisohn sisters' philanthropic association with the Henry Street Settlement set up a different economic model, whereby those who have money and expertise donate them, and they work side by side with the poor and the immigrants served by the settlement. Settlements depended upon the philanthropy of wealthy donors like the Lewisohn family for their buildings and their upkeep, the cost of housing settlement residents, and program funding. Most of the residents came from the educated middle class, and most of those taking advantage of settlement programs were working poor or recent immigrants.

The Lewisohn sisters, whose father and many others in their social circle were the primary donors to the settlement, bought the land to build a theater for $70,000 and spent an additional $65,000 to build the theater. In addition, they traveled to Europe to learn the most recent trends in theater technology and avant-garde production. As a result, they installed the first plaster cyclorama in New York, and they built rehearsal rooms and workshops for costumes and properties, such that contemporary critics and historians describe their Grand Street facility as "second to none in the city."[16] The Lewisohns' addition of workshops, classrooms, and rehearsal space was unusual among theaters, but it probably derives from the settlement model of conveniently housing all activities under one roof. When expansions or repairs were necessary, or when the box-office returns for a season failed to make the expected income, the Lewisohn sisters made up the difference, in an effort to maintain creative freedom.[17]

It is interesting that even though Alice and Irene donated a large chunk of each year's operating budget and acted, danced, directed, and choreographed, they never wanted to be involved in the artistic management of the Neighborhood Playhouse. Helen Arthur ran all aspects of the theater's business, and, by the 1920s, she had hired a small staff to assist her. Agnes Morgan was paid to be stage director. Teachers received a salary, and, starting in 1920, actors in the company received a stipend of $50 per week.[18] All of these salaries were built into the annual budgets for the Playhouse, a striking contrast to the Provincetown's part-time hiring of a director and a carpenter starting in 1917. The Neighborhood Playhouse's income was far from substantial, due to the theater's small seating capacity and the economic constraints of the local audience. From the theater's inauguration in 1915, tickets were $0.50 in the orchestra and $0.25 in the balcony, yet the first season made a $900 profit.

Costs of production rose substantially in the early 1920s for all the little theaters. At the Neighborhood, the 1920–21 season came in $15,000 over the Lewisohns' budgeted subsidy of $30,000.[19] In the fall of 1921, ticket prices rose for a second time to $1.50 orchestra and $0.75 balcony, the office began a subscription drive, and the production programs demonstrate paid advertisements for the first time. With such expenses, and the limitations on income, there was no way for a season to break even. By the 1920s, the Neighborhood Playhouse and other little theaters were a recognized part of New York City theater, and as their productions came closer to professional standards, their managements were assailed by demands by unions and by taxing and licensing authorities, which insisted they follow the same policies as professional theaters.[20]

The New York little theaters as a group aimed to define a new and distinctly American theater aesthetic, whether the individual company's primary focus was on new texts like the Provincetown, new performance styles like the Neighborhood, or audience development like the Theatre Guild. Each of them introduced new playwrights, pioneered the New Stagecraft, and introduced new styles of acting and directing. When the little theaters began, live theater in the United States was vibrant, yet dominated by melodrama and vaudeville, a good percentage of which were written or adapted by American authors. The dominant visual style was a scenic realism that cluttered the stage with functional properties and set dressings, the epitome of which was probably David Belasco's *The Governor's Lady* (1912), which famously placed the interior of Child's restaurant on stage.

The innovations by European artists Edward Gordon Craig and Adolph Appia—simplified, symbolic use of scenery and use of lighting to intricately control mood—had been studied by some American designers before 1911, but it was in 1911 that the Irish Abbey Theatre toured America, followed closely by tours of the Ballets Russes, and Reinhardt's *Sumurun*. These simplified and symbolic visual styles took New Yorkers by storm and accelerated the New Stagecraft movement in America. Just as novel as the visual style were the styles of the productions' texts, direction, and performance. Robert Edmond Jones, as well as the Lewisohn sisters and Agnes Morgan, had seen European avant-garde scenery and staging, but no one had successfully presented it on the American stage before these influential tours.[21]

Along with new plays by European and native authors, the Neighborhood Playhouse developed lyric dramas every year that integrally combined the storytelling modes of words, movement, music, and visual effects. Macgowan wrote of new play production at the Neighborhood Playhouse: "There, in a rather masculine field, the Neighborhood Playhouse did least. And yet most—if we consider the theater, as we should, a union of all the arts, and remember the mingling of music, movement, dance, pantomime, and speech in *Salut au Monde*."[22] Lyric dramas were sometimes based on poetry (*Salut au Monde, Guibour*); sometimes based on existing dance dramas, such as those by the Ballets Russes (*Petrouchka, La Boite à Joujoux*); and sometimes based on folk or ethnic traditions (*Jephthah's Daughter, An Arab Fantasia*). In any case, the common thread among lyric dramas was that the spoken word took a secondary place in the storytelling to music, movement and dance, and design elements, which would be deployed in a unified manner to immerse the audience in the sights and sounds of another cultural tradition. Instead of locating playwrights, the Lewisohns and Morgan developed the script from ideas, and from music and dances, and they often hired specialists in a tradition, such as composers, choreographers, or performers. Since play scripts were not produced as end products of the lyric dramas, even outstanding reviews, contemporary critical praise on the importance of these experiments to the development of American theater, and the specific contributions of the Neighborhood Playhouse's repertoire have been largely lost to later historians.

The New Stagecraft movement in America can be defined by several principles, all derived from work that had been going on in Europe for at least ten years before it emerged on United States stages: a unity of all production elements, economical and suggestive use of visual elements, and subordination of all elements to a script or director's concept. Robert Edmond Jones, who has come to dominate historical narratives of the New Stagecraft, is most heavily identified with the Provincetown Players, though he designed for all three little theaters under discussion. The Neighborhood was to employ many designers, launching careers for Warren Dahler and Alice Beer, and later and more notably for Aline Bernstein and Donald Oenslager. At the Neighborhood Playhouse, the subordination of text to idea and elevation of visual elements, backed by workable budgets, skilled craftspeople, and on-site workshops, made their implementation of the New Stagecraft unusual. By the 1920s, the aesthetic goals at the Playhouse eclipsed the social goals, as evidenced by the installation of a professional acting company, increased staff, higher budgets, and a greater commitment to lyric dramas. Although details of lighting designs are slim, the use of the plaster cyclorama is mentioned in reviews of many productions, and Thomas Wilfred's "color organ" was presented several times at the Playhouse against its cyclorama. The architectural design of the Neighborhood Playhouse suggests the intent to use simple, sculptural scenery, as there was no fly space and little room in the wings. Many examples of simple, symbolic sets exist, with one of the best being the large circular false proscenium used in *Salut au Monde*, which the poet Whitman stood in front of while all of the elements he salutes in the poem passed by upstage of the circular opening. When the producing staff increased from four to six, Alice Beer and Aline Bernstein, longtime designers with the organization, joined the governing body. Both had substantial careers in design after the close of the Playhouse.

While training in performance was introduced at many little theaters, at the Neighborhood Playhouse it predated the theater's founding; the Lewisohns had offered acting and dance training at the Henry Street Settlement and directed showings of work from these classes for approximately ten years. Early reviews point to an impressive level of technique in many performers but also state that performance quality was uneven. No theater experimented as consistently or radically with performance style as the Neighborhood Playhouse. Perhaps other theaters' focus on the text, American or European, as the central unifying production element, whereas the Neighborhood's declared ideal of lyric drama, with its decentered text, was one reason. Certainly the settlement environment, in which various cultures interacted, finding both common ground and differences, encouraged a breadth of cultural perspectives in the theater productions and encouraged modes of communication not dependent upon English fluency.

The bias of both Lewisohn sisters, but particularly Irene, toward new dance expressions, such as they observed by the Ballets Russes and at Hellerau, as well as in the dance dramas of Japan and India, led the Lewisohns to a belief in the power of movement, music, and design to create a complete and compelling story in an all-encompassing environment. To create the complete environment, with all of its visual, musical, movement, and textual components, rehearsals for lyric programs could last for months as the artistic staff developed the material working directly with performers.

Beginning in 1920 with John Galsworthy's *The Mob*, the Neighborhood Playhouse added a professional company to the two amateur organizations, the Neighborhood Players and Festival Dancers. Major roles across the season were given to this professional, salaried company, while the amateur groups filled in small roles and offered only a small number of performances annually. However, the mere decision to pay actors did not mean that actors could be found suitable to the new dramas produced by the little theaters. Alice Lewisohn describes,

> The rank and file of Broadway actors who applied, though they responded with enthusiasm to the idea, were trained to exploit obvious stage types rather than individuality of character. Their techniques were based on theatrical effect rather than upon relationship to the inner experience. . . . To find professional players willing to search beyond the obvious form and character of the part—in short, to enter into rapport with the orchestral values of a production—soon seemed like a quest for the Golden Fleece.[23]

Those trained in little theaters, or the untrained with shared values, were often better suited to present the new dramas than were trained New York actors. Other little theaters expressed similar casting difficulties. All of them ran into the same economic problems based on their commitment to noncommercial, innovative fare: it was impossible to sustain an active season that depended solely on amateur actors; if actors and directors have day jobs, they are easily burned out producing full seasons of theater on top of those jobs. However, the financial restrictions of the theaters (small size, low ticket costs, experimental fare) meant they could never support a fully professional company.

In Alice Lewisohn's book, *The Neighborhood Playhouse: Leaves from a Theatre Scrapbook*, she states that she and her sister funded the Neighborhood Playhouse in order to remain entirely free of market pressures. At one point, she asks "without the freedom to fail, to court adventure with all its recklessness, without the privilege of discard and discovery, how could the Playhouse be fed? How exist if fear and doubt lurked behind every gesture, and each production needed the shelter of success?"[24] The answer to her questions was a sizable subsidy from the sisters, which included their initial purchase of the land; research into theater architecture in the United States and abroad; hiring the architect and having the theater built; paying the artists, administrators, and teachers; and keeping up with necessary maintenance of the theater. In the 1920s, the Neighborhood had to meet changing economic needs, including unionized labor and paid actors and business staff. The Playhouse was unique among little theaters in its financial freedom, coming from the Lewisohns' observation of settlement work, which led to great aesthetic freedom.

By the late 1920s, the costs of continuing the Neighborhood Playhouse's unique lyric experiments were too heavy. Lyric programs were the most expensive to mount, yet they increasingly dominated the Playhouse repertoire as the producing staff defined the lyric ideal as their unique contribution to the Little Theater Movement. The Lewisohns found themselves gradually increasing the Playhouse's subsidy. In addition, Alice married designer Herbert Crowley in December 1924 and became less of a presence at the Neighborhood. The Playhouse's financial basis, with roughly two-thirds of operating expenses paid by Alice and Irene, could not continue indefinitely; their addition of $10,000 to the first year's operating budget had grown to $105,000 by the last year.[25] Late in the 1926–27 production season, Alice and Irene announced that they would suspend their financial subsidy and give the Neighborhood Playhouse theater to the Henry Street Settlement. They cited several reasons, including the realization that the small playhouse's out-of-the-way location, combined with low ticket prices, could not be profitable. In a speech to the company quoted in the *Herald Tribune*, Alice Lewisohn lamented, "Deeply as we deplore this step, we are forced to realize that economically and from the working angle and in view of our geography and the psychology of an audience, our present system is not conducive to the further development of creative expression."[26]

In response to a direct query, Alice told reporters that she and her sister had already spent more than $500,000 on the Neighborhood Playhouse, which reporters then headlined rather than highlighting any other reason for the theater's closing. Alice responded angrily to this coverage: "the sum named represents a mere fragment of the amount which should be indicated if we could estimate in terms of money the real endowment of the Neighborhood Playhouse: the endowment of the gifts of service, time, creative imagination and talent which have been brought not only by the immediate members of the group but by many, many others—many of them distinguished artists and craftsmen."[27] Alice moved permanently to Europe with her husband. The Neighborhood Playhouse School of the Theatre was founded, moving uptown under the direction of Irene and Rita Wallach Morgenthau. Irene continued work as a choreographer with "orchestral dramas" and began the Museum of Costume Art, now part of the Metropolitan Museum of Art. Agnes Morgan, Helen Arthur, and several other company members joined to found Actor Managers, which brought their successful *Grand Street Follies* uptown and produced several other shows into the early 1930s. The Provincetown Players succumbed to similar financial pressures in 1929, leaving only the Theatre Guild—by 1930, virtually indistinguishable from other New York producers—to survive the decade of the Great Depression.

Throughout the Neighborhood Playhouse's active years, its continuing dedication to experimental production, particularly to fostering movement, music, and visual elements as key elements of dramatic storytelling with its lyric ideal, influenced the stylistic experiments of the next decades. Direct descendants can be found in artists who worked at the Playhouse in their early years, such as designers Aline Bernstein and Donald Oenslager and dancers Helen Tamiris and Anna Sokolow. By the 1920s, Broadway audiences accepted the stylized productions of Arthur Hopkins, and American expressionist writers Elmer Rice and Sophie Treadwell had their work staged. Stylistic experimentation flourished in the 1930s in many units of the Federal Theatre Project, for example. Although it is harder to trace the historical influence of nontextual production elements, Alice and Irene Lewisohn certainly opened doors for later stylistic experimentation with their work at the Neighborhood Playhouse. The Lewisohn sisters' contemporary critics, like Dickinson, hailed them for their work; theater historians now, using a more complicated definition of a performance "text," can appreciate their unique contributions to the American Little Theater Movement.

Notes

1. Thomas Dickinson, "Ten Years of the Neighborhood Playhouse," *American Review* 11 (March–April 1924): 134.

2. Irene Lewisohn, "The Repertory Idea," Neighborhood Playhouse publication, 1927, Billy Rose Theatre Collection, Neighborhood Playhouse gift, New York Public Library for Performing Arts.

3. Kenneth Macgowan, *Footlights Across America* (New York: Harcourt, Brace, 1929), 50.

4. Thomas Dickinson, *The Insurgent Theatre* (New York: B. W. Huebsch, 1917), 75.

5. Alice Lewisohn Crowley, *The Neighborhood Playhouse: Leaves from a Theatre Scrapbook* (New York: Theatre Arts Books, 1959), 4–7.

6. Crowley, *Neighborhood Playhouse*, 12. Alice and Irene Lewisohn left many scrapbooks and substantial folders of scripts and other memorabilia to the New York Public Library for the Performing Arts, which can be found in the Billy

Rose Theatre Collection and in the Dance Collection. Although the narrative and interpretive voice one encounters in Alice's book is missing, one can discern a great deal about the work of the Playhouse by viewing these artifacts. The collection is difficult to navigate, as it is spread out under the names of the artists, the show titles, and in two large collections of scrapbooks. For example, Neighborhood Playhouse Gift, MWEZ + n.c. 10,288, folder 5, contains material on the earliest club performances like *Three Impressions of Spring*, from 1906, and *Hiawatha*, from 1908.

7. Ibid., 7.

8. Ibid., 9.

9. Ibid.

10. There are handwritten photograph dedications in the Lewisohn collection (MWEZ + n.c. 16,904: *The Grand Street Follies,* New York Public Library, Performing Arts Branch), and Clare Coss cites an interview with Playhouse performer Paula Trueman from May 19, 1985, in Clare Coss, *Lillian D. Wald, Progressive Activist* (New York: Feminist Press at CUNY, 1989), 8–10.

11. Macgowan, *Footlights*, 48.

12. Jack Poggi, *Theater in America: The Impact of Economic Forces, 1870–1967* (Ithaca: Cornell University Press, 1968), 17.

13. Dickinson, *Insurgent Theatre*, 19.

14. Doris Fox Benardete, "The Neighborhood Playhouse" (Ph.D. diss., New York University, 1959), 368. All specific references to the Lewisohns' endowment are drawn from Benardete's dissertation. I have found no substantiation for her figures except in the earliest years, when records of the Lewisohns' contributions to the Playhouse were included in the Henry Street documents, and in a meeting to plan for the 1920–21 season, when the Lewisohns' projected endowment was $30,000. See Neighborhood Playhouse Gift, MWEZ + n.c. 10,292, folder 1, New York Public Library for the Performing Arts, for complete club records from 1917 to 1918. I have found a few records of salaries and production expenses, mixed in with production memorabilia and minutes of meetings; these records substantiate Benardete's writing. Since Benardete and her husband worked in the Playhouse business office for years (see Benardete, introduction and note in Neighborhood Playhouse gift, MWEX + n.c. 10,292, folder 7, New York Public Library for the Performing Arts), she likely had access to documents that have not survived, and I do not question her figures. Her discussions of the Lewisohn endowment appear on pages 60–61, 326–30, 367–68, 448–53, 573–75.

15. Lawrence Langner, "The Magic Curtain," in Theatre Guild, *The History of the Theatre Guild, the First Fifteen Years, 1919–1934* (New York: Artcraft Litho. and Ptg., 1934), 102, and Poggi, *Theater in America*, 122.

16. Dickinson, "Ten Years," 135. Others echo Dickinson's remarks; see also Macgowan, *Footlights,* or books by Constance D'Arcy MacKay, Sheldon Cheney, or Oliver M. Sayler.

17. Benardete, "Neighborhood Playhouse," 368.

18. Ibid., 323–30.

19. Ibid., 367.

20. Theaters were subject to licenses, which the Neighborhood Playhouse at first avoided because of its settlement connection. Avoiding licensing as a theater allowed the Neighborhood Playhouse great freedom; for example, it could perform Sundays. The stagehands' union was the first one to which the Neighborhood Playhouse capitulated, paying union wages to workers. As indicated in her book, Alice did not like the loss of freedom of the stage that attended union regulations, and she particularly bemoaned taking any stagehand the union chose to send rather than cultivating stagehands as part of the company.

21. Winthrop Ames tried to introduce the New Stagecraft in 1909, but his endeavor at the New Theatre in New York failed.

22. Macgowan, *Footlights*, 50.

23. Crowley, *Neighborhood Playhouse*, 100.

24. Ibid., 219.

25. Benardete, "Neighborhood Playhouse," 575.

26. Percy Hammond, "Neighborhood Playhouse to Suspend Work," *New York Herald Tribune*, April 11, 1927.

27. Alice Lewisohn, "Letter to Percy Hammond," *New York Herald Tribune*, April 24, 1927. For initial coverage of the closing announcement, see Percy Hammond, "The Theatre," in *New York Herald Tribune*, April 11, 1927, and April 17, 1927; John Anderson, "Two on the Aisle," *New York Evening Post*, April 11, 1927. Clippings in Alice Lewisohn Crowley Scrapbooks, MWEZ + n. c. 9666, New York Public Library for the Performing Arts.

3

WHEEDLED, BULLIED, OR CAJOLED: BANKING ON EVA LE GALLIENNE

Robert A. Schanke

> It must be remembered that in 1926 there was no cultural explosion. There were no foundations, great or small, set up to help the arts. . . . Before the Great Depression, rich people were immensely rich and could do what they liked with their money—even keep it. No high taxes limited their fortunes. . . . One had to wheedle, bully, or cajole—and I did all three shamelessly. [I had] no qualms about asking rich people for their money. [1]

Such was Eva Le Gallienne's humble confession of how she struggled in 1926 to find patrons to fund her Civic Repertory Theatre: namely, Alice De Lamar, Otto Kahn, and Mary Bok. A few years earlier, in 1920, she had opened on Broadway to rave reviews for her performance in Arthur Richman's comedy *Not So Long Ago*. Soon after, she stunned the critics once again with her poetic and sensitive acting in Ferenc Molnár's *Liliom*. When she starred in Molnár's *The Swan* in 1923, she was hailed as one of the major artists of the American theater. Still, regardless of all the great accolades, Le Gallienne became restless when the long run of *The Swan* ended. She simply yearned for a theater without stars, without long runs, without high ticket prices, and without typecasting.

Also troubling her were the shortcomings she saw in her future career on Broadway. Critics had begun to mention her inability to play feminine passion. As one reporter described it, she "seldom rings true in scenes where she is called upon to reciprocate masculine ardor. The soft, feminine note is missing."[2] Questions whirled in her mind: Were the critics using her sexuality against her? Were they offended by her lesbianism? Was she going to be blackballed by the male-dominated Broadway establishment that considered her lesbianism a threat to its masculine superiority? Maybe she needed to stop bowing to the patriarchal Broadway system, she thought, and instead strike out on her own. If she was refused entry into their club, why not start her own? But how to finance it?

Since 1921, when Le Gallienne had embarked on a romantic relationship with Mercedes de Acosta, an aspiring playwright, the two women had often talked of producing de Acosta's script about Joan of Arc, with Le Gallienne starring as Joan. The plan was to premiere the play in Paris, followed by productions in London and New York. Their ultimate goal was then to open their own theater in New York, which they would name after the great actress Eleonora Duse. The owner of a theater in Paris was interested in the play, but with one condition: the women must find American backers. Mrs. Harold McCormick (Edith Rockefeller), of Chicago, initially expressed interest, but in November 1924, when she met de Acosta and Le Gallienne and learned that the two women were lovers, she quickly withdrew her support. At virtually the last hour, de Acosta suggested that they approach Alice De Lamar, a lesbian millionaire whom she had met a few years earlier. Le Gallienne agreed. If they could persuade Alice to love the project, Le Gallienne wrote, everything would work out beautifully.[3]

Alice De Lamar

When her father died in 1918 and left her $10 million (close to $200 million today), Alice De Lamar became one of the wealthiest young women in the country. In 1878, her father, known as the Captain, conceived the idea that ultimately created his fortune. When the silver fever broke out in Leadville, Colorado, he visited several mines and eventually purchased and mined his own claim. Later, he discovered and mined a vein of rich gold and silver in Idaho as well as a nickel mine in Nevada. In fact, mining towns in both Nevada and Idaho are named after him. He served as a senator in the Idaho state legislature. In 1891, he sold half of his interest in his Idaho mines for $2 million and subsequently moved to New York City.

Soon after that, the Captain married Nellie Virginia Sands. They lived most of the time in Paris, and on April 23, 1895, their daughter, Alice Antoinette, was born. After her parents' divorce three years later, Alice returned to New York and lived with her father. Undoubtedly to show the city's upper-crust elite that he had "arrived," in 1902, when Alice was seven years of age, the Captain built a lavish mansion, at a cost of $250,000, in the heart of the fashionable Murray Hill district and directly opposite the J. Pierpont Morgan estate.[4] The Captain built still another mansion ten years later. Called "the greatest estate ever built," Pembroke was an eighty-two-room estate built in the French neoclassic style in Glen Cove, New York.[5] It was in good company. Among Glen Cove's other palatial Gold Coast mansions were those of financier J. P. Morgan and five-and-dime magnate F. W. Woolworth.

The Captain endeavored to see his daughter accepted into New York's elite. From the age of twelve, Alice attended the Spence School, founded in 1892 by Clara B. Spence as a sort of college-preparatory school for young ladies. Spence described her school as "a place not of mechanical instruction, but a school of character where the common requisites for all have been human feeling, a sense of humor and the spirit of intellectual and moral adventure." Alice later wrote that the school "brought me the first sense of security I felt since I was five."[6] Often during winter holidays, she accompanied her father on his travels to inspect his mining investments out west. She graduated in 1914, and the next year became vice president of the Spence Alumnae Society.

On February 1, 1915, the Captain hosted a large debutante ball for Alice with four hundred guests at the elite Sherry's Hotel, where the ballrooms were designed to resemble reception rooms in a French palace, and tall mirrored doors reflected the dancers. Records show that in 1916, Alice attended another sumptuous party at Sherry's that Otto Kahn and his wife sponsored for their daughter Maud. Entertainment featured artists Enrico Caruso, Yvette Guilbert, and Mlle Pavlova. Among the one thousand guests was Mercedes de Acosta, who six years later became Eva Le Gallienne's lover.[7]

Alice De Lamar in 1927. Photograph by Arnold Genthe; courtesy of the Library of Congress, Prints and Photographic Division.

In spite of the Captain's aspirations for his daughter, she did not enjoy the ostentatious social events. Her longtime friend Eve Chevalier observed that Alice "never approved of the night-club, multi-marriage, jet-set lives of many of her contemporaries."[8] Wanting to escape from the oppressive Murray Hill mansion, she moved into her own apartment at 375 Park Avenue. She seemed almost relieved when World War I broke out, so she could escape from New York by volunteering for the Red Cross American Women's Ambulance Corps in France.

When the Captain died unexpectedly of pneumonia in 1918, no one had really anticipated the extent of his wealth. Newspapers around the country reported that the Captain had left an estate of $32,282,927. Of this, he established a trust fund of $10 million for Alice, with the provisions that the trust "shall not in any way be subject to the management or control of any husband of hers or of any other person whatsoever. . . . [B]ut, if my said daughter should die without leaving any lawful issue her surviving, then it is my wish and I do direct the principal of said trust fund so held in trust for my said daughter shall fall into and become part of my said residuary estate."[9] He also bequeathed to Alice his country estate.

Except for the modest amounts that he granted to friends, family, and employees and $300,000 to the New York Association for Improving the Condition of the Poor, the remaining bulk of his estate, which included his Murray Hill mansion, he divided equally among Harvard University Medical School, Johns Hopkins University, and the College of Physicians and Surgeons of Columbia University, "for medical research into the cause of disease and into the principles of correct living."[10] Each university received close to $5 million.

A few years after Alice had inherited her fortune, Le Gallienne and de Acosta asked her to back their production of the play about Joan of Arc. Good fortune was with them—they succeeded in gaining Alice's financial support. However, once they arrived in Paris, complications pursued them endlessly.[11] Since the theater they had been promised was too small for the sets designed by Norman Bel Geddes, they had to go elsewhere, reluctantly settling on another theater that cost them $7,000 for thirty days. Le Gallienne and de Acosta had raised a total of $12,000 before leaving New York, mainly from Alice, but out of desperation they had to ask her for an additional $28,000. Historian Kathleen D. McCarthy claims that in those days "Women played a far more limited role as donors . . . in part because they often controlled more limited resources. Even when they did inherit substantial fortunes, these bequests were often hemmed in by restrictive trusts and the executors' whims, checking their access to liquid resources."[12] Luckily for Le Gallienne and de Acosta, Alice was quite the exception. She had total control of her money. Being an acquaintance of de Acosta's certainly contributed to Alice's decision to finance the project. After all, as Teresa Odendahl suggests in her book *Charity Begins at Home*, individuals are more likely to give to individuals, in other words, to people they know.[13] But Alice's motivation was clearly more entangled. She was not only attracted by Le Gallienne's talent; she was clearly in love with her.

When the production closed, Alice invited Le Gallienne to her villa in Italy—without de Acosta. Eventually, as Le Gallienne and de Acosta sailed back to New York, it was clear that their own relationship had ended. Looking back at their breakup more than thirty years later, de Acosta reflected, "I learned many lessons from it [the production of *Jehanne d'Arc*] and it served a number of purposes. Not the least being, that a circumstance during its run opened the way for Eva to have her Civic Repertory Theatre and made the project financially possible for her."[14] Apparently, closer bonds with the wealthy Alice De Lamar showed more promise for achieving Le Gallienne's professional goals than did continuing her relationship with de Acosta.

Soon after Le Gallienne returned to New York, she began working on plans for opening her own theater, choosing to inaugurate the new venture by producing Ibsen's *John Gabriel Borkman* and alternating it in repertory with *The Master Builder*. In a speech at Yale University in December 1925 to promote her theater, Le Gallienne stated her goal for the American theater: "Of the stage and its condition today we might use the words of Christ of the ancient temple: 'This was a house of prayer and ye have made it a den of thieves.' Let us make the theatre of America stand free and high up, with no world peers."[15] Determined to realize her goal, Le Gallienne contacted her second major patron for help, philanthropist Otto Kahn. She certainly knew how he had already supported several other New York theater ventures, and she undoubtedly realized that Kahn knew Alice De Lamar, who had already pledged financial support for her scheme.[16]

Otto H. Kahn

Kahn was considered the modern Medici; Will Rogers called him "The King of New York."[17] Theresa M. Collins provides more information about Kahn and his philanthropy in another essay in this volume. Tortured by ambition and shunned by many of the New York elite because he was Jewish, he built a lavish mansion on Fifth Avenue, hoping it would bring him acceptance. Located directly opposite of what is now the Cooper-Hewitt Museum, the mansion boasted a massive stone fireplace, a recital hall that could seat 150 people, and a dining room for 40. It is now the Convent of the Sacred Heart School.

Eva Le Gallienne must have known that Kahn was an old friend of her father's, English poet and novelist Richard Le Gallienne. They had occasionally dined together in London in the early 1920s. Their friendship may have opened some doors for Eva Le Gallienne, but, more important, her dream of presenting the European classics in a repertory system echoed Kahn's dream of making New York a cultural capital of the world. He had seen the Elizabeth Robins's productions of Ibsen in London (probably accompanied by Richard Le Gallienne) and was thrilled that his friend's daughter planned to champion the playwright in the United States.

At his suggestion, Le Gallienne embarked in the spring of 1926 on a tour with her two Ibsen productions, traveling to major East Coast cities and as far west as Chicago. Kahn believed her proposal would benefit from the tour's publicity, so he lent her $5,000 to act as a "small backlog for the tour in case of need." The tour was so successful that she was able to pay it back quickly. When she returned to New York, she put five crisp, $1,000 bills into an envelope and addressed it, "To Mr. Kahn from Mr. Ibsen with many thanks."[18] Kahn was impressed: "The loans I make are seldom repaid," he said, "and this is the very first time I've been repaid in cash." He knew that the tour and fund-raising were grueling, but he told her that he was pleased that her "faith continues both unabated and militant."[19] He backed up his enthusiasm by lending her an additional $18,000 and guaranteeing the annual rent of $20,000 for the theater she planned to use on Fourteenth Street.[20]

Plans began immediately to sponsor a benefit dinner for Le Gallienne's Civic Repertory Theatre at Kahn's Cold Spring Harbor mansion. A few years earlier, Kahn had built the second-largest home in the country. On a 443-acre lot, the 127-room mansion boasted a mammoth sweeping marble staircase, 20 lavish bedrooms for guests, 49 fireplaces, and a 2,500-square-foot ballroom. Currently, this mansion is in the process of being restored and converted into a luxury health spa. In 1941, Orson Welles filmed the exterior and gardens to serve as home for Citizen Kane. Visitors could relax at the indoor pool, play tennis or golf. More than one hundred servants were always on duty. "Everyone is very anxious" to be invited to the benefit, Le Gallienne told him.[21] The guest list included Alice De Lamar.

All the visitors boarded Kahn's private yacht at the New York Yacht Club pier at 3:30 P.M. the afternoon of August 26, 1926, just in time for afternoon tea, and sailed northeast along Sands Point and into Long Island Sound, arriving at Kahn's castle in time for cocktails and dinner.

The evening must have been a success, for headlines announced that Le Gallienne had won pledges of support amounting to $68,000, much of it coming from Kahn and De Lamar.[22] The prospect of her dream certainly looked secure but was cinched when she learned that Mary Bok wanted to be included among the donors.

Mary Bok

Mary Curtis Bok, Philadelphia's Lady Bountiful, was another unique exception to Kathleen D. McCarthy's claims about women philanthropists, perhaps because Mary's father, like Alice's, was a self-made man who had not inherited his fortune. Cyrus Curtis was born in Portland, Maine, in 1850. He was of a middle-class family that lived in a small wooden house. By the age of twenty-two, however, he had begun to build his publishing dynasty, when he founded his first periodical, *The People's Ledger*, in Boston.[23] Seven years later, he moved his family to Philadelphia and launched the weekly *The Tribune and Farmer*. The women's column that his wife wrote for the weekly became so popular that it led to their establishing *Ladies' Home Journal* in 1883. By the end of the century, circulation had surpassed one million.

Curtis founded the Curtis Publishing Company in 1890 and bought *Saturday Evening Post* in 1897 for only $1,000. In less than a decade, its circulation increased from two thousand to more than a million. Advertising revenue topped $1 million per year. He began purchasing newspapers: Philadelphia's *Public Ledger* (1913), Philadelphia's *Press* (1920), *New York Evening Post* (1924), and the Philadelphia *Inquirer* (1930). His reputation was so renowned that he entertained President Calvin Coolidge and his wife on his yacht in 1927. To house all his company's publications under one roof, Curtis built the Curtis Center, at a cost of $3 million. Located on Independence Square, the twelve-story building was hailed as an architectural and engineering masterpiece. For the lobby of the new building, he commissioned a large mural forty-nine feet long and fifteen feet high. Maxfield Parrish designed the image of a dream landscape, and then Louis Tiffany created an intricate glass mosaic consisting of hundreds of thousands of pieces of colored glass.

Cyrus Curtis was a monumental philanthropist. In 1928 and 1929, he made two gifts totaling $300,000 toward the construction of a new science building for Ursinus College. Two years later, the Curtis Clinic

Building at the Jefferson Medical College of Thomas Jefferson University, in Philadelphia, was opened because of his generosity. That same year, in 1931, he gave $300,000 to Drexel University for the construction of a new residence hall. Because he was such an extraordinary benefactor of Camden, Maine, the town named a lighthouse and an island after him in 1934.

Mary Curtis was born August 6, 1876, two years before the family moved to Philadelphia. Her formal education was spent at the Ogontz School for Young Ladies in Abington, Pennsylvania, where she excelled, especially in her studies of piano and organ. At the age of thirteen, she began to accompany her mother on extensive travels in Europe. When she was just sixteen years of age, she became engaged to Edward William Bok and married him on October 22, 1896.

Mary Curtis Bok in 1928. Courtesy of the Curtis Institute of Music.

Her husband had emigrated to New York from the Netherlands with his parents in 1870, when he was seven years old. The young Edward shouldered several jobs when he was not in school—cleaning shop windows, selling bakery goods, delivering newspapers, even writing a social column for the *Brooklyn Eagle*. He dropped out of school at the age of thirteen to become an office boy for the Western Union Telegraph Company. Wanting to become a journalist, he began writing a newsy, readable literary letter to supplement book reviews in the *New York Star*. His column, "Literary Leaves," was soon picked up by forty-five newspapers, including the *Philadelphia Times*, where Cyrus Curtis read it each week. On October 20, 1889, Curtis selected Edward Bok to become the new editor of *Ladies' Home Journal*, a position he held until his retirement thirty years later, in 1919. His autobiography, *The Americanization of Edward Bok* (1920), was a best seller and won a Pulitzer Prize.

As was his father-in-law, Bok was interested in music. In 1916, he informed the president of the Philadelphia Orchestra Association that he would guarantee the deficit of the orchestra for five years, but only if the gift remained strictly anonymous. Following his retirement, he devoted himself to humanitarian causes. In 1923, he established the American Peace Award of $100,000 and endowed the Woodrow Wilson Chair of Government at Williams College as well as the Woodrow Wilson professorship of literature at Princeton University. Mary and her husband had two sons and lived in Merion, Pennsylvania, a suburb six miles from the Philadelphia City Hall.

Following her father's lead, Mary Bok also became a major philanthropist. Her focus was the arts. In 1917, she donated $150,000 to erect a three-story building to house Philadelphia's Settlement Music School. The school's goal was to provide music training to young immigrant children. Seven years later, with a gift of $12 million, she purchased three buildings on the prestigious Rittenhouse Square and opened the Curtis Institute of Music. All students received full-tuition and merit-based scholarships. As pianist Josef Hofmann explained in 1927, when he was on the faculty, the goal was "to hand down through contemporary masters the great traditions of the past; to teach students to build on this heritage for the future."[24]

Soon after she opened the Curtis Institute, Mary Bok met Eva Le Gallienne and became the Civic Rep's biggest benefactor, "writing checks every year of twenty-five or fifty thousand dollars with no strings attached."

"She loved Le Gallienne," recalled her stepson, "and she had this deep admiration and understanding of what Eva was trying to do and what she needed."[25]

During the Civic's second season, Le Gallienne was able to expand her operation by opening a free school for actors, called The Apprentice Group and funded in part by Bok. Each spring, Le Gallienne auditioned some three hundred applicants and selected twenty to thirty students. Those who were accepted attended all rehearsals of the Civic Rep and played as "supers" in the productions. They were charged no fee, and though they were guaranteed no salary, they were not allowed to have outside employment. The four best apprentices each year were paid to remain for a second season, through a scholarship fund provided by Bok. Among the apprentices who started their careers in this school were John Garfield, Arnold Moss, Howard da Silva, Bobby Lewis, May Sarton, and J. Edward Bromberg. By the Civic's sixth season, five among the twenty-eight actors in the permanent company had come up through the apprenticeship program. No wonder Le Gallienne called Mary Bok her "fairy godmother."

Until the onslaught of the Great Depression, Le Gallienne was able to continue wheedling, bullying, or cajoling wealthy donors to subsidize her work. With the support of her three major patrons, dozens of the Civic Rep's productions were critically acclaimed, including productions of *The Cradle Song*, *Romeo and Juliet*, *Hedda Gabler*, *Alice in Wonderland*, *Peter Pan*, *Camille*, *The Three Sisters*, and *The Cherry Orchard*. By the end of the 1932–33 season, however, she had received only $43,000 in donations, about 75 percent of what she needed.[26] A major cause of her economic problems was losing the support of her angels. By 1933, the economic depression and ill health plagued Kahn. He had been unable to pay federal taxes in 1930, 1931, and 1932. He had resigned from the Board of the Metropolitan Opera and from the vice presidency of the New York Philharmonic Society. It is certain that he wanted to continue his support of Le Gallienne. In a letter written in 1930, Kahn wrote to her father, "As for your daughter Eva, she is one of the artistic treasures of New York, apart from being a rare and delightful person. I owe her much more than she owes me."[27] But he was in no position now to help her and her fading dream. He died in 1934.

The situation with Mary Bok was equally troublesome. Straining her usual financial generosity was the death of Mary Bok's father. In the spring of 1932, he was stricken with a severe heart attack that hospitalized him for three weeks. He never fully recovered and died in June 1933. Her stepmother died of heart disease exactly one week after her father's initial heart attack. Although Bok must have known she eventually would acquire millions, she also knew that the new tax law passed by Congress in 1932 to combat the Great Depression was bound to eat into her inheritance. The tax on high incomes had risen from 25 percent to 63 percent; the estate tax was doubled to the rate of 70 percent. Obviously, it would take weeks and months to settle the estate before she could assess her financial picture. Reluctantly, she informed Le Gallienne that she would not be able to continue her annual donation. She simply "did not have the cash" to give her.[28]

At the very time that Le Gallienne needed Alice De Lamar not only to continue but also to increase her support, De Lamar was also reluctant to help. Beginning in 1915, she had made regular winter trips to Palm Beach, Florida, where she had become close friends with architect Addison Mizner. Although Mizner had been the premiere architect of Boca Raton and Palm Beach millionaires, with his Moorish, Spanish revival architecture, by 1928 he was nearly bankrupt. Always his champion, De Lamar continued to assist Mizner financially until he died on February 5, 1933. And, like Mary Bok, she feared how much the new tax laws were going to eat into her wealth. She had not lost her money during the Great Depression, but she could not assume the burden of funding Le Gallienne's theater by herself.

Aware that she could not afford to open the theater in the fall of 1932, Le Gallienne sublet the building to another theater group and toured with her acting company for two years, before finally closing the books forever on the Civic Repertory Theatre. Rather than feeling defeated by the Civic Rep's demise, Le Gallienne and her patrons should have celebrated their many victories. During its ten years of existence, the Civic Repertory Theatre presented thirty-seven plays—including five by Ibsen, two by Shakespeare, and four by Chekhov. Its was the New York English-language premiere of *The Three Sisters*. In fact, Modern Library announced that the Civic Rep "undoubtedly has done more to familiarize America with the work of the great Russian dramatist than any other group."[29] The Civic Rep presented three world premieres, and one of the scripts it produced, Susan Glaspell's *Alison's House*, won a Pulitzer Prize.

Le Gallienne had, indeed, maintained her goal of repertory and low ticket prices. From the very beginning, the average attendance had been about 78 percent of capacity, but by the last season in the theater, the Civic Rep was playing to nearly 94 percent. One critic noted that the audiences were made up of "People who have come to the theatre not for something to do after dinner, but because they love the theatre. One really ought to go there about once a month just to recapture the feeling of theatregoing."[30] She was selected for the *Nation* magazine's roll of honor for 1927 and 1930 and was on the cover of *Time* magazine. Le Gallienne herself had come to be regarded as a "Young Goddess, an inspiration," said Burgess Meredith. The high royalty of the American theater consisted of five people—Katharine Cornell, Helen Hayes, Alfred Lunt, Lynn Fontanne, and Le Gallienne. "To have a role in one of their plays was more than a privilege," he remarked. "It was a kind of knighthood."[31]

Epilogue

Even after Le Gallienne's Civic Repertory Theatre closed, Mary Bok and Alice De Lamar continued as patrons of Eva Le Gallienne. In 1935, Bok urged Le Gallienne to "keep on and not lose courage and give up" on her dream of establishing a repertory theatre. She gave Le Gallienne $10,000 as seed money to help fund any project that would allow Le Gallienne to "be her own master."[32] With added financial assistance from De Lamar, Le Gallienne conducted a national tour of *Camille* and a new production of Ibsen's *Rosmersholm*, ending with its limited engagement on Broadway. Two years later, Bok gave Le Gallienne an additional $50,000 to start up a new repertory company that would open at the Cape Playhouse in Dennis, Massachusetts. The plan was to premiere with Le Gallienne directing and starring in *Hamlet* and then to add Chekov's *The Seagull* to the schedule. By that time, De Lamar was living in Weston, Connecticut, near Le Gallienne's home, so she invited the company to live at her expense at the nearby Cobb's Mill Inn, which she also owned. After a few weeks of rehearsing, however, Le Gallienne abandoned the project, realizing that she had been unable to attract quality actors to the company.

When Le Gallienne, Margaret Webster, and Cheryl Crawford attempted to establish the American Repertory Theatre in 1946, Bok donated $10,000 to the project. When that scheme collapsed after two seasons, Le

Gallienne worried about money and plunged into a deep depression until she received an unexpected check from Bok. "What would I have done without her in my life?" Le Gallienne wondered. "Wonderful woman. Now I can stay here in peace & work on the Ibsen prefaces & the garden."[33] In 1950, Le Gallienne published the *Introduction to and Translation of Six Plays by Henrik Ibsen*. The following year, when Le Gallienne told Bok of her plans to write her autobiography as well as a biography of Eleonora Duse, Bok provided the funds for Le Gallienne to travel to Italy for research and additional funds so that she could commit herself totally to her writing. Bok assisted many artists. "Mary had a list," her stepson remarked. "Nobody knows the extent of the list. I was on it, my sister was on it, Le Gallienne was on it. I don't know how many others. Her interest was in creative people who needed her help."[34] When Mary Bok died on January 4, 1970, Le Gallienne reflected on "all I owe her through the years and my heart is full of love & sadness & immense gratitude."[35]

Alice De Lamar was even more considerate. During the 1950s, 1960s, and 1970s, she sent Le Gallienne checks whenever she knew that her friend needed money. "She really is marvelously good to me," Le Gallienne noted in her diary.[36] Undoubtedly, Alice's most generous gift to Le Gallienne came upon her death. Le Gallienne was breathless when the will was read. In essence, the will bequeathed to Le Gallienne one-fourth of De Lamar's entire estate. Le Gallienne's share totaled over $1 million.[37] "I knew her 60 years," Le Gallienne recalled. "She was one of the known good people. (She) donated an immense amount of good but she never wanted it known. She used her money in the best way possible. It is very sad for all of us to lose her."[38]

In 1986, when *American Theatre* magazine celebrated the silver anniversary of the nonprofit theater movement in America, it featured Le Gallienne and proclaimed that her efforts foreshadowed "a changing role for the theatre a generation in advance."[39] Along with Tyrone Guthrie, John Houseman, and Zelda Fichandler, Le Gallienne was credited for being one of the theater artists who "played a part in shaping America's nonprofit theatre."[40] Without the financial nod, however, from De Lamar, Kahn, and Bok, the genius of Le Gallienne might have gone unnoticed. Indeed, Eva Le Gallienne succeeded because she was blessed with a talent to wheedle, bully, and cajole . . . Simply, she did what it takes.

Notes

1. Civic Repertory Theatre manuscript, Beinecke Rare Book and Manuscript Library, Yale University.

2. Arthur Hornblow, "Mr. Hornblow Goes to the Play," *Theatre Magazine* 38 (December 1923): 15.

3. Le Gallienne to de Acosta, paraphrase of a letter, February 18, 1925, de Acosta Collection, Rosenbach Museum, Philadelphia.

4. The Polish Peoples' Republic purchased the building in 1973. On January 28, 1975, the Landmarks Preservation Commission designated the house as a Landmark.

5. Because of its expensive upkeep, Pembroke was demolished in 1968. The original carriage house is the only building that still stands. The estate now is the Legend Yacht & Beach Club, an exclusive gated enclave of forty-seven luxury waterfront homes.

6. *Palm Beach Life*, March 9, 1915, 10; undated letter from De Lamar to Addison Mizner and quoted in *Florida Architecture*, xv.

7. "The Three Dances Begin," *New York Times*, December 8, 1914; "Debutantes' Receptions," *New York Times*, December 10, 1914; "Alice De Lamar Makes Her Debut," *New York Times*, February 2, 1915; "Gorgeous Ball for Miss Kahn's Debut," *New York Times*, January 8, 1916.

8. Marilyn Burchfield, "DeLamar Created Artists' Haven Here," *Weston Forum* August 1985.

9. Extract from the last will and testament of Joseph R. De Lamar. Quoted in *Columbia Charters*, 1:575–76, Columbia University Archives.

10. "Gives $10,000,000 to Medical Work," *New York Times*, December 10, 1918. The three universities tried to sell the mansion as soon as the will was probated. The house valued at $1 million was finally sold to the National Democratic club for less than $300,000.

11. For a more thorough discussion of this production, see Robert A. Schanke, *"That Furious Lesbian": The Story of Mercedes de Acosta* (Carbondale: Southern Illinois University Press, 2003).

12. Kathleen D. McCarthy, "Twentieth Century Cultural Patronage," in *Alternative Features: Challenging Designs for Arts Philanthropy*, ed. Andrew Patner (Washington, D.C.: Grantsmakers in the Arts, 1994), 6.

13. Teresa Odendahl, *Charity Begins at Home: Generosity and Self-Interest Among the Philanthropic Elite* (New York: Basic Books, 1990), 37.

14. De Acosta, "First Writing," 181, de Acosta Collection, Rosenbach Museum, Philadelphia.

15. "Sees America Hope of Dramatic Art," *New York Times*, December 14, 1925.

16. De Lamar and de Acosta both attended the debutante ball for Kahn's daughter in 1916. Kahn and De Lamar owned houses near each other in Palm

Beach, Florida. Kahn and Alice's father were both members of the New York Yacht Club, and they both had mansions on the Long Island Gold Coast.

17. Ian Drake, "Modern-day Medici: Otto Kahn: Art, Money, & Modern Times," *The Philanthropy Roundtable* (May–June 2003), http://www.philanthropyroundtable.org/article.asp?article=947+paper=O+Cat=148 (accessed August 8, 2006).

18. Helen Sheehy, *Eva Le Gallienne: A Biography* (New York: Alfred A. Knopf, 1996), 138, 140.

19. Letter from Kahn to Eva Le Gallienne, May 5, 1926, Kahn Collection, Princeton University Library.

20. Memorandum in Kahn Collection, dated August 30, 1926. There was no indication of when the loan was to be repaid, but 6 percent interest per annum was suggested. This meant that the loan was payable upon demand but at no specific date.

21. Memo from Le Gallienne to Kahn, August 20, 1926, Kahn Collection, Princeton University Library.

22. For more detailed information about the Civic Repertory, see Robert A. Schanke, *Shattered Applause: The Lives of Eva Le Gallienne* (Carbondale: Southern Illinois University Press, 1992).

23. "Curtis Got Start as Maine Newsboy," *New York Times*, June 7, 1933; and "Cyrus H. K. Curtis Dies in 83rd Year," *New York Times*, June 7, 1933.

24. Maynard Good Stoddard, "A Legacy of Music—The Curtis Institute of Music in Philadelphia," *Saturday Evening Post*, January 2000.

25. Sheehy, *Eva Le Gallienne*, 142. Edward Bok died in 1930, and Mary Curtis Bok married Efrem Zimbalist Sr. in 1943.

26. Auditor's statement of May 6, 1933, Beinecke Rare Book and Manuscript Library, Yale University.

27. Letter from Richard Le Gallienne to Kahn, February 3, 1930; and letter from Kahn to Richard Le Gallienne, March 4, 1930, Kahn Collection, Princeton University Library.

28. Sheehy, *Eva Le Gallienne*, 217.

29. Pressbooks of the Civic Repertory Theatre, Beinecke Rare Book and Manuscript Library, Yale University.

30. *New York Times*, February 15, 1931.

31. Burgess Meredith, "A Marchbanks Fondly Recalls His Candida," *New York Times*, June 16, 1974.

32. Letter from Le Gallienne to her mother, April 24, 1935, quoted in Sheehy, *Eva Le Gallienne*, 237.

33. Eva Le Gallienne diary entry for April 30, 1948, quoted in Sheehy, *Eva Le Gallienne*, 298.

34. Sheehy, *Eva Le Gallienne*, 298.

35. Eva Le Gallienne diary entry for January 5, 1970, quoted in Sheehy, *Eva Le Gallienne*, 390.

36. Eva Le Gallienne diary entry for September 5, 1968, quoted in Sheehy, *Eva Le Gallienne*, 387.

37. Alice De Lamar, will, October 6, 1981, Westport Probate Office, Westport, CT.

38. "Alice De Lamar Supported Palm Beach Art Community," *Palm Beach Daily News*, September 8, 1983.

39. Peter Zeisler, "Toward Brave New Worlds," *American Theatre* 3 (November 1986): 5, 20.

40. Ibid.

4

QUEEN OF OFF BROADWAY: LUCILLE LORTEL

Alexis Greene

Attorney Street on Manhattan's Lower East Side is a short street by New York standards. Beginning at a wide thoroughfare, East Houston, it travels three blocks south before hitting the entrance and exit ramps of the Williamsburg Bridge, where it leaps the parkway and picks up for another three blocks until dissolving into Hester Street and the remains of a once-populous Jewish neighborhood. Most of the tenements that used to line Attorney Street have disappeared. Victims of fire, demolition, and the shifting patterns of urban lives, they have been replaced by garages and abandoned, garbage-strewn lots.

But on December 16, 1900, when Lucille Wadler was born at 153 Attorney Street, this was a bustling if poor neighborhood. Peddlers' carts filled the street from dawn until dusk; women stood on fire escapes and shouted across to their friends or hung laundry between buildings that were airless in summer and icy in winter. In a ground-floor shop at 153 Attorney, Lucille's maternal grandfather, Heiman Moskowitz, repaired watches and clocks. A few blocks further east, Lucille's father, Harry

Wadler, worked as a tailor, probably sewing men's cloaks and suits. Both Harry Wadler and Lucille's mother, Anny, had emigrated from Poland with their respective families when they were children, had married young, and were struggling to extricate themselves from the ghetto.

In 1900, the Lower East Side, where Lucille Wadler was born, and the New York theater, where, as Lucille Lortel, she would one day play a significant role, shared an aggressive approach to the world: each arena was rough-and-tumble and determined to survive. But after those similarities are taken into account, few places could have been farther apart than the overflowing tenements of Attorney Street and the profitable engine of the American theater known as Broadway. There the competitive, hardscrabble life of the stage was hidden behind glittering buildings, elaborate scenery, and glamorous costumes.

Broadway was the hub of the nation's theatrical universe. From its stages and producers' offices radiated the plays that took stars across the country, in seemingly endless circuits of big cities and small towns, to perform in opera houses; provincial halls; and the final stopping places, winter- and summer-stock theaters. As for "Off Broadway," the concept did not even exist in the United States in 1900, although within two decades the community theaters of the Little Theater Movement would begin to provide alternatives to Broadway's commercial productions.

How or when Lucille Wadler fell in love with theater is unknown. She studied dance as a youngster and, in later years, talked about how she always wanted to act in movies. Certainly her family possessed an artistic bent. Her mother Anny's two brothers were musicians, and Lucille's older brother, Mayo, was a child prodigy on the violin. Her sister, Ruth, became a painter. As Harry Wadler established his own dress-making business and made money, he moved his family from the Lower East Side to the Bronx, and finally, in 1914, to one of the elegant new apartment houses lining the upper stretches of Riverside Drive. By the time Lucille was a teenager, she had undoubtedly seen a good amount of theater and preferred theatergoing to school (she was a middling student at her finishing school, and there is no record that she graduated). Acting probably looked a likely career to an attractive, personable, somewhat spoiled, starstruck girl.

From 1920, when she entered the American Academy of Dramatic Arts' one-year training program, until 1931, when she stopped acting, Lucille Lortel immersed herself in theater (the stage name was a friend's suggestion; Lortel liked the alliteration). The academy promised to prepare a young actor for commercial productions, and Lortel, with her dark eyes, voluptuous figure, and long dark hair, was soon typecast as the exotic woman with a low reputation. Thus she went into David Belasco's popular production of Willard Mack's *The Dove*, a sultry melodrama set in Mexicana, Mexico; thus she toured with Florence Reed in John Colton's hit melodrama *The Shanghai Gesture*, acting the dissipated, half-English, half-Chinese girl Poppy. And she portrayed a half-Spanish dancer named Rosieta in a dreadful one-act called *The Man Who Laughed*, playing top vaudeville houses opposite silent film star Sessue Hayakawa. It was, she always believed, the highlight of her acting career.

Lortel toured with Hayakawa in 1928. In October 1929, the stock market plummeted, and aside from a couple of movie shorts and a comedy that closed out of town, Lortel could not find acting work. It was not in her nature to give up, but she had to face that she was nearly thirty years old and not the star she had dreamed of becoming. Theater, too, was being forced to change. "Wall St. Lays an Egg" screamed the famous *Variety* headline after the market crashed, and theater tumbled with it. The number of legitimate houses outside New York declined, and so did the tours that had kept hundreds of actors like Lortel employed.[1]

At some point in 1930, Lortel met an up-and-coming businessman named Louis Schweitzer, whose Russian Jewish family had emigrated early in the century from Odessa to France and then to the United States. The Schweitzers manufactured cigarette papers, a market that Louis and his two brothers intended to dominate in the United States. On March 23, 1931, on board the S.S. *Leviathan* en route from Paris to New York, Lucille Lortel married Louis Schweitzer and, at his insistence, quit the stage.

The producer Ben Sprecher, who worked for nearly two decades as Lortel's general manager at the Lucille Lortel Theatre, once said that many women with Lortel's wealth might have been satisfied to spend their days shopping and meeting friends for lunch. "Lucille," he said, "got up in the morning and said, 'What are we going to produce today?'"[2]

For ten years of her marriage, Lortel tried the first approach. She vacationed with her husband; gave parties in their Manhattan apartment; and entertained at Fairweather, their eighteen-acre estate in Westport, Connecticut. But Lortel found the socializing dull and the marriage unfulfilling; she and Schweitzer did not have children, and clearly Lortel did not want any. There is evidence in her correspondence that during 1941 she considered starting a stock company but that the plan fell through. Shortly before the United States entered World War II, Lortel and Schweitzer bought a white barn and moved it to their Westport property, intending to keep horses. But the war aborted that scheme, and instead the empty barn hosted celebrity-studded auctions for Russian Relief. At one such event, the comedian Danny Kaye reportedly looked around and said, "You know, this could make a nice little theater."[3]

Like many incipient theatrical producers, Lortel began by investing in Broadway productions. Then, in early summer 1947, when Schweitzer was in Europe on business and, Lortel suspected, carrying on an affair, she attended a backers' audition in somebody's New York City apartment. The place was crowded and hot. It was hard to see or hear the actors, let alone focus on the script for which the producers were trying to raise money. Lortel thought she could easily do the same in Westport and more comfortably besides.[4]

The result was the first summer of the White Barn Tryout Theatre and Lortel's induction into the art of producing. With help from her brother Mayo and theatrical friends eager for their plays to be heard, Lortel put together a summer season of what would now be called staged readings. The second floor of the empty barn acquired a platform at one end, black drapes, and as many folding metal chairs as the room could hold. On a pleasant Sunday evening, July 27, 1947, with only a table and chairs decorating the stage, a cast that included the African American star Canada Lee read a torrid drama about circus life called *Painted Wagon*, by the actors Philip Huston and Elizabeth Goodyear. The script was unmemorable, but the White Barn Tryout Theatre received a warm welcome from both the audience and the press. Even Lortel's husband, away in France, offered support, perhaps from a sense of guilt, perhaps finally realizing that his wife needed a project to occupy her. Indeed, for the rest of their married lives, Schweitzer would funnel both money and business advice to Lortel's theatrical enterprises.

The White Barn proved a valuable training ground for Lortel, especially during its first ten years, when it grew from a season of Sunday-night readings to rehearsed but minimally designed productions on Saturday and Sunday evenings. At the White Barn, Lortel nurtured and exercised her taste in plays, and there she also developed her particular producing style.

The White Barn's first season displayed a conventional roster of superficial Broadway hopefuls, but, by the following year, Lortel was adding plays of some artistic merit: Sean O'Casey's poetic urban drama *Red Roses for Me*, which she tried to move to Broadway; William Saroyan's surrealist *Jim Dandy*; and a play called *A-Day* by the screenwriter Robertson White, who, if not in O'Casey's or Saroyan's league, at least had tried to write a serious drama about the atomic age.

For the 1949 season, Lortel sailed with her husband to Paris, where she saw plays by avant-garde dramatists such as Jean-Paul Sartre and Armand Salacrou. In London, Lortel was exposed to the private "club theaters," a concept that she soon borrowed for the still-evolving White Barn (briefly renamed the White Barn Club Theatre). That summer in Westport, she imported British playwright Shirley Cocks's *Gingerbread House*, about a young artist dominated alternately by his mother and a homosexual attorney, and she also brought in a young American director named Sidney Lumet to stage Federico García Lorca's *Don Perlimplin and Belisa in the Garden*. In November, during a short-lived attempt at a fall season, Lortel presented a non-Equity group called the People's Drama Company in one performance of *They Shall Not Die*, a play about the Scottsboro case.

What influenced Lortel's eclectic taste? From her brother Mayo, who was an advocate of modern music, she perhaps absorbed an appreciation for the avant-garde. From her theatergoing during the 1930s, when she must have seen the plays of Clifford Odets and Sidney Kingsley, who became a close friend, she possibly felt the pull of dramas that possessed truthful human relationships and strong social impulses. She saw that the American National Theatre and Academy (ANTA), of which Lortel became a member around the time she started the White Barn, was desperately trying to bring plays of quality to the American theater.

Lortel's detractors—and there were many—liked to say that she took whatever material canny advisers sent her way. But even if she did entertain other people's suggestions—and how could she not, given the volume of slots to be filled and, eventually, the quantity of scripts she received?—ultimately she relied on her instincts. Colleagues such as the theatrical designer Ralph Alswang always cited Lortel's eagerness to go anywhere to find new work, even if she had to ferret out a downtown loft and climb five flights to do it. Long before her poor eyesight made reading difficult, Lortel did not read scripts, and her explanation suggests she may have been slightly dyslexic. "I find it difficult to read a lot of plays," she told a gathering in Westport in 1993. "I have to go over and over."[5] Instead, throughout her producing career, she required that plays be read out loud to her, or that she see a play in performance, and then she would respond to what she heard and saw.

After choosing plays, the aspect of producing about which Lortel felt most confident was publicity. Probably it was a skill she had developed as an actor, when she needed to corner a production's press agent to get her name in the papers. Certainly, hers was a hands-on approach, even after she hired publicity mavens to help. A fearless promoter, she used every means available to tell the world about herself and what she finally called the White Barn Theatre: press releases announcing that a play or playwright was being presented for the first time (even if not the case); parties in New York at the Plaza Hotel, where she and her husband then lived during most of the year; parties in Westport; interviews on radio and in the printed press. She always invited celebrities to attend her Sunday nights at the White Barn and insisted on being photographed with them for local newspapers. Her skill at attracting names, both onstage and off, fed on itself. The more talent scouts, movie and theater producers, and advertising executives she could round up for the audience, the better the actors who agreed to appear onstage; the better the onstage talent, the greater the number of agents, producers, and celebrities who made the train- or car-ride from New York.

As for Lortel's handling of money, her first years producing at the White Barn ingrained the habits that she would take to Off Broadway. Unlike most producers of summer theaters, she did not have to worry about profits at the box office, because her husband financed the theater at about $20,000 to $30,000 a season. Even after the State of Connecticut granted the White Barn charitable foundation status in 1951, Lortel never raised funds from outside sources; the Schweitzers used the charitable designation for tax purposes. Reliance on her husband's money gave Lortel artistic and managerial control, but later, when she produced commercially, she proved relatively ineffectual (as she herself admitted) when it came to raising money from other angels; it was always easier to write a check herself. Reliance on Schweitzer's money also brought her the reputation of being a rich woman dabbling in the theater, a description that distressed her and that she was never able to shake.

Lortel was rich and frugal. "Tight as the skin on an onion," was how Ralph Alswang's daughter Hope described her.[6] Certainly Lortel defended the payment arrangement she had engineered for the White Barn with Actors' Equity Association: in lieu of paying her performers Equity's summer-stock salary, the White Barn Foundation donated $125 to Equity Library Theatre for each White Barn production and gave each actor only $10 plus room and board, a surprising arrangement, perhaps, from a woman who once had struggled to earn a living on the stage. It is apparent also from the records of the White Barn and the Theatre de Lys that Schweitzer kept a close watch on how his money was being spent. He was often the one who negotiated contracts, approved purchases, and paid bills—aspects of producing that Lortel would turn over to others after Schweitzer died.

But no personality is cut and dried, least of all Lucille Lortel's. Generosity frequently balanced thriftiness. As a commercial producer, Lortel would often keep a show open with her own money. As owner of the Theatre de Lys, she would often forgo a production's rent if the producers were unable to make their weekly nut. And rarely did she profit financially from what she produced. Lortel produced theater out of enthusiasm for new plays and a need for personal recognition—not from a desire to make money.

When Lucille Lortel was growing up, alternatives to Broadway started appearing on the fringes of the city's theatrical life. The Neighborhood Playhouse set up shop on Grand Street in 1915, the same year that Lawrence Langner established the Washington Square Players in Greenwich Village. In 1916, a band of theater artists who had started the Provincetown Players in Massachusetts launched themselves from a small space in a Greenwich Village brownstone. During the 1930s, politically leftist theaters sprang up, and in 1939 the German director Erwin Piscator came to New York and established an experimental base with his Dramatic Workshop at the New School for Social Research. These organizations often contributed invaluable artists to the American theater, but the companies themselves tended to dissolve, or regroup and join the mainstream, as the Washington Square Players did in 1919, when it became the Theatre Guild.

During World War II, alternatives to Broadway generally evaporated. When the war was over, however, a fresh generation of theater artists was feeling locked out by Broadway's style, values, and financing, and turned, perhaps because of its lingering bohemian aura and low rents, to Greenwich Village. Starting around 1947, this neighborhood of small buildings and oddly angled streets became the crucible for a new theatrical movement: Off Broadway.

Stuart W. Little, who chronicled Off Broadway from his perch at the *New York Herald Tribune*, described the new phenomenon as "a state of mind, a set of production conditions, a way of looking at theater at every point at odds with Broadway's patterns."[7] Off Broadway meant miniscule production budgets, intimate and even grungy theaters, unknown actors working for little or no money, and audiences willing to take a chance on an untried American or avant-garde European author. For a producer such as Lortel, who felt passionately about new plays and also liked to be at the forefront of artistic events, Off Broadway offered an ideal opportunity.

In a sense, the story of Lucille Lortel and Off Broadway began on the night of October 28, 1952, when Lortel and her husband attended the opening—and the closing—of a musical called *Frankie and Johnny*, at the newly established Theatre de Lys on Christopher Street. That night, according to Lortel, Louis Schweitzer, perhaps scenting a disaster in the making, decided to buy the handsome 299-seat theater for his wife, so that she could have a foothold in New York and give plays the extended runs they could not receive at the White Barn. The theater's lease owner and producer, a combination visionary and con artist named William de Lys, left New York in the wake of his fiasco, and after three years of legal wrangling, Schweitzer paid around $100,000 to buy both the lease and the theater building. The Schweitzers took possession during the summer of 1955.

But what to install as the first production? The previous year, while the de Lys was in ownership limbo, an interim manager had briefly rented the theater to an acclaimed production of Bertolt Brecht and Kurt Weill's 1928 masterpiece, *The Threepenny Opera. Threepenny*'s producers, Stanley Chase and Carmen Capalbo (also the director), ran into Louis Schweitzer and suggested that they bring the show back to the empty Theatre de Lys. Schweitzer and Lortel agreed, and Lortel signed a rental contract that gave her "in association with" billing on all advertising, publicity, and programs, setting a precedent that Lortel would follow on every production that came into her theater, whether she produced it or not.

Lucille Lortel at the Lucille Lortel Theatre, circa 1991. Jules Alexander photograph.

In fact, Lortel did not produce *The Threepenny Opera*, which reopened on September 20, 1955, and enjoyed a seven-year run. But since that run was in her theater, and she did talk the show up and excuse its rental if box office receipts were low, Lortel became permanently identified as the production's *alma mater*. Few people knew that before *Threepenny* moved into the de Lys, Lortel had been eyeing a British play called *The River*

Line, which she later produced Off Broadway, only to see it close after fifteen performances.

Threepenny was the best thing that could have happened to Lortel, for the show's longevity (it finally closed in 1961 after 2,707 performances) required that she produce elsewhere. She helped bring a concert reading of Sean O'Casey's *I Knock at the Door* to Broadway in 1957 and coproduced his *Cock-a-Doodle Dandy* Off Broadway in 1958. She coproduced Jean Genet's *The Balcony* in 1960 with Circle in the Square.

But from 1956 until 1975, the most productive outlet for Lortel's energy and insights as an Off-Broadway producer was the ANTA Matinee Series, minimal productions that she presented at the de Lys at two-thirty on Tuesday afternoons for the American National Theatre and Academy.

ANTA had been born in 1931 in Philadelphia, where the conductor Leopold Stokowski brought together prominent citizens to advocate for the sort of arts movement that had once started the city's renowned symphony orchestra. Their politicking succeeded, and, in 1935, the seventy-fourth Congress passed a law granting a federal charter to create a people's theater called the American National Theatre and Academy.

ANTA soon ran into difficulties, however. For one thing, Congress did not appropriate any money with its charter, although one year later it funded the Federal Theatre Project, which soon overshadowed ANTA. Then the United States entered World War II, and federal concern about art fell by the wayside. ANTA essentially did not function until 1946, when a group of actors, directors, and producers reconstituted the organization in the hope of making it a resource for the American theater. Relying on members' dues and small private donations, and setting up chapters around the country, ANTA arranged for guest artists to work with university and community theaters and provided technical advice and a personnel service. For two seasons, ANTA sponsored the Experimental Theatre, which produced noncommercial plays on limited budgets, and then, in 1950, the group launched a sequel called the ANTA Play Series. ANTA served as the United States Centre of the International Theatre Institute. The organization's aims were idealistic and, given its inadequate fund-raising, overreaching: it wanted to unify the American theater and bring excellent, affordable productions to all American audiences.

Around the time Lortel acquired the Theatre de Lys, ANTA's New York chapter—the organization's largest and most active branch—was entertaining high-flown thoughts of establishing an acting company that would put on readings, workshops, and productions. As Lortel recollected years later, she cut through that grandiose thinking and said, "In the meantime, until you've raised your money, you could have my theater."[8] She and Henry Hewes, drama critic for the *Saturday Review* and an active ANTA member, organized a staged reading of *Cry, the Beloved County*, Felicia Komai's adaptation of Alan Paton's acclaimed novel, and on May 15, 1956, with a cast that included Clayton Corbin, Henderson Forsythe, Earle Hyman, and Rosetta Le Noire, and with the expressionist drops for *Threepenny* as background, they presented it to an enthusiastic audience. The audience was so responsive, in fact, that beginning in fall 1956, Hewes and Lortel, who billed herself as the Matinee Series' artistic director, organized eight more presentations for that theater season. Hewes soon dropped from the scene, realizing, no doubt, that Lortel was going to take charge and do things her way. After all, the de Lys was her theater.

The Matinee Series echoed aspects of the White Barn, which certainly was its model. Like the one- or two-night presentations in Westport, the Matinee Series was of a scope that Lortel could lay her hands on and control, unlike commercial productions, where she usually turned the nitty-gritty of management over to someone else. She again cajoled Actors' Equity Association into being flexible about fees; she spent days and nights hearing and seeing plays; she funneled information to a press agent but added her own personal brand of public relations, which included getting on the phone to critics, journalists, friends, and fellow producers—anyone who could spread the word, bring in an audience, or move a play to an actual run. She was well known for keeping a sharp eye on seating arrangements, both at the White Barn and at the Matinee Series. A patron only received an actual ticket at the door, so up until curtain time, Lortel could arrange seating to give the most influential people the best spots. After the performance, there might well be a discussion with the playwright and invited theater critics.

Lortel's work paid off: critics and people in the business came regularly, as did subscribers to the inexpensive series. Unfortunately, many of the plays Lortel presented received merely that single performance, and she urged ANTA to produce tours of the best work. But ANTA simply did not possess the resources. So, Lortel capitalized on a contact with the Library of Congress, and from 1960 until 1975, she brought at least one Matinee

Series production to Washington, D.C., usually for two performances in the Coolidge Auditorium. In April 1962, following a performance and discussion of Eugene Ionesco's *The Shepherd's Chameleon* and Edward Albee's satiric one-act *Fam and Yam*, the *Washington Post* theater critic Richard Coe wrote a positive review and dubbed Lortel "The Queen of Off-Broadway."

The Matinee Series built upon the White Barn's shrewd, eclectic mixture of art forms, unknown talents and revered stars, classic and avant-garde plays. The series' aim, written down before it began, was to have five categories of offerings: plays chosen because an actor wanted to try an unusual role; plays produced on minimal budgets, but with the help of actors and directors from the commercial theater; revivals of classics; readings; and presentations that brought together different art forms, such as adaptations of novels or poems for the stage.[9] A glance at the 1958–59 season, for instance, reveals a minimal production of Jean Giraudoux's *Song of Songs* (previously at the White Barn); a new play by Meade Roberts called *Maidens and Mistresses at Home at the Zoo*; dance dramas based on Federico Garçia Lorca's *Blood Wedding*, J. M. Synge's *Riders to the Sea*, and James Thurber's short story *The Catbird Seat*; *Curtain Up*, a one-woman show in which Ethel Barrymore Colt traveled the history of the American musical theater through song; Sophocles' *Philoctetes*, adapted by director Stephen Porter and actor Ellis Rabb, paired with André Gide's modern *Philoctetes*; and Tennessee Williams's *I Rise in Flames, Cried the Phoenix.*

But if Lortel modeled the Matinee Series on the White Barn, the Matinee Series differed significantly in terms of context. While the White Barn was both a showcase for artists and a source of local entertainment, the series functioned as a showcase and a consistent, highly visible contribution to the needs and identity of Off Broadway. This was a time when the American theater was playing intellectual catch-up with Europe. Off Broadway, by offering Ionesco, Brecht, O'Casey, Beckett, and their antecedents, was stepping in to close the gap. What is more, aside from Tennessee Williams and Arthur Miller, few American playwrights of high caliber had emerged since the 1940s; where were they going to come from—where did the theater exist to take the risk of airing their untried plays—if not Off Broadway? As Stuart W. Little himself pointed out, the idea of producing one entry a week, with minimal rehearsal and decor and with no commercial goals, sounded almost naive initially.[10] But over the course of nineteen years and more than one hundred presentations, Lortel's Matinee Series functioned as a kind of bellwether for a new American theater. Looking back over Lortel's programs, one finds the names of actors, directors, and authors who would feed the American theater for decades to come, as well as the names of many who simply contributed their talents and time to the creation of a vigorous new theater.

While the ANTA Matinee Series was progressing, Lortel's career and life were undergoing a transformation. After *Threepenny*'s orchestra played "Mack the Knife" one last time, on December 17, 1961, Lortel found herself, like most theater owners, with an empty house to fill. The long run had spoiled her, and she and Schweitzer now hired a general manager to bring rentals into the de Lys. She, of course, continued to look for new authors to produce, and one of the finest that she brought to light was the South African Athol Fugard, whose drama *The Blood Knot* she produced Off Broadway at the Cricket Theatre in 1964. Then, in 1971, Louis Schweitzer died, leaving Lortel an estate worth millions of dollars in stocks and real estate, and charging her to function as a philanthropist.

It took several years for Lortel to put her husband's injunction into practice. Among other things, Lortel had to recover from the depression of being alone. Her emotional recovery coincided with her decision, in 1975, to end the Matinee Series. Once again, she realized, the New York theater world was undergoing a sea change. Since the mid-1960s, a host of Off-Off-Broadway venues had arisen, all of which pursued a growing number of American dramatists. Lortel's pioneering efforts were being echoed in churches, cafes, and cubbyholes in Greenwich Village and beyond. Caffe Cino, Café La MaMa, Theatre Genesis, the Old Reliable—they drew young writers who, for the time being at least, scorned any semblance of established theater. Even though Lortel's base was Greenwich Village, to this new wave she represented an older, conventional generation, which did not automatically turn to the Matinee Series as an outlet for its work.[11]

The Matinee Series was also competing with not-for-profit institutions like the American Place Theatre and the Chelsea Theatre Center, which could afford to present full productions of the sorts of noncommercial plays to which Lortel was giving minimal productions. ANTA's dream of being the creator of a national theater had faded in the late 1960s, a victim of poor management, meager fund-raising, and perhaps being ahead of its time (the organization would survive as a not-for-profit producer of plays).

Bolstered by the establishment of the National Endowment for the Arts (NEA) in 1965, not-for-profit theaters funded by the NEA and by pro-arts foundations such as Rockefeller and Ford, were, in reality, becoming the national theater. "Theaters . . . subsidized by the government or by grants—will be where the future of the theater will be," Lortel astutely had told reporter Larry DeVine in 1966.[12] Long before Lortel shuttered her Matinee Series, she perceived that its function was being taken over by other kinds of organizations.

It was these not-for-profit organizations to which Lortel began making donations. To be sure, she did not abandon the White Barn or the de Lys (which would be renamed the Lucille Lortel Theatre in 1981), and on occasion she also produced commercially, notably Lee Blessing's *A Walk in the Woods* on Broadway in 1988. But in 1980, she established the Lucille Lortel Foundation, through which she donated several million dollars to the arts, particularly theater, between 1980 and 1999, when she died. Donations might be $50 or $5,000 or $1,000,000, depending upon the recipient's need, aims, and ability to reassure Lortel that her gift was special and would memorialize her, for as she became older, Lortel grew increasingly concerned that she and her work be recognized and remembered. She gave $100,000 to the Actors' Fund of America to create the Lucille Lortel Theatre at the fund's retirement home in New Jersey and, a fervent believer in the value of recording staged work, $1,000,000 to the New York Public Library for the Performing Arts to set up and run the Lucille Lortel Room/Theatre on Film and Tape Archive. Some donations had serious aims: $300,000 to Yale School of Drama and $225,000 to Brown University to foster the work of new dramatists. Gifts could also be quirky but have vital goals: $10,000 to build a gaily colored women's lavatory at the Players, the theatrical club on Gramercy Park that finally admitted women in 1989. A brass plaque on the bathroom door reads "Lucille's Loo."

More than in the past, Lortel became a conventional "angel," often helping not-for-profit companies produce plays or move productions to commercial venues. In this regard, she particularly supported Off Broadway's Circle Repertory Company and the dramas of Lanford Wilson, and, at one point, she arranged to leave both the White Barn and the Lucille Lortel Theatre to Circle Repertory after her death. But the disposition of her theaters was a source of great anxiety during the last two decades of her life. Ultimately, unnerved by Circle Repertory's uneasy financial state and faltering artistic direction, she changed her mind (Circle Repertory folded in 1996).

Lucille Lortel died on April 4, 1999, after a brief illness. Until the last, she kept abreast of what was being presented at the White Barn and the Lucille Lortel Theatre, and friends who visited her at the Sherry-Netherland, where she and Louis Schweitzer had bought an apartment shortly before he died, would still hear her talk up her shows, would still receive press releases with their tea. Lortel lived to be ninety-eight years old and to see the geographic heart of the American theater move from Broadway to Off Broadway to the regions and to know she had helped shape a new American theater that valued art before commerce.

Lortel left an estate worth approximately $37 million—$5 million of which went to the Lucille Lortel Foundation, along with the Lucille Lortel Theatre in New York and her Connecticut and New York City real estate, some of which the executors sold. She bequeathed more than $1 million to not-for-profit theater companies and other charitable organizations, including the Eugene O'Neill Memorial Theater Center, the Goodspeed Opera House Foundation, the Lee Strasberg Creative Center, and New Dramatists, each of which received $50,000. The Actors' Fund received $100,000 for her theater at the fund's long-term-care facility, and she designated $500,000 for continuing the Lucille Lortel Awards, which she had started in 1986 to recognize excellence Off Broadway.[13]

Before Lortel died, she had set up artistic advisory boards to help steer both her theaters, although the actual fiduciary and legal control—and the ultimate artistic decisions—were in the hands of men who had been her accountants, lawyers, and business advisers throughout her life. As though the executors of the Lucille Lortel Foundation really did not want the responsibility and the expense of running a summer theater (and a theater building that needed extensive renovation), the White Barn stumbled along with abbreviated seasons, first in Westport and then at the Lucille Lortel Theatre in New York. The final productions at Westport took place during the summer of 2002.

Then, in a move that might have distressed the competitive Lortel, in December 2005, the Lortel Foundation awarded a $2 million capital grant to the Westport Country Playhouse, and a building adjacent to the Playhouse was named "The Lucille Lortel White Barn Center." The

Foundation also made a $500,000 operating grant to create the White Barn Theater Program at the Playhouse, "to create opportunities for new playwrights, composers, directors, actors and designers to showcase their talents and develop their craft,"[14] a mission that Lortel would undoubtedly have endorsed, although possibly not at her longtime Westport rival. These grants pave the way for the foundation to sell the White Barn itself.[15]

The Lucille Lortel Theatre has fared better. Lortel had enjoined that the theater on Christopher Street be used by not-for-profit companies, and that dictate has been followed. In addition, the Lucille Lortel Foundation reports that since 2002 it has distributed more than $1.5 million in operating support grants to theater companies in New York City and maintains an Internet Off-Broadway Database.[16]

Finally, Lortel is an intriguing example of how a patron's personality lends an aura to her giving. She sincerely loved theater and had a reputation within the not-for-profit theater community of being approachable for donations. But she also had a reputation for wanting to be cosseted and praised in order to consider a gift and for withholding money if the potential recipient displeased her personally. Without Lortel on hand to make the decisions about monetary gifts, a good deal of the éclat surrounding her donations has evaporated. In its place, however, is a small foundation that, while lacking the personal touch, generally appears committed to carrying out its founder's wish to support pioneering artists in the American theater.

Notes

1. Alexis Greene, *Lucille Lortel: The Queen of Off Broadway* (New York: Limelight Editions, 2004), 52.

2. Ben Sprecher, discussion with the author, 2002, quoted in Greene, *Lucille Lortel*, 246.

3. Greene, *Lucille Lortel*, 78.

4. Ibid., 81.

5. Ibid., 104.

6. Hope Alswang, discussion with the author, 2001, quoted in Greene, *Lucille Lortel*, 33.

7. Stuart W. Little, *Off-Broadway: The Prophetic Theater* (New York: Dell Publishing Company, 1972), 13–14.

8. Greene, *Lucille Lortel*, 137.

9. Sam McReady, *Lucille Lortel: A Bio-Bibliography* (Westport, CT: Greenwood Press, 1993), 125–27.

10. Stuart W. Little, "Twenty Years: Lucille Lortel's Matinee Series at the Theatre de Lys," in McReady, *Lucille Lortel,* 231–32.

11. Greene, *Lucille Lortel,* 210.

12. Larry DeVine, "Off-B'way Dying, Producer," *Miami Herald,* April 9, 1966.

13. Greene, *Lucille Lortel,* 328–29.

14. Westport Country Playhouse, "White Barn Theatre Legacy Continues at Westport Country Playhouse," news release, April 24, 2006.

15. Frank Rizzo, "Lortel Spreads the Love," *Variety,* December 13, 2005, 12.

16. Lucille Lortel Foundation, "Lucille Lortel Foundation Announces Recipients of General Operating Grants for Small and Mid-Size Theatres," news release, http://www.lortel.org (accessed November 9, 2005).

5

PATRONAGE AND PLAYWRITING: RICHARD B. AND JEANNE DONOVAN FISHER'S SUPPORT OF CHARLES MEE

Jennifer Schlueter

In recent years, contemporary American playwright Charles L. Mee Jr. has garnered critical acclaim for works such as *bobrauschenbergamerica*, his Humana Festival collaboration with the SITI company in 2001, and *Big Love*, which has been regularly staged at regional theaters since 2000. Mee's work has fascinated for three main reasons. First, after writing a handful of Off-Off-Broadway plays in the 1960s, Mee moved into a career in editing magazines and writing popular histories and did not return to playwriting until the 1980s. Since then, he has produced a startling thirty plays, with four more under construction as of this writing. So the trajectory of Mee's career, and its relentless productivity, is highly unusual.

Second, Mee's playwriting technique is decidedly unorthodox. His plays are collages of his own writing and found material, sampled from a variety of texts, up to copyright law's three-hundred-word limit for fair use. Mee also maintains a Web site (http://www.charlesmee.org) from which his playscripts can be downloaded for free. He does so because, he says, he "borrows" material from the culture at large for his creations, and so he returns what he creates to the culture again. He encourages readers to take the plays he has created, make radical alterations, and then attach their own name as authors. And if a small company with limited financial resources wants to stage one of his plays as written, he doesn't charge royalties. "That," he explains, "seems only fair to me."[1]

Mee's laissez-faire attitude toward finances has led cynics to scoff, wondering how, if his works are available for free, he survives. In fact, he does charge some royalties, asking professional theaters and universities that can afford to pay to do so. But the real answer to that question is the third element of his uniqueness, as extraordinary as the plays themselves: since 1999, Mee has been fully supported by Richard B. and Jeanne Donovan Fisher, who act as his patrons. In perpetuity, he will be paid a generous stipend, so that he is able to devote his time fully to writing. The arrangement, which has coincided with the most prolific portion of Mee's career, is without parallel or precedent in American theatrical philanthropy. The Fishers' support, which is unhampered by stipulations or expectations, makes, Mee says, "the Medicis look like nitpicking cheapskates."[2]

The Medicis as analog to the Fishers is not hyperbole. Richard B. Fisher, who retired as chair emeritus at the investment powerhouse Morgan Stanley, spent four decades at the company. In that time, he participated in, and then presided over, phenomenal institutional growth, amassing a personal fortune in the process. Then he set about disbursing that fortune in a string of uncommonly generous philanthropic gifts in contemporary art, theater, and education. He supported, with his time as well as with his wallet, Bard College, Rockefeller University, the Brooklyn Academy of Music, *The Paris Review*, the SITI Company, the Urban Institute, the Tate Modern, and the Museum of Modern Art. Some of his gifts were staggering: $25 million went, in 2000, to Bard College for a performing arts center designed by Frank Gehry. He gave $10 million in 2004 as a leadership gift to the BAM endowment, which spurred the growth of that organization's endowment from $18 million to more than $50 million, and he gave $10 million to Rockefeller University for enhancement of the Rockefeller Research Building. Along the way, he endowed university chairs, supported a host of other institutions, and lent his time and expertise to the Urban Institute, a nonpartisan think tank for which he served on the board and as chair from 1987 to 2004.

Fisher's support of Charles Mee, then, is one small strand in a far larger philanthropic weave. But in the panoply of individuals and organizations that benefited from Fisher's generosity, Mee's case is a very special one indeed. Long before Fisher was a Wall Street titan or Mee was an avant-garde icon, the two men had forged a deep friendship. It stretched from the summer of 1971, when the two were young fathers just embarking on their careers, through decades of steady upward mobility (in Fisher's case) and fitful seeking (in Mee's), all the way to Fisher's death in December 2004. Fisher's support for Mee's playwriting was, and still is, Mee says, "like one brother supporting another—and that's hard to generalize to the impersonal world of philanthropy; it's more like a family relationship."

To track the relationship between these two extraordinary men is to see, in a microcosm, the difference between going into what Mee terms "the moneymaking business," in Fisher's case, and "the money-losing business," in his own.[3] It is also to understand a philanthropic arrangement that is both a one-in-a-million confluence of luck and timing as it is "a standard for arts patronage that no one else has ever achieved. It should be a model for everyone else." Ultimately, this is a story of two men whose lives resonated and intertwined: of a groundbreaking playwright and of a very generous friend.

"It's no one"

When Richard "Dick" B. Fisher was born in Philadelphia on July 21, 1936, his rise to president and chairman of Morgan Stanley could not have been predicted. The eldest of two sons of an adhesives salesman for what became the 3M Corporation, Fisher contracted polio at age eight. In its aftermath, he was left paralyzed from the hip down on his right side. With stamina and determination, he relearned how to walk with crutches and, later, a cane.

In 1957, Fisher earned a bachelor's degree in history from Princeton University. That same year, he married his first wife, Emily Hargroves. Uncertain about career aspirations, Fisher took a position in retail sales at Eastman Dillon, Union Securities and Company, where he worked on commission. While there, Fisher became fascinated with the intricacies of corporate finance, admitting, "I think I was the only person in the office who enjoyed reading company prospectuses."[4] This interest spurred Fisher to pursue graduate study in business, and, in 1959, he entered Harvard Business School. Between his first and second years in the M.B.A. program, he interned at Morgan Stanley's New York headquarters. Upon graduating in 1962 as a Baker Scholar with high distinction, Fisher returned to Morgan Stanley as an associate. From then on, he steadily rose within the company's ranks.

When Fisher joined the company, one portion of the historic "House of Morgan," it had long been regarded as a peerless investment-banking firm that counted among its exclusive clients fifteen of the world's twenty-five largest industrial companies. Fisher started on the bottom rung of a carefully policed corporate ladder. In later life, he recounted an anecdote to prove it: "Fisher drove up to Canada with one of the partners to work. . . . At the border, an immigration official, peering at Fisher in the backseat, asked the partner, 'Who's that in the back with you?' 'I'm traveling by myself.' The partner answered. When the officer gestured toward the person sitting in the backseat, the partner said gruffly, 'It's no one. It's a statistician.'"[5] Fisher would not remain "no one" at the company for long. As the 1960s turned into the 1970s, younger partners, including Fisher and the five others in a group that old-timers dubbed the "irreverent six," complained of a stodgy, lumbering organization that continued to grow in size as its management and planning remained mired in decision making by disordered, if collegial, discussion. Most important, they said, the firm did not have a trading operation, a lack rooted in the long-standing company perception of traders as inferior to bankers. So in 1970, the year the "statistician" Fisher was elected a partner and managing director in the company, Morgan Stanley was on the brink of major change.

"We saved not a penny"

Charles Mee's childhood and education were not so different from Richard Fisher's. Born in Chicago on September 15, 1938, Mee was the son of a Commonwealth Edison vice president. In 1953, he suffered a debilitating bout with polio. After six months in the hospital and many months of physical rehabilitation, Mee, like Fisher, learned to walk again with the assistance of crutches and a cane. In this time, Mee discovered that writing offered him solace. He says, "I became a writer before I had any plan about it. It felt good, and so I kept doing it. . . . I had nothing to say; it was just something I could do sitting down. It wasn't until years later that I discovered that writing is not about saying something, it is about discovering something."[6] Henceforward, Mee never ceased discovering through writing. Books, articles, essays, plays, polemics: the form might change, but the scribbling impulse did not.

Mee attended Harvard University, graduating in 1960 with a bachelor's degree in English literature. Although he had been involved in theater in his high school years, it was in college that he delved deeply into "that arena of warring passions and voices that seemed to be my natural life. I acted in plays—to hell with it, I played old men—and directed plays, and wrote plays."[7] When directing *The Good Woman of Setzuan* for the fiftieth anniversary of the Harvard Dramatic Club, Mee precociously traveled to New York to meet with Eric Bentley to discuss Brecht's work. During their interview, Bentley dispensed some surprising advice: "[he] said to me, if you want to write you should get a job that has nothing to do with words. You should get a job on Wall Street." Though in later years he would come to believe Bentley was teasing, upon graduation, Mee most dutifully heeded the recommendation of the expert on Marxist Brecht. Mee headed into the heart of capitalist America and got a job at Merrill Lynch. He lasted just six months as an investment analyst trainee. Unlike Fisher, who delighted in financial statements, Mee discovered that Wall Street "was not a job I knew how to do well."

In what would become a recurring theme in his career, Mee cobbled together writing work that would pay the bills. In 1961, he started at American Heritage, doing text and photo research. The job supported his forays into a diverse New York theatrical scene. In 1962, the same year that Fisher began his climb at Morgan Stanley, Mee became the editor of *Playbill* magazine. He also joined the foment of Off-Off-Broadway theater, seeing his plays staged at the Writers' Stage Company, St. Mark's in the Bouerie, and La MaMa ETC.[8] Mee also contributed to the movement through his work at the *Tulane Drama Review* (now *TDR*). Under Richard Schechner, Mee wrote articles for the journal in 1962, became an advising editor in 1963, and then its associate editor in 1964.[9] Of this rich time, Mee said, "We had a wonderful time. Suzi [Mee, his second wife] was an actress and I wrote plays for her, and we would hang around with friends of hers from the Strasberg Actors Studio, and we went to the theater all the time. . . . We spent time backstage. We spent time at Sardi's and Downey's. We had tea in the Palm Court at the Plaza Hotel and drinks in the Oak [R]oom and lunch at the Hotel New Weston. . . . I wonder where all our money came from. God, we had a wonderful time. We saved not a penny."[10] In fact, these joyfully profligate years could not last.

Mee juggled editing and playwriting through 1964. But between 1965 and 1970, with two small children to support, he drifted away from playwriting. In 1967, he became an editor at *Horizon*, American Heritage's hardcover magazine devoted to art, history, and archaeology. He also began writing books for the same publisher. Some of these, like *Daily Life in the Renaissance* (1970), were extensions of the work he was doing at *Horizon*. But the work he coauthored with Edward C. Greenfield, *Dear Prince: The Unexpurgated Counsels of N. Machiavelli to Richard Milhous Nixon* (1969), flagged Mee's growing discontent with the Nixon presidency that would coalesce, in the coming years, into agitation for impeachment. In 1971, however, Mee was focused on his promotion to editor in chief at *Horizon*. And that summer, he rented a house in Haines Fall, New York, as a rewarding rest for himself and his young family.

"It was idyllic"

In the summer of 1971, Richard Fisher had the same idea. With their three children, Richard and Emily headed to their summer house in Haines Falls. It had been an exceptionally busy year at Morgan Stanley. In 1971, pressed by partner Robert H. B. Baldwin and supported by Fisher's "irreverent six," the company had broken with long-standing tradition and offered sales and trading services. So the summer's respite in the foothills of the Catskills was welcome. While there, Emily Fisher, who had obtained her master's in education from Harvard in 1961, coordinated a summer recreation program for the community, in which the Fisher's own children took part.

Charles and Suzi Mee enrolled their two children in Emily's program. It was through them that Mee and Fisher met, two men just getting started in their lives in New York. And they found they had many interests in common. "We liked each other right away," Mee says. "We both liked to read fiction and poetry. We liked to talk about politics. He loved music and the theatre. We both loved painting. We loved a lot of the same artists of the twentieth century, in particular post [World War II] American artists. We loved our kids." Polio, the "viral accident" that was part of each man's life, marked common ground but went undiscussed: "[There were] maybe a dozen words over twenty five or thirty years. . . . [W]e understood each other without words," Mee explained. So they sat by the pool together and talked about books: "It was idyllic," Mee remembers.[11] The friendship between Fisher and Mee deepened and grew over successive summers at Haines Falls. Their careers, however, continued to diverge, as did the gap in their annual income.

"Ambition is ordinary"

Bright, sociable, and gracious, Fisher climbed at Morgan Stanley in the 1970s. Leon Botstein, president of Bard College, said of Fisher's rise, "He cultivated the requisite ambition that is indispensable to the dramatic success he enjoyed in his work. Ambition is ordinary. But ambition coupled with tolerance and patience and an elegant talent for focusing attention on others is extraordinary."[12] It was precisely these attributes, especially his reputation as a remarkable listener, that made Fisher stand out at the firm.

Like Fisher, Morgan Stanley was ambitious, though perhaps not as gracious as the man who would one day become its president. In the early 1970s, the company set up Wall Street's first mergers and acquisitions department. Though it had long disapproved, like other Wall Street firms, of unsolicited buyouts, in 1974, Morgan Stanley facilitated International Nickel's hostile takeover of ESB. The move shocked analysts and paved the way for increasingly frequent and vituperative mergers throughout the corporate world.[13]

In 1974, Mee was still working as editor in chief at *Horizon*. But much of his focus was on his National Committee on the Presidency (NCOP), an organization founded in 1973 that lobbied for the impeachment of Richard Nixon in response to the Watergate break-in. Increasingly politicized, Mee resigned from his position at *Horizon* in 1975.

So while Fisher continued on with Morgan Stanley, Mee made another career shift, into a decade focused on writing popular history books. The books Mee wrote tended to take up charged events in American political history, including the peace conferences following World Wars I and II, the corrupt Harding administration, and the Marshall Plan. Consciously writing for a popular audience, Mee suggested in 1981 that he hoped, through the books, "to talk politics with my fellow citizens."[14]

Meanwhile, Morgan Stanley was continuing its voracious expansion. Between 1975 and 1977, the company added portfolio management, government-bond trading, automatic brokerage, and retail brokerage to its cache of services. In the dawning 1980s, it dabbled in junk bonds. And in 1983, Robert Baldwin, who had set the firm's tremendous growth in action by advocating the trading division, retired. The company moved fully into the hands of the "irreverent six," with Richard Fisher ascending to its presidency in 1984.

As president, Fisher led with candor and integrity. The *New York Times* described him this way: "Under Mr. Fisher, Morgan Stanley had been a place where anybody could walk into the boss's office and disagree with a decision—and Mr. Fisher would hear them out, and sometimes even agree. . . . [He] roamed the halls, talking to traders, investment bankers and executives up and down the ranks. He chatted up clients. He made people feel good about themselves, and about the firm."[15] Fisher's leadership style was the linchpin in the company's continuing success, which multiplied on his watch. One of the last remaining private investment houses, Morgan Stanley began trading on the New York Stock Exchange in 1986. Just 20 percent of its stock was made available for public sale. The remaining 80 percent—then worth $800 million—was held by its 114 managing directors and 148 principals. On the first day of trading, the stock shot from $56.50 to $71.25 per share. Richard Fisher, who held 729,275 shares that day, was suddenly worth more than $53 million.

Charles Mee, on the other hand, found himself in dire financial straits in the 1980s. His interest in writing works of history wore thin. He wanted to return to creative writing, and so, in 1981 and 1982, he worked on a never-published novel. And he descended deeply into debt.

> I received a pink piece of paper saying that the sheriff's office was going to auction off all my furniture for nonpayment of back taxes. . . . I looked at the novel and realized it was absolute junk. . . . I threw [it] away. And then I thought: that was stupid, because there were things in there that I wanted to remember for myself, for my own writing. So I decided to make some notes on some of this stuff, and the notes took the form of a trilogy of one-act plays. . . . And I looked at them and I thought, Oh, I get it: if you're just writing for yourself, for your own sake . . . this is the form it takes. So that's when I went back to writing plays.[16]

As he moved back into playwriting, Mee pulled himself out of debt by returning to editing as a source of regular income. For Rebus, Mee edited an art history series and medical journals. He eventually became the publishing house's editor in chief.

Then came a breakthrough: in 1986, the same year that Richard Fisher became a very wealthy man, Mee's *Vienna: Lusthaus* was produced at the Public Theatre. This collaboration with choreographer Martha C. Clarke was Mee's first piece to be staged since the 1960s. It won an Obie for best play. In 1986, by virtue of two very different successes, Mee and Fisher found themselves at key turning points in their lives.

"A third way"

The late 1980s on Wall Street were epitomized for many by Michael Douglas's pronouncement in Oliver Stone's 1987 film *Wall Street*: "Greed, for lack of a better word, is good." But when most of Wall Street crashed that year, entangled in its greed-fueled stratagems, Morgan Stanley was the only publicly traded house to actually boost earnings. The fact that the company weathered the downturn better than most was often attributed to Fisher, who, Mee says, "could see through walls."

Fisher was a rare financial leader: both ambitious and humble, competitive and cooperative, his ethic permeated his company. Even as he grew steadily more wealthy, he never embodied the greed-is-good caricature. Instead, he possessed, as Leon Botstein suggests, "the capacity to resist the corruption of success, the deformation of character, intentions, and principles that wealth, power, and fame seem to bring. He was utterly singular in our contemporary world in that he retained simplicity of manner, unaffected grace, and an elegant sense of humor and irony."[17] Thus, as Fisher became uncommonly wealthy, he also became uncommonly generous. He embarked on a remarkable philanthropic career. While still leading Morgan Stanley's highly successful foray into international markets, he joined the boards at Rockefeller University, Bard College, and the Urban Institute, and he championed fund-raising at the Brooklyn Academy of Music. Fisher remained committed to them all to his death.

In 1991, Fisher became the chair of Morgan Stanley's board. And then, in the wake of restructuring following the celebrated 1997 merger with Dean Witter that he spearheaded, Fisher gracefully stepped aside to allow the newly formed company to grow on its own. He was named chair of the executive committee.[18] From then on, more and more of Fisher's time focused on his philanthropic interests. In 2000, he became chair emeritus and devoted himself even more fully to this arena.

Meanwhile, from 1986, when *Vienna: Lusthaus* revived his playwriting career, into the late 1990s, Charles Mee's plays were steadily produced by directors such as Robert Woodruff, Anne Bogart, and Tina Landau. Yet he was not a high profile playwright: despite a buzz surrounding his work, Mee still needed to work at Rebus to support his family, which had grown to include two more school-age daughters by his third wife, playwright Kathleen Tolan. Over the years, Mee had steadily "bought back" his time from Rebus, in order to stay home in the mornings and write. But, Mee says, the work "wasn't what I loved, and I wanted to spend all my hours with what I loved." So, in 1996, he left the company and paid the bills by teaching playwriting at Brown University in 1997 and 1998. He kept writing.

In 1998, Mee circled back to Bertolt Brecht, the author who had launched his theatrical career. He wrote *Full Circle*, an ambitious version of *Caucasian Chalk Circle*, which upends Brecht's Marxist worldview as it refuses to settle for an American capitalist alternative.[19] Its characters seek a "third way":

> some middle ground
> to get rich, like in the West
> and to share like in the East
> Because this choice that we are being given
> this should not be our only choice.[20]

Throughout the piece, Mee grapples with financial need, oblivious wealth, failed revolution, avarice, mendacity, and, most dangerous of all, the seeming inability of art to make any difference at all. He writes:

> You have all these artists who like to say of themselves
> well, I am changing the world
> and if they like to say it
> there is no harm in it
> except that it is not true
> and it gets an artist in the habit of lying
> and expecting his lies to be accepted
> so that, when his lies are not accepted
> he is in a snit.

Or not, or not
it may be that a work of art contributes
to the common discourse of a culture
and so, in some modest way,
supports or undermines the status quo
but really so what?
I mean if you really care
whether this fellow on the street has no food or clothes
the most useful thing to do is not to put on a play
but give him food.[21]

The play sprawls, overreaches, and takes big risks. It is Mee at his best, raising difficult questions that entrap and implicate him in the very issues he examines. And the most challenging question raised in *Full Circle* is one that could be asked of both Mee and Fisher: in an inequitable world, what are the political responsibilities of art and wealth?

The question is amplified when art and wealth dally together, as they do in every patronage arrangement. In "When in Trouble, Start More," his 1990 address to the Theatre Communications Group (subsequently reprinted in the *New York Times*), Mee was pointed when it came to the willingness with which contemporary artists accommodated themselves to the preferences of their financial backers: "We are not presently in the position of writers in previous centuries who, if they wanted to publish a book, submitted the manuscript to church authorities to receive a *nihil obstat* and an imprimatur. . . . These days the *nihil obstat* comes from the National Endowment for the Arts; and the imprimatur comes from the Rockefeller Foundation, the Ford Foundation or Philip Morris. We are not against this. On the contrary, we insist upon the Government's support as our right."[22] Instead of bemoaning the philistinism of an NEA that slashed funding, Mee argued that theater practitioners should embrace their status as "canaries in the cave," as first challengers of consensus. And, he says, they should watch where their money is coming from: "In the golden triangle of government subsidy, the favor of rich patrons, and the fortunes of the marketplace, we preserve our freedom best by becoming addicted to no single source."[23]

So artists must remain vigilant against the temptation to pander to their funders' tastes. For Mee, though, the responsibility does not belong to artists alone. Philanthropists also must resist the desire to eschew controversy.

In *Full Circle*, Mee lampoons the middle-of-the-road sensibility when he has Heiner Müller, cast as the spineless artist director of the Berliner Ensemble, grovel before Erich Honecker, former secretary general of the East German Communist party. Müller's abjection is double edged; his bridling against an imperative to produce state-ordained propaganda is linked with a pointed critique of American philanthropy.

> . . . we are grateful for a government that ensures the public order and nurtures the public good, sometimes even by giving grants to cultural institutions, god knows! even though to be sure it is easier to give grants to ballet companies or to art museums rather than to theatres where words are used and because words have meaning, this or that word might offend someone even without meaning to although we make every effort to delete every offensive word we are able to locate so that the government will be able to give us a grant—although your excellency, in all honesty, I must say that you have cut our grants in recent years. I mean not you, not you yourself, of course, but your granting agency.[24]

But Mee's forceful arguments against philanthropic indolence and bloodlessness jangle uncomfortably against his next career move.

By 1998, when *Full Circle* was being staged at Chicago's Steppenwolf Theatre, Mee had become completely frustrated by the exigencies of chasing after money and the constraints the pursuit of it placed on his ability to write for the theater. So he did what few artists have the connections to do: he wrote a letter to his old friend, a multimillionaire. In the letter, Mee detailed a business proposition, a merger quite unlike any that Fisher had ever brokered for Morgan Stanley. Mee suggested that they form a playwriting company. Fisher would put in the capital, and Mee would furnish the product.

Fisher and his second wife, Jeanne Donovan Fisher, waved away Mee's good capitalist offer of a joint venture. Instead, they proposed an arrangement in which they would, twice yearly, write Mee a check for an amount sufficient for his family's needs. Mee could then do as he wished. Mee describes the rare arrangement in this way: "Dick said to me, 'I want to see what you do if you don't have to worry.' And then you need to try to imagine that he really meant what he said, that he and Jeannie really intended to give me complete freedom to do whatever I wanted to do, without even the hint of a remark that would in any way inhibit me, that they were patrons of the arts in a way that neither you nor I can quite conceive." Unlike the granting agencies that Heiner Müller debased himself before in *Full Circle*, the Fishers supported Mee with no strings attached. Unlike the theater groups that bend to accommodate their funders' tastes, Mee now writes only for himself. And there is no "company;" that is, Mee retains full rights over his work, though he does gratefully note, on every play, that the work is "made possible by" the Fishers. What Mee does with his time is his own decision; there are no stipulations about quantity or quality of work. Any royalties are Mee's to keep. Most important, the Fishers do not commission, criticize, or censor Mee's work. The arrangement is an idiosyncratic miniature of, and as close as anyone has yet gotten to, the utopic "third way" sought in *Full Circle*.

To this date, work has flowed out of Mee at an astonishing clip.[25] Since the Fishers began supporting him in January 1999, he has written an average of three plays a year. His work has been staged all over the world. And the plays he writes, while certainly not abandoning his lifelong desire to "talk politics with [his] fellow citizens," are, for better or for worse, decidedly lighter in tone, as his series of plays on love—*Big Love*, *First Love*, and *True Love*—make plain.[26] Some of this has to do with the fact that Mee had himself recently fallen in love with, and married, actress Michi Barall. There's no denying it: Charles Mee is, finally, a very happy man. Who wouldn't be?

Of course, when we recall Mee's 1990 admonishment to TCG—"In the golden triangle of government subsidy, the favor of rich patrons, and the fortunes of the marketplace, we preserve our freedom best by becoming addicted to no single source"—Mee's comfortable settling-in to just such single-source addiction can seem problematic. That the Fishers never impinged on his freedom by placing demands on his playwriting is true. But, as a result of his more comfortable life, Mee himself might have begun to place fewer: the lighter tone of Mee's work since 1998 can also suggest that the easy comfort of writing with patronage has allowed him to indulge in self-reflexivity and nostalgia.

Perhaps it is churlish to criticize the still-evolving outcome of the Fishers' generous gift. Certainly, when Richard Fisher died in December 2004, of complications from prostate cancer, he left behind him a rare legacy of colossal business success coupled with wisely generous philanthropy. Leon Botstein described Fisher's uncommon life in this way: "He was an idealist and a dreamer. He was a lifelong believer in social justice and that now unpopular cause, liberal and secular democracy; in business governed by enlightened, ethical, and visionary self-interest, neither naïve nor self-serving—in which greed and vulgar materialism are tempered. . . . With quiet dignity, Dick returned to the public sphere the gift of his life more fully than anyone I have ever known."[27] Without exception, those organizations with which he had a sustained relationship all spoke of Fisher's lasting impact. All acknowledged that his leadership would be sorely missed.

For Charles Mee, too, Fisher's influence will not fade. There is, of course, the matter of money: Fisher provided Mee with a bequest to allow him to continue to write, and Jeanne Donovan Fisher is committed to continuing that support into the future.[28] But Fisher continues to support and sustain Mee in more important ways, as well. The two men shared a love of American art, and, lately, Mee has been working on plays inspired by works by Joseph Cornell and James Castle in Fisher's private collection. Above all, it is the model of Fisher's fully lived life that Mee clings most tightly to. He says, "I think all the time, all the time of how game and ready for some new engagement with life Dick was. It inspires me, truly, a dozen times a week, whenever I am flagging, whenever I am overcome by the difficulties of life and work, I think of him, and re-engage as he would."

Notes

Special thanks to Charles Mee and Jeanne Donovan Fisher, for their forthright answers to my many questions about the late Richard Fisher. Thanks also to Tom Postlewait, for his always helpful editorial guidance. Finally, thanks to Scott T. Cummings, who is a fount of knowledge on all things Mee. His book *Remaking American Theatre: Charles Mee, Anne Bogart, and the SITI Company* (Cambridge University Press, 2006) treats Mee's work in far more detail than I have done here. Any errors are, of course, my own.

1. Richard Christiansen, "Playwriting Has Been Mainly Greek for Mee," *Chicago Tribune*, October 28, 2001.

2. From his interview with the author, conducted via e-mail on April 10, 2005. Unless otherwise noted, all further quotations from Charles Mee are from this interview.

3. Douglas J. Keating, "Charles Mee: Steal This Play; I Did," *Philadelphia Inquirer*, March 23, 2003.

4. "Richard B. Fisher," *Working Knowledge*, July 2, 2001, Harvard Business School, http://hbswk.hbs.edu/puitem.jthml?id=2344&t=special_reports (accessed July 21, 2005).

5. Ron Chernow, *The House of Morgan: An American Banking Dynasty and the Rise of Modern Finance* (New York: Simon & Schuster, 1990), 581. Even though the leadership at Morgan Stanley (including Richard Fisher) refused to participate in Chernow's study, the book is definitive and was indispensable as I attempted to reconstruct Fisher's career.

6. Charles Mee, *A Nearly Normal Life: A Memoir* (Boston: Little, Brown, 1999), 184.

7. Charles Mee, *A Visit to Haldeman and Other States of Mind* (New York: M. Evans, 1977), 174.

8. Erin B. Mee, "Shattered and Fucked Up and Full of Wreckage: The Words and Works of Charles L. Mee," *Tulane Drama Review* (hereafter *TDR*) 46, no. 6 (Fall 2002): 102.

9. These include two pieces, not entirely complimentary, on the Living Theatre, "The Becks' Living Theatre," *TDR* 7, no. 2 (1962): 194–205, and "Epitaph for the Living Theatre," *TDR* 8, no. 3 (1964): 220–21. He also wrote a polemic "Theatres—Not THEATRE," *TDR* 7, no. 4 (1962): 86–95. Finally, Mee's play *God Bless Us, Every One* found its way in, *TDR* 10 (1966), no. 1: 162–206.

10. Mee, *Visit to Haldeman*, 35.

11. Charles Mee, David Fisher, Robert G. Scott, and Leon Botstein, "Memorials for Richard B. Fisher," read at memorial service for Richard B. Fisher, The Riverside Church, New York, January 12, 2005, published by Princeton University Class of 1957, http://www.princeton57.org/dynamic.asp?id=memorials2 (accessed July 16, 2005).

12. Ibid.

13. In *The House of Morgan*, Ron Chernow describes the seismic change the company instigated in this way: "Morgan Stanley entered the 1960s a model of civility, then turned itself inside out" (580).

14. Robert Dahlin, "Charles L. Mee, Jr." *Publishers Weekly*, June 26, 1981, 12.

15. Joseph Nocera, "In Business, Tough Guys Finish Last," *New York Times*, June 18, 2005.

16. Erin B. Mee, "Shattered," 102.

17. Mee et al., "Memorials," 2005.

18. The merger with Dean Witter has had troublesome fallout recently. Analysts suggested that the merger would be a clash of cultures, between "Main Street," Dean Witter with its Discover Card and small-time brokers, and "Wall Street," Morgan Stanley with its "white shoe" reputation. But also, the merger did not prove as fruitful as hoped, with Dean Witter's products and services steadily underperforming Morgan Stanley's. As revenues fell, temperatures rose. Philip Purcell, the Dean Witter executive who demanded the position of chief executive officer of the merged companies, and eight former Morgan Stanley

executives publicly struggled for control of the organization. Richard Fisher's memorial service in January 2005 became a hot spot of resentment and plotting by executives, with current leadership paling compared with that of Fisher. "The group of eight," as they dubbed themselves, pushed for Purcell's ouster in the first half of 2005. Though Purcell's hand-picked board resisted, he was finally shown the door in June 2005. For a delightful comic book–style summary of this turf war, see Peter Arkle and Jon Gertner, "Morgan v. Stanley v. Morgan Stanley," *New York Times*, June 5, 2005.

19. *Full Circle* was first produced as *The Berlin Circle* at the Steppenwolf Theatre, under the direction of Tina Landau, in November 1998. In 2000, it was staged by Robert Woodruff at ART, and the title was changed to *Full Circle.*

20. Charles L. Mee, *Full Circle*, 78, http://www.charlesmee.org (accessed February 2, 2003).

21. Ibid., 89.

22. Charles L. Mee, "When In Trouble, Start More," *New York Times*, July 8, 1990.

23. Ibid.

24. Mee, *Full Circle*, 8.

25. For a study of Mee's career, aesthetic concerns, and working technique, see Jennifer Schlueter, "'This is what it is to be human': The Drama and History of Charles L. Mee" (master's thesis, Ohio State University, 2003).

26. Jeanne Donovan Fisher produced Mee's *True Love* in 2001 at the Zipper Theatre in New York as the inaugural, and eponymous, performance of the production company she shares with Laurie Williams, Mee's former partner for whom the lead role was written. True Love Productions has gone on to underwrite several recent Broadway and Off-Broadway successes, including *Retreat from Moscow*, with John Lithgow and Eileen Atkins (2003–4) and the American run of the Abbey Theatre's acclaimed *Medea*, starring Fiona Shaw (2002–3). The company has also backed the BAM run of Mee's *bobrauschenbergamerica* (2003) and the New York Theatre Workshop's remount of his *Vienna: Lusthaus* (2002). Donovan Fisher was vice president and director of worldwide corporate communications at Morgan Stanley and later a partner in the consulting firm Citigate Sard Verbinnen. She wed Richard Fisher on May 31, 1997. In addition to her work at True Love Productions, she is a philanthropist in her own right, serving on the boards of the Sundance Institute, the Bard Performing Arts Center, and the Environmental Defense Fund.

27. Mee et al., "Memorials," 2005.

28. "At least until Chuck wins the Nobel Prize and can support me," Donovan Fisher writes. From an e-mail interview with the author, August 2, 2005.

6

EVERYONE'S AN ANGEL

Dan Friedman

The voice of this chapter is not the usual scholarly or journalistic third person, but the subjective first-person plural. While I hold a doctorate in theater history and have made use of the discipline and methodology of a historian, I am also a founder of the Castillo Theatre of which I write and, thus, am an active agent in the story I relate. While I make no claim to objectivity, I have worked hard to assure accuracy. At times, for narrative purposes, I refer to Castillo as *it*, but primarily I have chosen the plural *we* to convey the collective building of Castillo, of which I am a part—one of its builders and the teller of our story.

The Castillo Theatre in New York City raises money like no other theater in the United States. It is a nonprofit theater with an annual operating budget of $900,000 that takes no funds from federal, state, or municipal arts councils.[1] It has no individual or family patron upon which it depends. Nor does it rely on foundation or corporate funding. Instead, the Castillo Theatre has organized, over two decades of intensive outreach, a broad base of individual contributors. Over the twenty-two years of its existence, roughly half a million people have contributed to the All Stars Project Inc., the nonprofit cultural organization of which the Castillo Theatre, the All Stars Talent Show Network, and related performatory youth programs are a part. Currently, five thousand people contribute anywhere from $35 to many thousands of dollars on an annual basis.

What makes this all the more remarkable is that Castillo is a radical theater, producing what it calls "postmodern political theatre."[2] The core of its repertory is the work of its artistic director and playwright-in-residence Fred Newman, whose topics include America's legacy of slavery and racism, African American and Jewish relations, and the limits of identity politics. Castillo is the major producer in the United States of the East German avant-gardist Heiner Müller and has also produced other political playwrights such as Bertolt Brecht, Peter Weiss, Aimé Césaire, Ed Bullins, and the Israeli Josef Mundi.

Despite the political and experimental nature of the theater's work, the band of angels who make Castillo financially possible is not limited to those who share the views of its artists. Those who contribute to Castillo—and make up its audience—range from Wall Street executives to African American church ladies, from same-sex couples in Chelsea to suburban families from Connecticut, from unreconstructed communists to blue-blooded Republicans.

Castillo and the All Stars Talent Show Network, which produces talent shows with young people in inner-city communities, were launched in 1983 by a small group of community organizers and political activists, some with arts backgrounds, others without, all of whom wanted to find ways to create cultural projects that could reach out to and involve people who usually did not think of themselves as theatergoers or creators of culture. This group concluded that culture—the organization of how we, the human species, see—was seriously neglected by social change activists and was determined to do something about it.[3]

Since this group of organizers did not have the financial resources to fund the projects on their own, and since the group was interested in creating a theater that would function as a community social forum, the funding and the building of the Castillo Theatre and the All Stars Talent Show Network were entirely interwoven from the start. In the case of Castillo, the founders faced the same challenge that all nonprofit theaters in the United States face, namely, the need to fill the unavoidable gap between what can be taken in by the box office and the cost of production. The solution Castillo developed during the first decade of its existence would set it apart from all other nonprofit theaters in the country and would bring into being an unusually close relationship between the theater and its audience, many of the members of which are also Castillo's numerous modest "angels."

For the founders of the Castillo Theatre—including myself—bridging the gap raised political as well as economic issues. On the practical level, it was obvious that the usual funding sources for nonprofit arts projects, the liberal foundations and the National Endowment for the Arts under the newly elected Ronald Reagan, could not be counted on to financially underwrite the kind of theater—with mostly untrained community people as performers in plays with radical political content—that we had begun to produce. On the principled level, we were committed to doing theater for and with communities that usually did not go to the theater. Therefore, we were determined to find a way to give the people in these communities a stake in seeing (and in creating) theater.

The nine people who in 1983 constituted themselves as the Castillo Collective initially came together through community organizing and political activism. We were attracted to a progressive political movement, led by Fred Newman, in which cultural and emotional change was considered as important as political and economic transformation. This movement was seeking ways to express itself culturally, and Newman encouraged the formation of Castillo. With Newman's leadership, the Castillo Collective began the search for an independent way to bridge the gap between box-office income and production expenses as well as building an intimate and active interface with its audience and community.

That we were able to begin the search without resorting to government arts councils or corporate foundations was because the political movement we were a part of had already been active for a decade and was able to provide us with both the beginnings of an audience drawn from community and political organizations around New York City and in-kind resources. In particular, the Castillo Theatre originated as a project of the New York Institute for Social Therapy and Research, an organization of radical developmental psychologists, psychotherapists, and social workers founded in 1979 by, among others, Newman and Lois Holzman. The Institute was busy developing social therapy, a nonpsychological approach to human emotionality and development, and establishing social therapy centers around the New York City metro area. However, the Institute perceived its mission as broader than therapy. It wanted to engage both the psychological and the cultural establishments as a means of furthering individual and social development. So the Institute was happy to help Castillo get started.[4]

For the first five years of its existence, the Castillo Theatre performed rent-free in a large room in one of the Institute's locations, a loft on East Twentieth Street between Broadway and Fifth Avenue. The early years were characterized by rough-hewn theatrical experimentation. Among the early experiments were the following: *A Demonstration: Common Women, the Uncommon Lives of Ordinary Women* (1986) which brought together nonactors from the community—specifically welfare activists, mostly African American women, and white radical lesbians—for a performed confrontation that spun off into a montage of scenes, poems, songs, and video clips; *From Gold to Platinum* (1986), a political science-fiction play about a second American revolution that was compiled and written through a series of meetings and improvisations with community organizations throughout New York City; *All My Cadre* (1987), a soap opera about a group of young and restless leftists in New York City; and a seven-hour interactive production of Heiner Müller's *Description of a Picture/Explosion of a Memory* (1992). In 1986, Castillo produced its first play by Newman, *Mr. Hirsch Died Yesterday*; since then, it has staged some thirty Newman plays and musicals, and in 1989, Newman became the theater's artistic director.

During these first years, however, the direction Castillo would take was far from clear. As the sampling of works suggests, the Castillo was moving in a number of directions at once. Some of the members came out of political street theaters of the 1960s and 1970s, others from the European avant-garde, still others from the feminist stand-up comedy scene, so just what kind of theater we would produce was a matter of dispute. In this regard, our strength was that we practiced our differences rather than just arguing about them. One thing was clear, however: the setup with the Institute was temporary, and Castillo, if it were to last, would need to find a way to be self-sufficient.

In 1981, the activist community of which Castillo and the Institute were to become a part had established a nonprofit organization, the Community Literacy Research Project (CLRP), which, as its name implies, was established to fund literacy classes for adults. During the 1980s, the CLRP evolved into a nonprofit that raised money for the community's nascent cultural and youth projects. In 1989, the CLRP made a major investment. With the financial help of Judy Penzer—a painter, Castillo founder, and daughter of a commercial real estate investor—the CLRP purchased a nine-thousand-square-foot loft at 500 Greenwich Street in the far west of Soho. The nonprofit rented part of the space to the East Side Center for Social Therapy, which practiced the social therapy developed by the New York Institute. The rest of the space was rented to Castillo and a collection of politically oriented periodicals. Part of the space was outfitted as a small theater for Castillo and the rest as a newsroom and print production facility. By 1994, the publications had all been closed and the Castillo Theatre was flourishing.[5] The move ushered in a new era for Castillo. Castillo now had to not only finance its shows but also pay the rent every month.

What we wound up doing was taking up the model of community outreach that we knew from our earlier political organizing. All of us had worked street corners for independent political candidates in the 1980s. Some of us had canvassed, raising money for the Washington, D.C.–based Rainbow Lobby. Given our political history, what we did to ensure the survival of our theater made perfect sense: we set up tables on street corners and started talking to passersby about Castillo. When it got too cold on the street, we moved to the subway platforms. We eventually set up a canvassing operation, going up and down halls in apartment buildings and knocking on every door. We worked neighborhoods all over the New York metropolitan area. The tables on the street were supplied with a poster and some flyers, and the Castillo volunteers would approach strangers, saying something like, "Hi, my name is So-and-So. I'm an adjunct professor (or a costume designer or an office manager or a social worker or whatever), and I'm volunteering today to raise money for a theater that doesn't take government or corporate money. We're building an independent theater because we want a place where we can take artistic and political risks without always looking over our shoulder worrying if someone is going to pull the plug on us."

Of course, most people did not stop. Some were downright nasty. But a few folks would stop and listen, and a certain percentage of those who listened, who held conversations with Castillo's organizers, would make a contribution. In the early days, they often said something like, "I don't think this has the chance of a snowball in hell of working, but I like that you're out here trying, so here's ten dollars."

The Castillo organizer would typically respond, "Thanks, that's great. I'd love to take your name and phone number so we can call you back, invite you to a play, and ask you for more money." The person who had just given a donation would usually smile or chuckle and give us their phone number. (And we, indeed, did call them back within a few months to sell them a ticket to a play and ask them for more money.) That exchange repeated countless times is how at the end of Castillo's first decade it had a database of the tens of thousands of people who had given $10 or more, their phone numbers, and permission to call them.

"In the early years what was significant was that we were out there; that's what organized people," recalled Gabrielle L. Kurlander, an actress with Castillo since 1986 and president since 1990 of CLRP (now known as the All Stars Project Inc.). "We were selling visions and ideas. As we moved further along in our history, we actually had small but visible accomplishments, but in the early days people on the street were responding not so much to our product but to our spirit. In a certain sense we were selling hope. What is significant is that people bought."[6]

Gladys Janava, who has been a regular donor to Castillo since the mid-1990s, put it this way: "I first gave money to a volunteer on Montague Street in Brooklyn. I used to give money whenever they were out there because I liked what they were saying. . . . I used to subscribe to the theatre season but never used my tickets. One day I decided to go see a play at Castillo and I fell in love."[7]

The street operation was up and running seven days a week. All Castillo Collective members were volunteers, and the street organizing was done in the evenings after paying jobs and on weekends. We set ourselves quotas. Castillo needed a certain amount of money to pay the rent and produce the season, and so if we didn't, for example, make the goal set for a particular Saturday in eight hours, we stayed out ten or twelve or whatever it took.

Everyone involved with Castillo during this period—actors, directors, designers, playwrights, and nonartists who believed in the project's importance—participated in this outreach. It was extremely demanding and time consuming, and there were those in the Castillo Collective who were

Castillo volunteers organizing on the streets, circa 1990.
Courtesy of the All Stars Project Inc.

conflicted or who openly resisted the street work. "As a political artist, I, of course, support our independence," they would say, in effect. "I agree we shouldn't take government or corporate money. But I'm a director, not a fundraiser. You raise the money and I'll direct the plays." There were intense disagreements about this, and some of Castillo's founders and early builders, rather than keep doing this work, left. The remarkable thing, perhaps, is that more people joined than departed. People met on the street, and people who came to see Castillo's shows asked how they might help in addition to giving money or buying a ticket. Castillo's handful of organizers grew, by the mid-1990s, to scores of people deployed to the streets on a regular basis.

This was also the period during which Newman became Castillo's artistic director and playwright-in-residence, and the theater's work became increasingly identified with his plays. Newman, who started out and has remained a radical political leader, explores in his plays ethical and political issues of concern to both his political movement and the larger world. *Sally & Tom (The American Way)* (1995), for example, is a musical that looks at the relationship between Thomas Jefferson and his slave Sally Hemings, a thirty-five-year relationship that embodied the contradiction between democracy and slavery and the legacy of racism that continues to define so much of American history and culture. *Lenin's Breakdown* (1994) portrays Lenin, leader of the Russian Revolution, as an old homeless man who checks himself into Bellevue, a mental hospital in New York City, looking to understand the failure of his life (and of twentieth-century communism). In *Sessions with Jesus* (2002), Jesus returns to the earth (the Upper West Side of Manhattan, to be precise) looking for a therapist. He needs a therapist because he is hearing the voice of Osama bin Laden asking for forgiveness. Jesus, of course, is all about forgiveness, but he's having a hard time forgiving the mass murderer.

While the form and style of Newman's plays have varied a great deal over the years, for the most part, they have come to approximate conventional realist plays—at least in their beginnings. They then tend to evolve—or devolve, depending on your perspective—into philosophical conversations that resolve none of the conflicts raised by the play. As Richard Schechner put it in an interview in the early 1990s, "I would call Fred Newman's theatre a New York '90s working class style of performing. It's not the style of Stanislavski to Strasberg to Adler to you. Newman's work is the display of contradictions. There is no attempt to resolve and therefore the question becomes: What future do you want to construct?"[8]

This period following the move to Greenwich Street also coincided with a virtual blackout of critical response to Castillo's work. The involvement of Newman and other Castillo leaders in independent, left-of-center politics (from 1979 to 1994, with the pro-socialist New Alliance Party) made us an anathema in particular to the *Village Voice*, leftist gatekeepers of avant-garde and alternative theater in New York City. The weekly was born in the 1950s as the "voice" of the reform Democratic Party clubs—which by the 1970s had become the Democratic Party establishment in New York City. That establishment apparently felt threatened by the small successes of the New Alliance Party in the city's African American, Puerto Rican, gay, and liberal Jewish communities. In a *Voice* article about the opening of Castillo's new space on Greenwich Street (attended by JoAnne Akalaitis, Richard Foreman, Bill T. Jones, Judith Malina, Richard Schechner, and Robert Wilson, among others), Alisa Solomon declared that Castillo was not a theater at all, but a fund-raising scam for the New Alliance Party.[9] After that issue (which included a slam of Castillo's first production of Müller's *The Task*),[10] the *Voice* never again reviewed a Castillo production, and without the imprimatur of the *Village Voice*, none of the dailies would consider a review.

Although there have been dozens of pieces about Castillo productions in local community weeklies over the subsequent fifteen years, it would take Castillo's move to Forty-second Street, in 2004, to get a review in the *New York Times*. In a lackluster review of *Stealin' Home (A Baseball Fantasy)*, Newman's play about Jackie Robinson, critic Eddie Goldstein wrote, "*Stealin' Home* has much to share on racism, hero worship, cultural changes in the United States and latent homosexuality in the locker room. Perhaps the most valuable insight on contemporary role models is that only heroes in tights and capes can live a lifetime in the public eye without regrets."[11] During the first two years on Forty-second Street, the *Times* has reviewed three productions by Youth Onstage! (the All Stars Project's new youth theater) as well as *Day of Reckoning*, a play about the nineteenth-century anarchists Albert and Lucy Parson, by Melody Cooper. The other dailies have continued to keep their distance.

At a celebration of Castillo's move uptown, held at Sardi's in September 2004, Castillo was welcomed to the commercial theater district by Julio Petersen of the Shubert Organization; Tim Tompkins, president of the Times Square Alliance; Ken Cerniglia, associate dramaturg at Disney Theatrical; and Ben Cameron, executive director of the Theatre Communications Group—all of which is testimony to the power of the Castillo funding model. Despite the virtual boycott by the city's press, the years of intensive street fund-raising and audience building succeeded in what it set out to do: bridge the ongoing gap between ticket sales and production costs without resorting to government, corporate, or foundation money while, at the same time, winning the respect of many fellow theater producers and artists. Throughout the period of street work and canvassing, Castillo produced full seasons of up to nine plays a year, often filling the house without either a review or a penny of government funds and virtually no foundation money. At the end of its first decade, Castillo had proved that an alternative funding model for nonprofit theater in the United States was possible.

The years of street work and canvassing accomplished something else as well—a diverse audience with a close and active relationship with the theater. Castillo had started with a core audience of political activists and others whom they were organizing, primarily from the African American and Puerto Rican communities around the city. The street outreach expanded the Castillo audience dramatically, and over the years, it came to include elements of the younger, hip crowd that attends Off-Off Broadway, along with over-fifty upper-middle-class Broadway aficionados. It also includes a large proportion of African American, Latino, and other working-class people from the boroughs; businesspeople who do not usually attend theater, and international visitors.

People come to Castillo because, for the most part, they met Castillo on the street or on the phone. They come because they or someone they know is a Castillo investor, a Castillo angel. They may have given $5 on the street ten years ago; they may have contributed $5,000 last month. They may never have given money but have volunteered on house staff for the last two years. Whatever the specifics, it is *their* theater. Attending a show is, for most Castillo audience members, a social and civic activity. "I feel like there is a loss of community in New York and in America. The value of neighbors—the ability to share—is being lost," said Mike Grannum, explaining why he donates to Castillo and attends plays regularly. "Castillo's work of bringing people together to build community is extraordinarily important. It's a way we're talking to one another."[12]

Castillo's audience comes to see the issues and concerns of New York City and the larger world explored and played with, and this laboratory of the social imagination is theirs—it is funded and sustained by them. "I moved to New York City in 1992, and soon after I was walking down Eighty-sixth Street when a nice young lady with a clipboard appeared," said retired health-care administrator Michael Dean, recalling how he first encountered Castillo. "I've continued to support it all these years because it's a theatre that takes very seriously addressing the inequalities of our society. While I'm not always entertained by Castillo's productions, I feel an obligation to be supportive of this kind of work so that it can keep getting better."[13]

In this sense, Castillo is a community theater, although its community is neither geographical nor ethnic. The Castillo community is an open and self-defining community that Castillo itself has helped bring into being through its ongoing grassroots outreach. Here it is helpful to broaden our lens, for the community of which Castillo is a part was not built by Castillo alone. It is doubtful, given the conservative political atmosphere of the last twenty-five years, that it could have reached its current level of financial security as a freestanding political theater, no matter how extensive its street operation.

While Castillo was being built without government or corporate money, other activists from the same political movement were building other cultural and political organizations in the same manner. This network of organizations and projects became Castillo's larger community. The All Stars Talent Show Network (ASTSN) has been of particular importance in the growth and development of Castillo. The ASTSN was launched in the same year as Castillo. Its initial impetus came from members of the New York City Unemployed and Welfare Council who asked Castillo's founders to organize something positive for their kids to do. The ASTSN was originally produced by Castillo in church basements and community centers in some of New York City's poorest communities.

In 1989, the same year that Castillo moved to its Greenwich Street location, Pam Lewis, an actress and singer who had been performing with and building Castillo since 1985, became the producer of the ASTSN. Under her leadership, the program grew from a project of the Castillo Theatre to a large, self-sufficient cultural program for youth that outpaced Castillo in terms of both the number of participants (performers and audience) and the amount of money it was able to raise. Today, the Talent Show Network involves many thousands of young people each year in New York City and hundreds more in Newark, New Jersey. Elsewhere, the ASTSN is being produced by local organizations in Atlanta, Oakland, Los Angeles, and Amsterdam. In New York, a typical show attracts some 300 performers (dancers, singers, rappers, poets, and instrumentalists between the age of 5 and 25) and 1,500 audience members. Community centers have long since given way to high school auditoriums, the only venues large enough for a show of this size in most working-class communities.

As progressives, some of those organizing and fund-raising on the street and at the door for the Talent Show Network in the early 1990s were pleasantly surprised to learn that the appeal of a community-based youth development program crossed political and ideological lines. Not only liberals and progressives but also conservatives were willing to support a performatory youth program based in the city's poorest communities. For many conservatives, that the program did not take government money was a plus.

"No one ever went to conservatives and said to them, 'You have to support an effort to do something about the poverty and underdevelopment of Black and Hispanic people,'" points out Kurlander:

> People went to liberals and progressives for that, mostly through the funding conduits of the Democratic Party. We've learned that you don't have to be a progressive or a liberal to realize there's something wrong in this country, to feel that people and communities are underdeveloped and to want to do something about that. . . . We work to win conservatives, and all other donors, over to creating a social connection between themselves and their networks and people from other strata of society—with poor people, the young people in the Talent Show Network, and with the people who have built the All Stars and Castillo, people who are progressive political activists.

In 1998, Castillo joined the ASTSN as a program of the CLRP, and the following year, the CLRP changed its name to All Stars Project Inc. The All Stars Project now includes, in addition to Castillo and the Talent Show Network, two newer programs, the Development School for Youth and Youth Onstage![14] Donors now were organized around the totality of the work. Chris Street, the All Stars Project's director of development, recalls it this way:

> During the transition period, when the theatre and the All Stars ceased being separate non-profits, there were donors who had originally given to the talent show who questioned why we did the theatre. . . . We said, "We think it's important to do both, and we make this whole thing work, so at the very least you have to have a discussion with us about that. . . . If you like the development work we're doing, then you have to take a look at the fact that we think a politically engaged, independently funded theatre is an important part of the creative mix of this community."[15]

That initial resistance notwithstanding, funding levels have continued to rise, and even people who like neither the art nor the political perspective of Castillo's artists continue to give—and to attend the productions. Kurlander explained the phenomenon: "Business people have investment portfolios—stocks and bonds—and they put maybe five percent of their investments into experimental, really risky stuff. Philanthropically, that's us. . . . We say to the donors, 'Give to the traditional stuff. Give to the opera and ballet and your alma mater, but you have to up the percentage you're giving to the culturally experimental, the offbeat, the change-the-world effort.' That's compelling to people, not everybody, of course, but to a lot of people."

In 2003, the All Stars Project Inc. was able to purchase and renovate—at a total cost of $11.7 million—a performing arts and education complex at 543 West Forty-second Street, not far from Times Square. The complex contains three theater spaces, rehearsal rooms, costume and set shops, dressing rooms, and offices. This new All Stars Project headquarters is now home to Castillo and Youth Onstage! and contains the offices of the ASTSN and the Development School for Youth.

Throughout their histories, the ASTSN and Castillo have maintained a close relationship. In the earliest days, Castillo produced the talent shows—setting up and running the sound system, painting the backdrops, hanging and running whatever lights were available, and so on. Under Lewis's leadership, Castillo artists and technicians taught these skills to young people in the program, who have, for more than a decade now, run all tech, stage, and house management themselves. In the 1990s, there were a number of Castillo productions that involved young performers from the ASTSN. The opening of the new space on Forty-second Street has significantly deepened the cross-fertilization between the two projects. It has allowed for the formation of the Youth Onstage! youth theater and for much more interaction between Castillo and the young people in the other programs of the All Stars Project. A new theatrical form, the Hip-Hop Cabaret, featuring alumni of the talent show, has emerged at the All Stars' Forty-second Street complex. It combines the energy and creativity of hip-hop with the European political cabaret tradition. During the 2004–5 season, in addition to two plays and two Hip-Hop Cabarets produced by Youth Onstage!, two Castillo productions—*Have You Ever Seen A Dream Rapping?* and *License to Dream* (with the David Parsons Dancers)—featured young performers from Youth Onstage! and the Talent Show Network.

Kurlander likens the relationship between Castillo and the All Stars youth programs to the relationship in many nonprofit professional theaters between their productions and their education departments: "The Public Theatre, the Roundabout Theatre, all the major non-profit theatres have education departments. They get particular kinds of grants from particular kinds of sources to run programs for young people that help support their overall staffing of the theatre, and some of the theatre's activities that are harder to support. We're kind of like an education outfit with a theatre department. Another way to put it is that we take our education department very, very seriously."

The development of All Stars Project Inc. as a nonprofit that included both the Talent Show Network and Castillo took place under Kurlander's leadership and coincided with a vast expansion of the fund-raising capacities of both entities. During their first decade, the Castillo Theatre and the All Stars Talent Show Network had gathered a database of some one hundred thousand people (and their phone numbers) who had given at least $10. Given that base, we were able to gradually transition to a primarily phone operation, although street work has never ceased to be a part of the mix for Castillo.

In 1989, when Castillo and the Talent Show Network were both still primarily street operations, they raised a total of $250,000. In 2000, nearly six years after Castillo had transitioned to a primarily phone operation and had learned how to organize people to give larger sums, All Stars Project Inc. brought in $3.8 million in donations. Since then (the last five years), it has raised $31 million in private donations and $4 million in 2004 alone, a 17 percent increase over 2003. In addition to giving money, of the approximately five thousand people who give to the All Stars each year, some of them are businesspeople who actively reach out to friends and coworkers to give to the All Stars, thus themselves becoming volunteer fund-raisers and producers of the Talent Show and Castillo.[16]

In 1994, CLRP (now the All Stars Project Inc.) started the President's Committee, consisting of those who gave $1,000 or more annually. Today, the committee involves five hundred business leaders and concerned citizens in seventeen states. Counted among its members are seventy-five managing directors and partners in major Wall Street firms, hedge funds, *Fortune* 500 companies, and national law firms.[17] Learning how to ask for larger sums was a challenging process. "People won't give you $1,000 if you don't ask for it," notes Kurlander. "We didn't know how to do it before we did it. I literally went and asked some people for $50,000. It didn't work at first but I became someone who *could* ask for that kind of money and we soon found the people who could give it." In 2004, the largest single donation to the All Stars was $250,000—the total amount raised fifteen years earlier.[18]

Also contributing to this transition was the fact that a number of early All Stars volunteer organizers and fund-raisers—in particular, Jeff Aron and Bonny Gildin—found jobs as professional fund-raisers at other nonprofits in the mid-1990s. "We didn't know most of the traditional ways things got done, so we learned a lot from their experience," recalls Street. As the All Stars grew, it was able to hire a number of these former volunteers as full-time fund-raisers. "One big thing it did it was it gave them confidence," continues Street. "Our method is the method we developed—grassroots, in your face. Jeff [Aron] helped to develop that approach and then came back with the experience of a very successful traditional fundraiser as well. It gave them a worldliness that has been an important part of our success."

While the size of some of the donations has grown considerably and the number of people giving at any one time has gotten smaller, the broad base of the outreach and fund-raising remains the dynamic through which Castillo and all the projects of the All Stars Project continue to grow. Street explains:

> The key is that we are always bringing new people in. The top end is always looking to see if you're bringing new people in, otherwise they leave. That's critical and that's why we work to bring new Castillo donors in at $35 year, so the $100,000 donors know that they are not alone and that the theatre is healthy. . . . One tenth of one percent of those $35 donors goes on to give you $100,000 someday, but even if they never do, it's part of deepening the community and people see that you're busting your ass, that you're still on the street. They see that all sorts of people are supporting this with their money. It's just that some of them have more money and some have less money. If you have more money, you can give more money, but we at Castillo relate to everyone as an angel.

Notes

1. Figures supplied by Dolores Cepeda, comptroller of the All Stars Project Inc.

2. The phrase began to appear in Castillo's promotional material in the late 1990s. The collection of scripts by artistic director Fred Newman is *Still on the*

Corner and Other Postmodern Political Plays by Fred Newman, ed. Dan Friedman (New York: Castillo, 1998).

3. For more on the history of Castillo, see Eva Brenner, "Theatre of the Unorganized: The Radical Independence of the Castillo Cultural Center," *Drama Review* (Fall 1992) (T135): 26–60; Dan Friedman, "Castillo: The Making of a Postmodern Political Theatre," *Theatre Symposium* 8 (2000): 130–40; Pedro R. Monges-Rafuls and Laureano Corces, "Fred Newman: A Man of Many Ideas," *Ollantay Theater Magazine* 5, no. 1 (Winter/Spring 1997): 83–97; Fred Newman, "Surely Castillo Is Left—But Is It Right or Wrong? Nobody Knows," *Drama Review* (Fall 1992) (T135): 24–27.

4. For more information on the Institute, see http://www.eastsideinstitute.org.

5. Castillo and the publications were briefly affiliated as New Alliance Productions. This association proved significant both in terms of the political, and sometimes topical, orientation of Castillo's plays and in terms of the development of new leadership who helped further develop Castillo's work. For example, Diane Stiles, who was the production manager of the weekly newspaper, went on to become, and remains, Castillo's managing director.

6. All quotes from Gabrielle Kurlander are from an interview conducted by Dan Friedman, August 21, 2005.

7. Interview with Gladys Janava by Diane Stiles, Summer 2002.

8. Richard Schechner, ". . . New York '90s Working Class Style of Performing. It's Castillo' Own Style," *National Alliance* 12, no. 15 (April 8, 1991), 1.

9. Alisa Solomon, "Caught NAPing," *Village Voice*, October 17, 1989.

10. Robert Massa, "Reign of Error," *Village Voice*, October 17, 1989.

11. Eddie Goldstein, "A Baseball Legend Playing a New Position: Flawed Human," *New York Times*, November 20, 2004.

12. Interview with Mike Grannum by Diane Stiles, Summer 2004.

13. Interview with Michael Dean by Dan Friedman, November 11, 2005.

14. The Development School for Youth is a leadership-training program for inner-city teens between the ages of sixteen and twenty-one. Executives from major corporations teach workshops (e.g., Dressing for Success, Capital Markets 101, Resume Writing and Public Speaking) during a thirteen-week core training program and sponsor students in eight-week paid summer internships. Youth Onstage! produces politically engaged theater with young actors, aged fourteen to twenty-one, and provides a free after-school performance-training program taught, on a volunteer basis, by theater professionals.

15. All quotes from Chris Street from interview by Dan Friedman, August 21, 2005.

16. Figures from All Stars Project Inc. Annual Report 2004 and interview with Kurlander, August 21, 2005.

17. Street interview, August 21, 2005.

18. Ibid.

7

AN ALTERNATIVE THEATER ANGEL: GRANT GOODMAN

David A. Crespy

When one thinks of the typical theater investor, what comes to mind are those hopelessly starstruck entrepreneurs—say, corporate executives or investment bankers—who, out of personal vanity, rather credulously drop large sums of money into a Broadway show so they can see their names in the *Playbill* for the latest Broadway hit. And as the Broadway musical hits the $15 million mark for production budgets, in many ways only the super rich, super elite can afford to drop a few hundred thousand on these kinds of projects. But there is another theater in America, one that I have written about in my book, *Off-Off-Broadway Explosion*, and that is the regional alternative theater, which is largely funded by the generosity of a very different kind of theatrical investor. This kind of regional Off-Off Broadway lives in the community centers, libraries, and community-college and high school theater auditoriums. Here, the costs are low enough and the ideals high enough to allow to exist theaters that challenge prevailing tastes and mores and attempt to present the kind of plays that were once done in the small art theaters. These are not community theaters in the conventional sense of the phrase, doing endless productions of *Nunsense* or *Gypsy*. The regional alternative theater movement carries on the traditions of Paul Fort's Théâtre D'Art and Lugné-Poe's Théâtre de L'Oeuvre in the nineteenth century, the Provincetown Playhouse and Washington Square Players in the early twentieth century, and the Caffe Cino and La MaMa Experimental Theatre Club in the 1960s.

Across the country, these theaters, like Annex Theatre in Seattle or First Run Theatre in St. Louis, have found some funding through government sources, but they owe their existence to individual benefactors who are also theater members—putting in long hours of labor in addition to the money they invest. By the late 1990s and early 2000s, under the more conservative funding policies and economics of the Bush administration, these small theaters became more reliant upon these individual investors than ever. Theater artists presenting nontraditional work in places outside of New York, Chicago, or Los Angeles are still subject to the kind of backlash that Southwest Missouri State University in Springfield, Missouri, received when it produced Larry Kramer's *The Normal Heart* in 1989—a boycott by local conservatives and an attempt to shut down a theatrical production. Theaters have found it increasingly more difficult to find funding to present alternative theater. The theatrical entrepreneurs of this not-for-profit regional alternative theater movement are very different from rich dilettantes who do not actually participate in the day-to-day tasks of running a theater. They differ, too, from the kind of corporate investors like Disney, which consider the $10 million to $20 million it costs to produce a Broadway show a drop in its budgetary bucket.[1]

This essay examines one particular alternative theater angel and the events that led him to a lifelong commitment to theatrical investment. Professor Grant K. Goodman, an emeritus faculty member of the University of Kansas, has, since 1989, donated to the English Alternative Theater (EAT) of the University of Kansas in Lawrence anywhere from $10,000 to $15,000 a year for its artistic director, Paul Stephen Lim, to use any way he sees fit. Goodman describes his working relationship with Lim: "I've given him carte blanche—he tells me he's doing this or that or the other. I don't question his decisions. He's a very bright capable person and this gives him free reign to do as he sees fit. KU, accordingly, has the only English Department in the United States with a theatrical component. And that excites me as an academic."[2]

Since a full history of English Alternative Theater would be a separate essay, my focus is on the aspects of Goodman's life that led him to his initial investment in EAT and the vital roles he continues to play in that theater company. In addition, this essay explores Goodman's partnership with playwright, director, and playwriting teacher Paul Stephen Lim and how the two have worked together to provide a support system for theatrical writers in their community.

Goodman's investment effectively created English Alternative Theatre and sustains Lim's project, which is to produce alternative theater by artists who are often marginalized by mainstream tastes. Uniquely affiliated with the English department and independent of the theater department of the University of Kansas (with which it now coproduces original plays), EAT deliberately explores plays outside the realm of traditional community theaters while keeping very close ties with its own community. EAT's productions have included plays that deal with African American and Asian American culture, Native American drama and ritual, as well as plays of interest to scholars in the field of English literature. EAT has been and is one of the most important academic producers of new plays and new playwrights in the Midwest, many of which have been produced and published through the national and regional Kennedy Center American College Theatre Festivals.[3] In addition to original work, EAT has sought to stimulate the intellectual tastes of its Lawrence, Kansas, audiences by producing provocative new plays as a second stage and established plays of the Western canon in challenging new ways.

There was no alternative theater in Lawrence, Kansas, until Goodman provided Paul Stephen Lim with the opportunity to give voice to his talents as a producer, director, writer, and designer. In a state where science of evolution is questioned and the religious Right has fanned the flames of hatred and homophobia by the likes of Far-Right religious fanatics such as Reverend Fred Phelps, it is of the utmost importance that a theater like EAT have the opportunity to produce plays that challenge the status quo and raise important and controversial issues. And since its inception, in many ways, EAT has been a victim of its own success, having spawned since its inception in 1989 many other small theaters with which it now shares its Lawrence theater audiences.[4] Lim, however, does not believe that EAT really competes with any other group in Lawrence but attempts to

Grant Goodman and Paul Stephen Lim. Courtesy of Paul Stephen Lim.

be a supportive part of the Lawrence theater community, believing that "the more people go to the theatre, the better it is for all of us."[5]

According to Lim, most of the competition that EAT has encountered is with its own demanding schedule and the limitations of Lim running a "one-man operation"—though with its new working relationship with the university's Department of Theatre and Film even that is changing.[6] After sixteen years of looking warily at each other, under the new leadership of English Department chair Dorice Elliott and Department of Theater & Film chair Chuck Berg, EAT and University Theatre joined forces in fall 2005 to coproduce *An Army of One*, by Zacory Boatright, one of Lim's students. Lim says that the alliance is producing some inevitable "birthing pains," but, if all goes well, the two organizations can only help each other in continuing to create a more vital theater, one that begins with the playwright, preferably a playwright who is still alive and in our midst.

Grant Goodman was born on October 18, 1924, in Cleveland, Ohio. His parents, Elaine and Lewis Goodman, imbued him with a love of theater from a very early age. His father graduated from the Wharton School of Business at the University of Pennsylvania in 1921, and his mother graduated from then Western Reserve University (now Case Western Reserve University), also in 1921. Goodman's father went to work in his father's business, the buying and selling of textiles, and later he and Goodman's uncle, his father's only sibling, expanded into the manufacture of cloth polishing wheels, or buffs, as they were known. Despite his father's business focus, both of his parents were cultured and knowledgeable and kept him abreast of the world outside their lives in Cleveland. They kept a subscription to the *New Yorker*, and he traveled extensively with his parents and his father's mother throughout his youth. Goodman's parents were avid theatergoers, and they took him to New York frequently to see the Broadway theater. In addition, he attended the many road shows that came to Cleveland.

Goodman was a student at Shaker Heights High School, a progressive and rigorous high school in the 1940s, as it remains today. At Shaker Heights, Goodman was the editor of the school newspaper and was involved in dramatics as an extracurricular activity. He performed both the Player King and Osric in the high school's production of *Hamlet* in the 1941–42 academic season. He remembered the performance as being "an exciting and stimulating experience," and his high school experience in general as "wonderful and very fulfilling in every way."[7] In the fall of 1942, Grant Goodman was accepted into Princeton University; he was the first Shaker Heights student to be accepted to the school. He quickly sought out the dramatic arts at the school and was cast in drag as Gloria Glocoat in the Princeton Triangle Club Show, *Ask Me Another*, its first show in revue format. The drag performance was the norm for the Princeton Triangle Show that featured only male performers, and during the course of the Second World War, its operations ceased, briefly ending Goodman's burgeoning theatrical career.[8] In the spring of 1943, Goodman was interviewed for the Army Intensive Japanese Language Program and was selected to begin one full year of study at the Army Intensive Japanese Language School at the University of Michigan.

However, the study of Japanese did not curtail Goodman's theatrical activities. During that year in Japanese language training, some members of the first class wrote an original musical show titled *Nips in the Bud*. The students who created the show were a very unusual group in Goodman's opinion: "These were very, very bright guys who wrote songs—and it was a fantastic show."[9] *Nips in the Bud* was performed at the Lydia Mendelssohn Theatre at the University of Michigan, and it was a huge success. In retrospect, one of the curious things about the production is that the Army Intensive Japanese Language School program was, according to the documentation that now exists, supposed to be secret. Ironically, *Nips in the Bud* was so successful that the production moved to a run at the commercial theater in Ann Arbor, the Michigan Theater, and Goodman performed two small roles in that show.

Nips in the Bud was about the goings-on at the language school, about the interaction between the lower levels and the higher levels of students at the school. According to Goodman, one of the performers did a "wonderful" Geisha dance that he learned from one of the teachers. The show consisted of two acts and fifteen scenes, and it included such songs as "Strummin' on the Old Benjo" (*benjo* being the Japanese word for "toilet") and a grand finale with the title number and a patriotic march called "Off Toward the Rising Sun," with its stirring opening lyrics: "Hey, hearken to the Doughboys, / Off toward the Rising Sun; / Say, sad about the foe boys, / They're full of scare, / We'll soon be here, / They'll swear in old Nihon-go." By Goodman's own estimates, the production raised a million dollars' worth of war bonds, which at that time was considered a big deal. Although *Nips in the Bud* would be considered an offensive title now, it was deemed a very clever show at the time, and the audiences loved it.[10]

Goodman left Ann Arbor in the spring of 1944, after studying Japanese for a year, and went into infantry training for two months at Fort McClellan, Alabama. He then had six months of training of military Japanese in Fort Snelling, Minnesota, outside of St. Paul. In the spring of 1945, he went overseas as a second lieutenant in military intelligence and landed in the Philippines approximately two months before the Japanese surrender. Goodman had the extraordinary experience of working as an intelligence officer on General Douglas MacArthur's staff, translating captured documents and interrogating Japanese prisoners in Manila. He boarded ship three different times to invade Japan, only to discover it was a drill each time. In each case, Goodman had to climb landing nets with a full field pack and all his dictionaries and guns. "I thought I would never make it," he recalled. "I don't know how I did it to this day."[11] His producing partner, Lim, has often reminded Goodman during some of the more trying times of producing theater with the English Alternative Theatre that at one point in his life he climbed the sides of ships to fight for his country—no small achievement considering the enormous size of the dictionaries he was required to carry.[12]

When the atomic bomb was dropped, Goodman remembers that he and the others on MacArthur's staff were tremendously thrilled and relieved and believed correctly at the time that "that was about it for the Japanese." However, the invasion plans were always real, despite that they were never carried out—this was Operation Olympic—and were very well planned, although Goodman remembers saying to his fellow officers, "If we ever landed on the shore of Kyushu, any little old lady with a broom stick could have knocked us over the head because we were so burdened with these enormous dictionaries. You don't know how huge those dictionaries were in those days. I had Japanese-English, Japanese-Japanese, and military dictionaries in Japanese; they're physically very heavy and big and I still have them. I kept them after the military service."[13]

On September 2, 1945, Japan surrendered formally, and before the surrender there were negotiations with MacArthur, who wanted to have a complete order of battle from the Japanese. It was brought to the Philippines, and Goodman's team worked forty-eight hours straight translating all of it. For Goodman and MacArthur's staff, that was the end of the war.

Goodman finally did sail for Japan and landed on October 1, 1945, walking ashore at Yokohama because there was no port left standing to land in. His company had to make its way to the beach using landing craft. At the time, Goodman remembers being utterly appalled—he had never seen such destruction in all of his life, and no one in his company could understand how the Japanese had continued to fight—because, according to Goodman, "they had been bombed into smithereens." Goodman remained stationed in Japan for a year during its occupation by American forces—from October 1945 to October 1946. In the winter of 1945, the American forces sponsored a production of Gilbert and Sullivan's *The Mikado*, which had never been produced in Japan. The production of *The Mikado* was part of the effort to democratize the Japanese, and, since that production, the show has rarely been produced in Japan, because, to a certain extent, the opera was considered insulting to the Japanese.[14] It was produced at the largest surviving theater, which was the Takarazuka Gekijo, the theater at which the Takarazuka girls' troupe appeared. It was a huge theater, and the production was costumed with royal robes supposedly borrowed from the imperial household.[15] *The Mikado* was the only large theatrical production that Goodman experienced in Japan during his stay there.[16]

In October 1946, Goodman came back to the United States. His goal was to return to Princeton, but there was the problem of being admitted in the middle of the year. Despite that problem, the Princeton University office of admissions permitted Goodman's late admission, because he had just recently been honorably discharged from the military. Although the Princeton admission office permitted him a January admission, he had a period of free time after his release from military service between October and January of 1946. It was at this point when Goodman seriously entertained the notion of entering the American Academy of Dramatic Arts. In fact, he went into New York City on his own and made it up to the front door of the American Academy of Dramatic Arts. At the last minute, he decided against enrolling. As he recalls, "I said to myself[,] forget it—you're not good looking enough to be a professional actor, and two, I didn't think being Jewish would be a plus, and three, I didn't think I could sustain the kind of commitment that I felt I needed. I had come out of a very different kind of atmosphere academically. I just turned around and never did it. I've never regretted the decision, but of course, my interest in theatre remained."[17] It was particularly important to Goodman, after he made this decision, to still keep a foothold in the theater, despite the fact that he didn't have "the fire in the belly," to be an actor in the same way he had a passion to be scholar—and that was the deciding moment for him.

In the spring of 1947, he was again enrolled at Princeton and found himself once more in the Princeton Triangle Show, this one titled *All Rights Reserved*. He particularly enjoyed the experiences, especially after a five-year hiatus—it was fun to be reunited and renew his friendship with students from the 1942 Triangle show who were also back from military service. Goodman graduated in 1948, and at his graduation the theatrical world struck again. The great American stage actress Katharine Cornell received an honorary degree that year from Princeton, as did President Harry Truman—and the excitement at that graduation was palpable. Knowing that he had to walk up on the stage where the celebrities were seated and receive his degree, Goodman made it his business to take a good look at Katharine Cornell before he stepped off the stage—a moment that perhaps presaged his addiction to the magic of theater celebrity.

That summer, he left immediately for Ann Arbor and began his graduate studies at the University of Michigan. At that time, in 1948, the best program in Japanese studies in the United States was at Ann Arbor. The university had a generous Carnegie endowment for Far East studies and boasted a very fine faculty. Goodman completed a master's degree in Japanese studies in 1949 and a Ph.D. in history in 1955, publishing both his master's thesis and his doctoral dissertation.[18] Goodman came to love Ann Arbor and its community; and his love for theater continued there as well. He and his then roommate at Ann Arbor, a wealthy heir to General Motors money, decided to throw elaborate soirees in their home for visiting theater artists, who were invited by the University to present road shows. At that time, Ann Arbor was on the circuit for the ballet, including troupes like the Ballets Russes de Monte Carlo—one of the most popular of the ballet companies in the world at that time. The company and its lead dancer, Leon Danelian, came to all their parties—and later modern-dance legend Alvin Ailey came to some of them as well. The parties gave Goodman a chance to still feel part of the Ann Arbor performing arts community while keeping a focus on his graduate studies.

After completing his degrees at Ann Arbor, Goodman found himself in several different positions before finally, in 1962, accepting a job at the University of Kansas. These included one year at the University of Washington (1955–56), two years at the University of Delaware (1956–58), and a Fulbright scholarship to the Philippines (1959–60). He taught at the University of the Philippines, his second time in the Philippines, and his first time since the war. When he came back to the United States, he accepted a position at SUNY Fredonia, near Buffalo, and spent two years teaching there. Following that, he accepted a position at the University of Kansas and began a career there that lasted nearly twenty-seven years.

Goodman has published voluminously over his fifty-year career on Japanese and Asian history and has, in fact, been one of major figures in the academic field of Asian studies in the United States.[19] His contributions to the field have done much to shape its scope and to nurture its growth over the forty years of his work as a researcher, scholar, and writer. Despite retiring nearly sixteen years ago from the history department at the University of Kansas, Goodman remains a leader in his field and continues to be active as a Japan scholar, giving papers and attending conferences even as he celebrates his eighty-second birthday. His yearly sponsored University of Kansas lecture series, the Grant Goodman Distinguished Lecture in Japanese Studies, has brought to Lawrence many leading scholars in Japanese studies.[20] In addition, he is the sponsor of the Grant Goodman Prize in Philippine History through the Philippines Studies Group of the Association for Asian Studies.

Soon after Goodman had begun his career at Kansas, he received another Fulbright-Hays to Japan and the Philippines in 1964–65. He spent the first semester in Tokyo and the second semester in Manila. It was then that he met Paul Stephen Lim for the first time, through mutual friends in Manila. Lim was twenty-one and the chief copywriter for the Philippine subsidiary of J. Walter Thompson, one of the world's oldest and largest advertising agencies. Later, Lim was pirated away by another Philippine advertising agency, one that paid him twice as much. Lim was a kind of boy genius, taking advantage of his work in advertising to have other entrées in the field of communications. He had his own television program, and he was involved in coordinating events in the Araneta Coliseum in Quezon City, an enormous showplace. Goodman reflected on his first impression of Lim in the mid-1960s: "Paul was just remarkable—I was blown away. I had never met anybody like that, and I thought he was a genius. I couldn't get over him—he had read the whole Modern Library—people don't do that in America, let alone in the Philippines. I mean he was knowledgeable about authors, philosophy, and movies—all at the same time. Moving from subject to subject—and managing a full-time career in copywriting at the age of 21. It was amazing. Amazing!"[21]

But Lim eventually became bored with the advertising world in the Philippines and decided he wanted to be a writer in New York. It was a happy coincidence that his brother was living in New Jersey. He came to the United States on a tourist visa, with the hopes that he would find employment in advertising in New York. Because of his work with J. Walter Thompson Philippines, he assumed the parent company would immediately offer to hire him. But because his youth seemed to contradict his enormous experience in advertising, and because he seemed overqualified for the positions he applied for, after several months he had no luck finding employment. His visa was running out, and his hope that an employer would go to bat to procure him a green card was fading.

At that point, Lim was in contact with Grant Goodman, who suggested that Lim become a student at the University of Kansas—and procure a student visa. And so Lim enrolled at Kansas in 1969 to finish his degree, which he had never finished in the Philippines because he had dropped out of school to work in advertising. He remained on a student visa from 1968 until 1978. Initially, Lim's brother discouraged him from going to Kansas, because he had been a student there himself and had a bad experience there—and Lim would have his own struggles with the university. But because of his close connection with Goodman, Lim decided to enroll. Goodman arranged for Lim to work with one of the associate deans who was particularly perceptive and a strong advocate for the support of international students. He evaluated Lim's transcript from the Philippines, gave him credit for several courses, and designed a very specific graduation plan. In a year and a half, Lim graduated Phi Beta Kappa. Goodman recalls Lim's rapid progress at the university: "Just remarkable. He just blew the courses away—and the professors were equally stunned. Paul was an English major and then he went into the MA program in English and he immediately started teaching in 1972. I think Paul has been teaching almost thirty years already—something like that—because he started teaching into his MA program and even back then, he was winning awards in the teaching of Freshman-Sophomore English."[22] At that time, Lim wasn't interested in playwriting—he didn't know anything about it until he wrote his first play in a class taught by Dr. Ron Willis. Then, in 1975, typical of Lim's precocity, that play, *Conpersonas: A Recreation in Two Acts*, went to the Kennedy Center through the American College Theatre Festival. It was produced by the university's theater department, performed by Kansas students, and directed by Kansas graduate student David Cook. When that play went to Washington, Grant Goodman, Goodman's mother and aunt, and Lim's mother all went and stayed at the Watergate; according to Goodman, they "had a wonderful time. It was just so exciting!"[23]

Adding to the festivity, and perhaps the over-the-top success of Lim's play, there was a message from Imelda Marcos, the wife of Philippine dictator Ferdinand Marcos, congratulating him at the time. The success with this one play gave Lim the impetus to think more about playwriting. Because there was nobody at the university who was particularly interested in it—and certainly the Kansas English department had never offered it—Lim decided to teach it himself.[24] According to Goodman, Lim had some problems with the various chairs of the English department in those days, because they felt threatened by his productivity and ambition and, perhaps, were also jealous of his sudden success in the field of playwriting—this despite the fact that he did not have a Ph.D. Lim discussed this experience:

> As late as 1989 (the year the department decided to hire me to teach playwriting full time), the big discussion was whether or not the department should hire "one of its own." It was then argued that whatever I had learned as a playwright was something I had learned from others *outside* the department and the university and that, as such, I was "self taught" and not "one of its own." This was how I was hired, when the opportunity came up to do a "direct minority hire." Although I have always been a hard worker all my life, I threw myself into my new full-time job at the University of Kansas with even greater energy than usual because I wanted to prove to everyone that I hadn't been hired simply for the shape of my eyes or the color of my skin. To this day, I have very ambivalent feelings about "affirmative action."[25]

It finally took the influence of an executive vice chancellor who interceded on Lim's behalf to see that he got a regular appointment, and, from that point on, Lim went through the ranks in no time. He was assistant professor, associate professor, and finally full professor in the minimum of years. Still, according to Goodman, it took them quite a while to give Lim the kind of recognition that he has subsequently received as a distinguished professor of playwriting. Lim has now been teaching at University of Kansas for more than thirty years, beginning with freshman-sophomore English in 1972.

Lim started his theater work in Lawrence by directing for the Lawrence Community Center and, by the late 1980s, had directed five or six shows for that group. He was teaching half time in the English department and then, in 1989, was scheduled to direct one of his own plays, which he was in the process of writing for the Lawrence community theater. Lim then came on board full-time in the English department. At first, Lim thought there was absolutely no interest on the part of the theater department to present original scripts. In addition, he realized that the kind of original, and often controversial, material he was interested in producing would not interest the Lawrence Community Center. Despite this disinterest in producing original work, Lim felt if he was going to be teaching playwriting it might be possible to develop new plays if the English department had its own producing organization. In the beginning, Lim thought that the organization would just perform staged readings and maybe one production a year. And that was the start of the English Alternative Theatre.

The very first show that Lim produced was a double bill of Susan Sontag's *The Way We Live Now* and Terrence McNally's *Andre's Mother*, designed by James Erdahl, who later died of AIDS and whose struggle with the disease inspired the production. Lim had wanted to offer the full hour-long version of *Andre's Mother*, but the script was not available, so he contacted Terrence McNally. McNally said he had written it as a ten-minute play as part of an evening of plays about AIDS, and that people from PBS came and saw it and loved it and contracted him to write the hour-long version, which was eventually on PBS. However, PBS owned the rights to the play—he had sold it as a work for hire and so could not give Lim the rights to the hour-long version—but he agreed that the university could have the rights for free to the ten-minute version.

Despite these difficulties, Lim produced a double bill of Susan Sontag's *The Way We Live Now*, which is about five people talking about a friend of theirs who is offstage dying of AIDS, and he put the two together as though it was one play, so that it was as though the five people were talking about Andre, and then the EAT company segued into *Andre's Mother*. Lim produced the two one-acts as EAT's first full production in late November 1990. *Two From the Hurt* raised over $2,000, and EAT turned over the proceeds to the Douglas County AIDS Project, which had just been founded at that time. Like many of EAT's productions, the play was performed in an alternative space—the inside courtyard of the Spencer Art Museum. Erdahl designed the colorful backdrop for the play, and EAT used an actual grand piano, belonging to Franz Liszt, as the primary piece of furniture for the production. Lim describes how the performance of *The Way We Live Now* and *Andre's Mother* influenced Goodman: "The audience sitting on three sides of the grand piano was absolutely in tears—there was one man whose entire t-shirt was just drenched—he was crying so hard. Grant was so impressed by this that he then contacted me and said, 'What would it take for you to keep EAT going and for you to continue to do productions like this one?'"[26] Subsequently, Goodman, who had not yet committed to funding EAT, decided to put his money into its productions and has done so ever since.

Goodman donates his money to the English department, annually dedicating it to the Paul Stephen Lim Playwriting Development Fund in the University of Kansas's Endowment Association. According to Goodman, the money is there for Lim to draw on throughout the year for productions, travel, scholarships, and whatever need arises. Goodman pays in on a yearly basis, because Lim does not know at what point he will need a break or when his interests may change to new projects. For Goodman, his investment in EAT is a deeply felt, very personal tribute to a close friend and talented colleague. Goodman states, "I feel like I've invested very well in something really worthwhile." Because of his generous annual contribution, English Alternative Theatre continues in its somewhat quixotic quest, giving voice to the kind of plays that no other theater in Kansas would dare to produce.

However, beyond the local significance of Grant Goodman's funding of the University of Kansas's English Alternative Theatre, there are regional and national implications as well. Goodman's support of EAT is a paradigm for the funding of regional alternative theater within a university setting. This funding has made EAT a model for new play development within the academy and demonstrates how an alternative theater can contribute greatly to the success of student work. Goodman's funding has made it possible for EAT to produce scripts and productions that compete nationally through the Kennedy Center American College Theatre Festival. In addition, through EAT's involvement with the festival, Goodman's funding of nontraditional, marginalized plays and playwrights has made a significant impact on playwriting in the Great Plains region and nationally as well. EAT's artistic director, Paul Stephen Lim, has served as Region V Chair of the theater festival's National Playwriting Program. He later served as a respondent for the festival's national selection team and was honored by the festival with a medallion for lifetime achievement for his work with EAT. Paul Stephen Lim and his English Alternative Theatre have become the benchmark for the production and development of new work in American university theater, producing more winning plays and playwrights than any other university in its region. And none of this would have been possible without Grant Goodman's funding, and his deep belief in the possibility for alternative theater to change not only Kansas but also the world.[27]

Notes

1. Michael Riedl, "Curtain Call," *Jungle Magazine*, July 8, 2004, http://www.mbajungle.com (accessed July 26, 2005).

2. Grant Goodman, telephone interview by author, Columbia, MO, January 3, 2005.

3. In its sixteen years of existence, English Alternative Theatre has presented twenty original plays at the Region V Kennedy Center American College Theatre Festival, and of those, six have achieved national recognition through the festival or the Association for Theatre in Higher Education (ATHE). In addition, EAT also had an Irene Ryan National Winner (a major acting award) in Megan Dillingham in 1999. More information is available at http://www.eat.ku.edu (accessed July 26, 2005). Award-winning plays include *Graf Spee*, by Ken Willard; *Canvas*, by Sarah Zercher; *The Beadsman*, by Brian Boies; *The Devil's Game*, by Bo Price; *Upright*, by James Hilburn; *Pterodactyls*, by Scott Ferree; *Bereft*, by Nick Woods; *Bunnies*, by Michael O'Brien (also performed at the Kennedy Center in Washington, D.C.); *Whiteout*, by Alan Newton (selected as winner of the Lorraine Hansberry Playwriting Award); *Big Envelopes*, by Matthew Hubbard; *Mourning Glorie*, by Kirby Fields; *Two Faces of Deception*, by David Huffman; *The Smog Also Rises*, by Paul Shoulberg; *One Last Time*, by Carol Dias-da-Silva; *Ketchup*, by Kristin Soper; *Attack of the Asians*, by Tim Macy (also performed at the Kennedy Center in Washington, D.C.); *Fatherland*, by Adam Merker (also a prize-winning play at the ATHE Conference in San Diego); *The Story of Izanagi and Izanami*, by Kristen Wirsig (also performed at the Kennedy Center in Washington, D.C., and selected as the national winner); *The Option*, by Elizabeth Dean; and *Weaving the Rain*, by Dianne Yeahquo Reyner.

4. Mitchell J. Near, "Independent theaters stage opportunities for KU students," *Lawrence Journal World*, August 11, 2001. Some of these small independent theaters presenting plays in Lawrence, Kansas (outside the university's theater productions), include Lawrence Community Theatre, Will Averill's Cardtable Theatre, E.M.U. Theatre, Rick Averil's Seem-To-Be Players, and the Lawrence Arts Center.

5. Paul Stephen Lim, "Lim's Part of Essay," personal e-mail to the author, September 26, 2005.

6. Ibid.

7. Grant Goodman, interview by author, Lawrence, KS, December 25, 2004.

8. Mary Ann Jensen, "Difficulties in the Depression Years," Princeton Triangle Club—History, http://www.princeton.edu/~triangle/content_page history.html (accessed July 26, 2005).

9. Goodman interview, January 3, 2005.

10. Gene Sosin, "The Army JLS Revue," *The Interpreter: The US Navy Japanese/Oriental Language School Archival Project*, no. 70A, December 15, 2003, http://www.UCBlibraries.colorado.edu/archives/collections/jlsp/interpreter70a.pdf (accessed July 26, 2005).

11. Goodman interview, January 3, 2005.

12. Lim, telephone interview by author, Lawrence, KS, May 14, 2005.

13. Goodman interview, January 3, 2005.

14. Sumiko Enbutsu, "Playing *The Mikado* in the town of Titipu," *Japan Times* (online edition), January 28, 2001, http://search.japantimes.co.jp/member/member.html?file=ft20010128a1.html.

15. Joseph Raben, "*The Mikado* in Japan," Gilbert and Sullivan Archive: The Mikado, http://math.boisestate.edu/gas/mikado/html/mikado_japan.html (accessed July 26, 2005).

16. Ibid.

17. Goodman interview, January 3, 2005.

18. Grant Kohn Goodman, "A Translation of Otsuki Gentaku's Ransetsu Benwaku," Occasional Papers, No. 3 (Ann Arbor: University of Michigan Press, 1952); Grant Kohn Goodman, "The Dutch Impact On Japan (1640–1853)" (Ph. D. diss., University of Michigan, 1955).

19. Goodman has written, edited, or coedited fifteen books and more than sixty articles. A selected list of Goodman's major publications includes *Japan: The Dutch Experience* (London: The Athlone Press, 1986); *Amerika* no *Nippon Gannen* (America's Japan: The First Year, 1945–1946) (Tokyo: Otsuki Shoten, 1986); editor, *Asian History* (New York: Markus Wiener Publishing, 1986); editor, *Japanese Cultural Policies in Southeast Asia During World War 2* (New York: Macmillan, 1991); and editor, *Asian History*, 3rd ed. (New York: Markus Wiener Publishing, 1993).

20. "Foreign relations expert scheduled to speak at KU," *Lawrence Journal World*, March 19, 2003. Scholars who have presented their work in the Grant Goodman Distinguished Lecture Series include Chalmers Johnson, Emiko Ohnuki-Tierney, Akira Iriye, and John Nathan.

21. Goodman interview, January 3, 2005.

22. Goodman interview, December 25, 2004.

23. Ibid.

24. Lim, telephone interview by author, tape recording, Lawrence, KS, January 8, 2005.

25. Paul Stephen Lim, "Lim's Part of Essay," personal e-mail, September 26, 2005.

26. Ibid.

27. The Web site for EAT is http://www.eat.ku.edu.

8

PRODUCER, BENEFACTOR, AND PLAYHOUSE MAKER: DAVID GEFFEN

John R. Poole

Mogul of the entertainment industry, self-made multibillionaire, adviser to artists and presidents, David Geffen has been referred to by many in the entertainment business as a "genius," a "ruthless cutthroat," "the ultimate seduction," "an asshole," "a shark," a "pig," and "hero."[1] Hollywood insiders and cultural critics must also add to the list Angelino by way of Brooklyn, leading West Coast philanthropist, supporter of the gay community, and patron of the arts. Enfant terrible of the 1970s and 1980s music industry, Geffen has shaped the music we have heard over the past forty years and thereby the popular culture of our time. Often referred to as "Hollywood's richest man" Geffen built a personal empire estimated by Forbes in excess of $4.5 billion by discovering, managing, or producing pop music icons such as Jackson Brown; Janis Joplin; the Eagles; Joni Mitchell; Crosby, Stills, Nash & Young; John Lennon; Bob Dylan; Aerosmith; Cher; Guns N' Roses; and Nirvana.[2] As a "bad-boy" record producer, he leveraged his way into Hollywood filmmaking by banking on then unknown actor Tom Cruise and producing top-grossing hits such as *Risky Business*, *Interview with a Vampire*, and *Beetlejuice*. The *G* in DreamWorks SKG, Geffen's more recent successes include *American Beauty*, *Saving Private Ryan*, and *Gladiator*, with partners Steven Spielberg and former Disney whiz kid Jeffrey Katzenberg. Unlike his mentors and peers who shunned professional theater, Geffen parlayed his celebrated instinct for what the public wants by developing a strong relationship with the Shubert Organization in New York City and by backing some of the biggest winners in Broadway and Off-Broadway history. *Cats*, *Little Shop of Horrors*, and numerous other Broadway hits have made Geffen "the only man in the history of cultural capitalism who has succeeded in three different industries—popular music, Broadway, and Hollywood."[3]

In the early 1990s, the David Geffen Foundation set the pace for a new philanthropic ethos in the land of convertibles, suntans, and palm trees, in part "fueled by ego, prestige, [and] civic pride."[4] He has donated millions to the nonprofit community in Los Angeles: a staggering $200 million donation to the University of California, Los Angeles, School of Medicine, "the largest gift of its kind," and now renamed the UCLA David Geffen School of Medicine; $1 million each to amfAR (American Foundation for AIDS Research) and APLA (AIDS Project L. A.), including $2.5 million to the David Geffen Center for H.I.V. Prevention and Health Education; $5 million for the Geffen Contemporary at the Museum of Contemporary Art; and two seismic endowments totaling $10 million to Los Angeles's newly minted David Geffen Playhouse.[5]

The man and his foundation are indistinguishable; one informs the other and provides a window into his support of those enterprises that strike closest to his sense of alienation as "an individual whose identity is in part constructed from his isolation as a gay man."[6] Indeed, if this impresario's unprecedented success in the music industry was fueled by unbridled insecurity—Geffen profiler John Seabrook wagged "the only long-term investment through the years had been himself"—his motive to produce Broadway shows appears to grow out of his deep affection for theater as the earliest refuge of his young life.[7] Elusive and enigmatic, Geffen adheres to film producer Ray Stark's dictum "high profile, broken nose" and, thus, frustrates chroniclers who fail to capture the sensibilities of the man behind the icon, preferring instead to focus on the juicy if polarizing elements of his character.[8] Insights as to what motivates Geffen's philanthropy in funding AIDS research as well as his support of the arts

David Geffen under the marquee of the Winter Garden Theatre before the Broadway opening of *Cats*. Chester Higgins Jr./The New York Times.

are to be found by looking at his early and recurring romance with the Broadway musical.

"I'm just a Broadway baby"

David Lawrence Geffen was born on February 21, 1943, the younger of two sons born to Abraham and Batya Geffen—both first-generation immigrants from Russia. As a middling student, there was little in his childhood that would suggest any potential for a successful career. He was "one of those kids you would shake down for a quarter on the playground, or you'd steal his slice of pizza in the schoolyard," recalls a junior high schoolmate. Unlike other boys in the rough-and-tumble world of Brooklyn, Geffen found escape in reading about celebrities, Broadway, and Hollywood, in the columns of Walter Winchell, Ed Sullivan, and Earl Wilson. Repeatedly watching favorite films such as *The Wizard of Oz* and *Singin' in the Rain* and devouring *Hollywood Rajah*, Bosley Crowther's biography of Louis B. Mayer, fueled his desire for a life far away from the streets of Brooklyn.[9] Batya recognized that David had the same drive and instinct as she had and would often buoy his spirits by referring to him as "King David," convincing him that one day he would be a great success. In the late 1940s, Batya expanded the shoestring operation she ran out of her Brooklyn apartment into a successful storefront business, Chic Corsetry by Geffen—"If you look buxom, try our bra that makes you look smaller and younger!"—and schooled her son in the art of negotiating the deal with suppliers and customers. Watching his mother run a small business would instill in him an entrepreneurial savvy that he would draw on for the rest of his life.[10] "My mother," Geffen told *Forbes* magazine, "taught me how not to get hustled."[11]

Independent and confident, young Geffen was soon drawn to the nearby world of Broadway. Unaccompanied, he fearlessly hopped the train to Times Square, where he went to see the great Broadway musicals of the 1950s, having paid on one occasion $2.90 for a balcony seat to see Rex Harrison and Julie Andrews in *My Fair Lady*. The future producer of *Little Shop of Horrors* and *Cats*, and of landmark plays *M. Butterfly* and *"Master Harold" . . . and the Boys*, got his first entrepreneurial experience as "something of a ticket shark," scalping tickets outside Broadway theaters on opening night . . . at the tender age of ten.[12] The stomping grounds of Broadway's Great White Way provided his first lessons in the distinctions between show business and business. In a thoughtful profile, Edmund White captures something of Geffen's understanding of how these two worlds intersect: "[Geffen's] personality marks that awkward point where art meets business, for if art is based on sympathy (compassion and understanding and above all empathy, a readiness to plumb one's own feelings, even the vaguest, and to divine other people's sentiments, even the most transgressive), then business is, more brutally, all about knowing when to cut one's losses, when to shut down the film if it's running over budget, how to fire a friend and how to distinguish between one's own taste and one's judgment about what will sell."[13] However much his personal tastes may have been reflected in his affinity for the Broadway scene, Geffen's hunger for success soon led him to realize that "a star is a star," whether on Broadway or in the evolving rock music industry. It would be in the latter that his chutzpah would make him a very rich man at a very young age.[14]

Rapidly ascending through the ranks of William Morris and other management agencies in New York, Geffen moved to the West Coast in the late 1960s to be closer to the action, where, over the next decade, he prospered, founding his own recording labels, first Asylum and later

Geffen Records. Geffen created a very successful niche for himself in Los Angeles working with whom he called "significant artists." He fostered an environment where an artist "creates their [*sic*] own music, records it, and produces it. As opposed to pop artists, who use other people's work and it's all fabricated. These people create and craft themselves."[15] Geffen's meteoric rise and financial fortune were made by founding and/or shepherding the careers of the Eagles and Crosby, Stills, Nash & Young and by reviving the stalled careers of Cher (with whom he had a brief and very public affair) and Bob Dylan. Even as he secured his financial fortune, the wunderkind recording producer attempted to make his mark as a film producer. The results were mixed. Except for his lone hit film *Risky Business*, his foray as a Hollywood producer was peppered with notorious flops, including *Personal Best*. With his career beginning to fizzle and battling a brief cancer scare (a purported benign tumor in his bladder was later revealed to be a misdiagnosis), Geffen retreated to New York. There, he more openly explored his gay identity while playing in the New York City nightlife; attending gallery openings; hanging out with friends Calvin Klein, Halston, and Steve Rubell at the latter's notorious Studio 54; and reconnecting with his first passion, Broadway theater.[16]

Just when it seemed the world was through with David Geffen, Bernard Jacobs, president of the Shubert Organization, approached him with the idea of backing a musical in workshop that was having some trouble. The production was *Big Dreams*, and this time the "significant artist" was not an up-and-coming rock star but choreographer and director Michael Bennett, creator of *A Chorus Line*.[17] Geffen bankrolled the production by investing several hundred thousand dollars to keep the project moving forward.[18] "David has this knight-in-shining-armour syndrome," a friend once observed. "He particularly liked it if he could rescue you from a compromising situation."[19] Attracted to more than just his money, artists valued "his intelligence, his deep and cutting sense of humor, shrewd eye, and love of gossip. He was an instructive presence: funny, bright, and formidable."[20] So, too, Bennett was attracted, warming to Geffen personally but also appreciating his contributions to *Big Dreams*; the musical workshop about the 1960s music business, for which Geffen had a special affinity, was an ideal first investment in a Broadway show.

The new backer did not meddle with the artistic details of the production, unlike the intrusive, micromanagement style some felt he adopted in music and film ventures. Rather, he preferred to underwrite artists of Michael Bennett's caliber who captured his imagination. Money and "the chance to make buckets of it" had usually been his motivation for a given venture. Such was still the case with the new musical. For the first time, however, Bennett's new project seemed not only to reflect a diversion away from "stoking the star maker machinery behind the popular song" but also to tap into a personal sensibility with which he identified.[21] When Bennett asked for Geffen's advice, it was given. Indeed, it is David Geffen who suggested that the musical's title *Big Dreams* be changed to *Dreamgirls*, and the art department at Geffen Records designed the now-famous logo and posters.[22] Besides bankrolling the new show, Geffen also secured the rights to release the Broadway cast album and to produce a movie version (released in December 2006 through DreamWorks/Paramount). Jennifer Holliday made an impression on the record mogul, and he offered her a solo recording contract. Indeed, Geffen's clever marketing of the *Dreamgirls* original-cast album would lead to two Grammy Awards.

After the critical and financial success of *Dreamgirls*, Geffen was again approached by the Shubert Organization to back Andrew Lloyd Webber's London smash *Cats* for Broadway. The production would cost an unprecedented $3.9 million. Geffen believed in the production's potential market value more than the other investors did and immediately signed on. As preproduction costs skyrocketed and the other backers became "jittery" over the ever-increasing budget, Geffen did not blink. He saved the imperiled production by backing a full third of the then-unknown commodity.[23] Twenty-nine years after hustling tickets as a ten-year-old kid, *Cats* opened in 1982, and for Geffen it became "the single best investment ever made in a Broadway show," expanding his fortune by approximately $6 million annually for the run of the show.[24] In a profile by the *New York Times* a few days before the production opened, Geffen immodestly crowed, "The record business is a disaster, Broadway is a disaster. Things are bad, but I'm doing well. . . . I'm Billy the Kid, the fastest draw. It's not arrogance. It's the truth. I'm good at deciding what people like. I'm gifted at knowing what will be a success before it is a success."[25]

Geffen's association with the Shubert Organization would lead to numerous other ventures: *"Master Harold" . . . and the Boys*, *Good*, *Miss Saigon*, and *Little Shop of Horrors*, a small Off-Broadway show that "most captured [Geffen's] imagination" and would become "the highest grossing musical in Off-Broadway history."[26] Perhaps feeling threatened by King David's Midas touch, Bernard Jacobs commented that Geffen was, in fact, just an investor in these plays, but that he gave so generously and so often that they let him wear the title of producer.[27] Quibbling aside, Geffen's business acumen in marketing Broadway musicals to America through his recording label helped revitalize "the fabulous invalid's" resurgence in the 1990s. Original-cast recordings of *Dreamgirls*, *Cats*, *Rent*, and *Little Shop of Horrors* proved highly successful, with *Les Misérables* alone selling more than a million copies.[28]

With his career on the upswing, Geffen was again a major powerbroker in Hollywood. He ceaselessly talked up *Little Shop of Horrors* songwriting team Howard Ashman and Alan Menken to Hollywood executives and introduced them to his friend Jeffrey Katzenberg, the up-and-coming executive in charge of the then-moribund animation production unit at Disney. Geffen felt that the reason Disney's latest animations were flat was primarily because of the music. He won Katzenberg over with the idea that the new animated features should have "Broadway-like scores." Katzenberg struck a multipicture deal with the songwriting duo and revitalized Disney animation and, eventually, the Broadway musical, with such hits as *The Little Mermaid*, *Beauty and the Beast*, and *Aladdin*.[29] Geffen enjoyed playing "the man behind the curtain," pushing ideas until they caught on. It was Geffen who harassed an initially reluctant Mel Brooks to create a Broadway musical treatment of *The Producers*: "David Geffen called me at my office and said, 'You know, I got a great idea. I've just seen *The Producers* on television and it was meant to be a musical.' I said, 'No. It's a good movie; let's leave it alone and forget about it.' He said, 'No!' and he wouldn't. . . . He was like a terrier. He grabbed a cuff of my trousers with his little terrier teeth and jaw and wouldn't let go until finally I said, 'Ok! Ok! We'll make it a Broadway musical.'"[30]

Beavis and Butt-head, Philanthropists

Civic pride in the City of Angels had long remained dormant. Not since the early 1960s, when Dorothy Chandler, the city's leading cultural patron, joined forces with Lew R. Wasserman, de facto "godfather" of Hollywood, to build the city's first major performing arts facility in the form of the Dorothy Chandler Pavilion had any kind of civic enterprise taken hold.[31]

Indeed, "for all their glitzy wealth and self-promotion" there appears to be "no sense of civic pride that obliges one to give in a sustained or systematic way."[32] Los Angeles's volatile entertainment industry; swelling immigrant populations; lack of proximity of cultural districts to wealthy neighborhoods; and myriad natural, economic, and political disasters over the years conspired to suppress any genuine sense of patronage on behalf of the city. With the rise in the early 1990s of the Hollywood "mogulocracy," powerbrokers Eisner, Ovitz, Spielberg, and others made philanthropy the ultimate sign of power. Industry mavens attribute the recent mania in high-profile art collections and philanthropic giving as parts "financial investment, social status, and aesthetic appreciation." In a business fraught with all manner of anxieties, acquisition, and appropriation, such largesse "gives [Hollywood executives and stars] a seriousness which their work doesn't, and it cuts them apart from the pack."[33] In truth, who could resist the allure of being the benefactor whose support draws such gushing, over-the-top press as in *Vanity Fair*'s coverage of the newly opened Getty Center in 1997: "with its colonnades, skylights, courtyards, and reflecting pools, this will be the Louvre of Los Angeles, its Uffizi, Tate, and Metropolitan. *And*, one feels, its Acropolis, its Vatican City, its Teotihuacán."[34]

Ego and jealousy have always played their part in spurring charitable giving, along with more altruistic motives, and they appear to be driving the new giving in Los Angeles on an unprecedented scale. Michael Eisner donated $25 million to jump-start a drive for the new $50 million Disney Concert Hall, which also benefits the California Institute of the Arts; Steven Spielberg established two new foundations to "promote Jewish life"; and Michael Ovitz earmarked $25 million to the UCLA School of Medicine.[35] David Geffen's long history of business conflicts with über-agent Michael Ovitz, founder of Creative Artists Agency and regularly touted in the 1990s as "the most powerful man in Hollywood," served as a catalyst for philanthropic gestures to the good fortune of the Los Angeles citizenry.[36] Fund-raisers in Los Angeles joked that then mayor Richard J. Riordan could solve the city's fiscal troubles simply by changing its name to Los Geffen.[37] "Hollywood giving is all about billing," and David Geffen would play second banana to no one.[38]

Such rivalries do not, in themselves, fully explain the generosity of Geffen's contributions in reshaping the cultural landscape of the Los

Angeles community. A confluence of events served to motivate Geffen to funnel his fortune into his adopted hometown. After years of struggling to maintain the appearance of a heterosexual life and after losing many friends and associates to AIDS, he made national headlines when, during an acceptance speech at the AIDS Project Los Angeles (APLA) ceremony honoring him for his contributions to AIDS charities, Geffen declared, "As a gay man, I've come a long way to be here tonight."[39] Coming to terms with his gay identity was the key to his early philanthropic gestures. While he enjoys a devoted circle of friends, as of this publication, Geffen has no significant other, no family beyond a very tenuous one with his estranged brother, no one with whom to leave his fortune. The City of Los Angeles perhaps more than any single person inherits his legacy, his fortune, and even his heart. Of the city he has said, "[It] is my home and I want to do my part in contributing to its future."[40]

In 1986, the David Geffen Foundation was established to emphasize giving in four major areas: populations affected by HIV/AIDS; civil liberties; the arts; and issues of concern to the Jewish community, particularly in California and New York.[41] In the merger mania of global entertainment conglomerates in the late 1980s and early 1990s, Geffen augmented his foundation's portfolio by selling David Geffen Records to MCA, which in turn was sold to the Japanese consortium Matsushita Electric Industrial (MEI). When the dust had settled on the mergers, Geffen netted a cool $600 million.[42] The Geffen Foundation continues to grow through profits on such dubious cultural but financially successful films as *Beavis and Butt-head Do America*. After watching the popular animated show on MTV, he proposed the idea of transforming the irreverent cartoon series into a movie and record album. Once again, his intuition about the cultural value of a given project proved infallible. The movie grossed more than $60 million in its U.S. theatrical release alone, with additional millions flowing in from the international release and its soundtrack and home video sales.[43]

Since 1990, Geffen has funneled his entire salary and 100% of the profits from his film, recording, and Broadway transactions to his foundation. The most savvy of Hollywood brokers, his deals ensure that he "receive 10% of a film's first dollar gross—which is distributed even before the studio recoups its costs."[44] To date, the total assets of the David Geffen Foundation are in excess of $182,921,433.[45] This figure does not include

Geffen's contribution to his foundation through the sale of DreamWorks SKG to Viacom in 2005 for $1.6 billion.[46]

"What is the city but the people?"

The people are indeed the city, as Shakespeare suggests in *Coriolanus*, yet in Los Angeles, theater was not developed for its own sake, nor for that of its citizenry, but as a tool in service to its hometown industry. If Broadway represents a lucrative avenue of economic exploitation by Hollywood, theater in Southern California has largely been more about showcasing talent for film producers and directors than about developing a genuine cultural mission to serve the community. In part, this is because of the peculiar nature that is the Hollywood machine. Unique to Los Angeles is the Equity waiver agreement, known as the ninety-nine-seat waiver or the Plan by Actors' Equity and the Screen Actors Guild. This code waives Equity rules in order to allow union actors (read, film and television stars) to perform without a salary contract.[47] One of the best-kept entertainment secrets in Los Angeles, audiences can see live performances by actors who they recognize from film and television while providing opportunities for young or established screen actors to generate exposure "between projects." The provision restricts theaters operating under this code from having more than ninety-nine seats and thus prevents the legitimate theater producer from staging more challenging productions or attracting a larger audience.

To be sure, there is a humming theatrical scene, particularly in Hollywood's so-called Theater Row, but on the whole, the ninety-nine-seat waiver operates to suppress the growth of the theater market. Randall Arney, artistic director of the Geffen Playhouse and former artistic director of Chicago's Steppenwolf Theatre explains:

> Young artistic grassroots companies that are producing in 99-seat houses is very different from the actors who don't care about their 99-seat houses: "I'm just doing this so my agent can see me and I can get an agent and get a film." Young theatres that are wanting to grow are kinda kept at 99 seats. There are more functioning theatres in Los Angles than any other city in the country when you count the 99-seat houses. [However,] no grassroots little group of actors bringing furniture from their parent's porches in 99-seat houses are able to take the step to 125 seats because the union then insisted you pay.[48]

In essence, ninety-nine-seat waivers, designed to protect actors in the film and television industry, inhibited the Darwinian evolution of working theaters in Los Angeles to expand to the next market level. Arney points to the success of Steppenwolf in Chicago's burgeoning theater scene which helped create a "middle class" of theater in town. "When we came to Chicago in 1980 there were only a handful of theatres, the Goodman among them. Today there are 180 or 200 of different sizes."[49] Successful theaters propagate other successful ventures.

In 1995, Geffen overcame the hobbling effects of the ninety-nine-seat waiver when his foundation stunned the Los Angeles theater community by giving $5 million to the former Westwood Playhouse (originally an old furniture store), making it "one of the largest philanthropic donations ever made to an already-constructed nonprofit theater." Owned by UCLA since 1993, the theater was promptly renamed the Geffen Playhouse in recognition of the sizable gift. "The largest [gift] the foundation has made in the arts arena" is all the more remarkable, as there were no conditions placed on the donation.[50]

Theater leaders hailed the generosity of the gift. "For such a long time, we've hoped there could be a relationship between Hollywood and the nonprofit theater, where so many of the people in Hollywood got their start," said Lindy Zesch, longtime deputy director of Theatre Communications Group in New York. Moreover, Zesch added that this kind of contribution is rare nationwide, "In terms of an outright gift, not related to the construction of a building, I don't think there has ever been anything this big." The gift provided for a yearly payout of $500,000 over ten years toward operating expenses and helped bridge the funding gap that must sustain the annual $4 million operating budget.[51] For Arney, the donation represents a watershed event, "By creating a 500-seat theatre on the west side of Los Angeles, David helped us land as a premiere theatre that sort of just joined the Pasadena Playhouse and Mark Taper Forum." "What he has done is open up a major chapter in West Los Angeles for theatre of a size that hadn't existed."[52] Five years later, in 2002, the theater's namesake again made another unprecedented donation of $5 million as part of the drive to raise $17 million for renovation, expansion, and endowment of the five-year-old playhouse.[53] In a press release, Geffen said, "I believe the theater is important to the cultural life of Los Angeles, and I'm proud of its association with the UCLA School of Theater, Film and Television."[54]

In the past ten years, the Geffen Playhouse has benefited the entire Los Angeles region, even as it has aggrandized its major benefactor. Since there were no conditions placed on the grants, the playhouse was able to funnel some of the funds into educational programs and develop a subscriber list of approximately fourteen thousand that reads like a who's who of Hollywood. Hollywood elite such as Dustin Hoffman, Tom Hanks, and Sharon Stone bring their families to various programs at the local playhouse, where they mingle with approximately one hundred thirty thousand attendees annually.[55] According to Arney, "There is obviously an audience for theatre that we've been able to tap into."[56]

Through the leading gifts of the Geffen Foundation, the Geffen Playhouse has created a venue for "a body of work that has changed the cultural landscape of Los Angeles."[57] In fact, Gilbert Cates, noted film director and producing director of the playhouse, wants it to be "a place where you see plays that you otherwise couldn't see unless you traveled thousands of miles[,] . . . a theater with a broad, risk-taking point of view."[58] The Geffen's programming is eclectic in that it produces a wide variety of projects that "have a real community impact here," says veteran Los Angeles theater director David Schweizer.[59] Productions include popular, contemporary plays such as Steve Martin's *Picasso at the Lapin Agile* and Richard Greenberg's *Take Me Out*, as well as new adaptations of *Hedda Gabler* (starring Annette Bening), *Little Shop of Horrors* and *By Jeeves*, which first premiered at the Geffen en route to Broadway. The playhouse recently produced Heather Raffo's *Nine Parts of Desire*; *Harriet's Return*, starring Debbie Allen as Harriet Tubman; Donald Margulies' *Collected Stories*; and new works by David Mamet, Sam Shepard, and Sandra Tsing Loh. Due to the playhouse's close association with Hollywood, it also offers a venue for noted screenwriters to produce world-premiere works, such as Lawrence Kasdan (*The Accidental Tourist, Grand Canyon*) and *Six Feet Under* and *West Wing* scribe Rick Cleveland. In the fall of 2005, the Audrey Skirball Kenis Theater at the Geffen Playhouse opened, providing an intimate space that serves as a site for new play development. The opening of this new space fills a potential vacuum in Los Angeles, in view of the Center Theater Group's announced elimination of four programs devoted to minority play development in 2005.[60] Actors who have worked at the playhouse include John Goodman, Uta Hagen, David Hyde Pierce, Frank Langella, Steve Martin, Beau Bridges, Jason Alexander, Peter Falk, and countless others.[61] The integration of professional opportunities in directing, acting, and writing for artists who populate the film industry is indeed unique.

However, the playhouse holds another unique and more far reaching position in Los Angeles theater: "For Geffen, it is outreach," according to Jennifer Edwards, the playhouse's director of grants and communication.[62] Debra Pasquerette, education director agrees, "The main stage may draw from West L.A., but education and outreach reach the entire metropolitan area."[63] A model for regional theaters, the diversity of programs reaching out to community and social service groups is unmatched in the city and rivals that of any regional theater in the country. The Geffen actively seeks organizations that focus their efforts on underserved or disadvantaged groups by introducing them to interactive workshops and seminars as well as offering complimentary tickets to all main-stage productions. Organizations such as Alternate Living for the Aged, Chinatown Service Center, Hispanic Seniors Club, Islands of Tolerance, Reading Is Fundamental of Southern California, and LA Shanti are enjoying access to live theater on an unprecedented level.[64] The impact of the theater's outreach program is evidenced by one youth's comment from GLASS (gay, lesbian, and transgender teens who have been abused), who, after a performance of *Looking for Normal*, said, "After seeing this play, I know now that other people feel the same as I do."[65] According to Pasquerette, the goal of this and other programs is "to diversify our patrons" from senior citizens to at-risk students, adding, "At any given night, you can have a [$10,000] donor and seated two rows back kids from a halfway house." The Geffen also enjoys a strong partnership with the Los Angeles Unified School District, the largest school district in America, by providing all eligible Title I, low-performing schools complimentary tickets and bus transportation to student matinee presentations. The Geffen is unmatched in the quality and reach of its outreach programs, providing for many disadvantaged youth their only exposure to the performing arts.[66]

Why does Geffen continue to support the playhouse and the development of theatre in Los Angeles? "I'm not sure," muses Arney. "He's been to some of our shows but not a lot of them necessarily. By the same token I have a feeling he likes when things are going well at the Geffen Playhouse. I have a feeling he likes that affiliation. He likes the fact that he has written a check and that it's impacting live theatre in Los Angeles."

Arney pauses for a moments and then adds, "He felt it important to plant a seed here."[67]

Planting seeds is David Geffen's contribution to the American theater both on Broadway and regionally in Southern California. Pennies from heaven, if you will. Geffen as "angel" is merely a manifestation of the uneasy relationship between commerce and art. Without this mogul's deep pockets, *Dreamgirls* would have never seen a Broadway opening; *Les Misérables* would not have enjoyed the same measure of international recording success; and young, nontraditional theater audiences would never have been introduced to *Rent*. More quietly, had it not been for Geffen's leadership and financial clout, the emergence of a more vibrant and accessible professional theater in Los Angeles would not have been possible. It is interesting to note, then, that in Hebrew, *Geffen* means "fruit of the vine."[68] Joni Mitchell, perhaps better than most, captures the amalgam that is Geffen's hybrid career of dealing in business and art in "Free Man in Paris," a song she wrote about him. He deals "in dreamers and telephone screamers," knitting together two inextricably linked cultures of creativity and commerce. Yet, out of the noise of *Cats*, Cruise, or Crosby, Stills, Nash & Young, the creation of his new playhouse remains the real David Geffen legacy in nurturing a new millennium of dreamers.[69]

Notes

1. Marlo Thomas in Tom King, *The Operator: David Geffen Builds, Buys, and Sells the New Hollywood* (New York: Random House, 2000), 269; Sonny Bono in Stephen Singular, *The Rise and Rise of David Geffen* (Ontario: Carol Publishing Group, 1997), 54; Peter Lampack, Geffen assistant and protégé, in David Rensin, *The Mailroom: Hollywood History from the Bottom Up* (New York: Random House, 2003), 126; Julia Phillips, *You'll Never Eat Lunch in This Town Again* (New York: Random House, 1991), 534; David Crosby in David Crosby and Carl Gottlieb, *Long Time Gone: The Autobiography of David Crosby* (New York: Doubleday, 1988), 140; Michelangelo Signorile, *Queer in America: Sex, the Media, and the Closets of Power* (Madison: University of Wisconsin Press, 2003), 302, 365.

2. *Forbes 400* 176, no. 7 (October 2005): 150.

3. John Seabrook, *Nobrow: The Culture of Marketing, The Marketing of Culture* (New York: Alfred A. Knopf, 2000), 180.

4. Mary McNamara, "The Changing Face of Giving; Philanthropy in America Is Not Dead; It's Just Evolved," *Los Angeles Times*, January 9, 2000, home edition, 1.

5. Linda Mackey, "David Geffen Lends a Hand," MedHunters.com, http://www.medhunters.com (accessed July 29, 2005); King, *Operator*, 484; Judith Miller, "In Los Angeles, a New Generation Discovers Philanthropy," *New York Times*, December 8, 1997, late news edition, sec. A, 14; Don Shirley, "New Geffen Gift Will Expand Playhouse," *Los Angeles Times*, June 4, 2002, home edition, sec. F, 1.

6. Miller, "In Los Angeles."

7. Seabrook, *Nobrow*, 180.

8. Bob Colacello, "The Art of the Deal," *Vanity Fair* 58 (April 1995): 317.

9. Singular, *Rise and Rise*, 4, 7, 11.

10. King, *Operator*, 14, 22.

11. Singular, *Rise and Rise*, 13.

12. King, *Operator*, 23.

13. Edmund White, *Arts and Letters* (San Francisco: Cleis Press, 2004), 343.

14. Fred Goodman, *The Mansion on the Hill* (New York: Random House, 1997), 121.

15. Goodman, *Mansion*, 143.

16. Goodman, *Mansion*, 327–29; King, *Operator*, 290–92.

17. King, *Operator*, 302, 303.

18. Singular, *Rise and Rise*, 98.

19. Goodman, *Mansion*, 236.

20. Ibid., 237.

21. King, *Operator*, 523; Joni Mitchell, "Free Man in Paris," sheet music, Crazy Crow Music BMI, 1973.

22. King, *Operator*, 332; Singular, *Rise and Rise*, 98.

23. King, *Operator*, 353, 354.

24. Ibid., 355.

25. John Duka, "The Ego and the Art of David Geffen," *New York Times*, October 3, 1982.

26. King, *Operator*, 351; Don Shirley, "Geffen Gives $5 Million to UCLA Stage Theater," *Los Angeles Times*, home edition, April 21, 1995.

27. Singular, *Rise and Rise*, 99.

28. Ibid., 351, 416.

29. King, *Operator*, 415; Singular, *Rise and Rise*, 200.

30. Mel Brooks, *Recording* The Producers*: A Musical Romp with Mel Brooks*, DVD (New York: Sony Music Entertainment, Inc., 2001).

31. Miller, "In Los Angeles."

32. Ibid.

33. Colacello, "Art of the Deal," 289, 290.

34. Ibid., 288.

35. Miller, "In Los Angeles"; Kim Masters, "Toe Tags of 2002," *Esquire*, January 2003, 106.

36. King, *Operator,* 325, 326. Indeed, as the following blurb from *Esquire* suggests, regardless of motive, recipients benefit when philanthropists collide: "Geffen has elevated revenge to an art form, especially with respect to longtime adversary Michael Ovitz. On the very day after Ovitz's company imploded last spring, Geffen announced a $200 million donation to the UCLA School of Medicine. It was a generous gesture—the biggest gift ever to a medical school. But the fact that Ovitz had earlier pledged $25 million to the same institution—and had reportedly been tardy with some of his payments—was hardly lost on Geffen's pals. They quickly noted that Ovitz would now have to make his checks out to the David Geffen School of Medicine. Nota bene: Geffen visits the Mayo Clinic for his annual physicals," from Masters, "Toe Tags," 106.

37. Miller, "In Los Angeles."

38. Ibid.

39. King, *Operator,* 489.

40. Mackey, "David Geffen."

41. The Foundation Directory, "David Geffen Foundation," http://fconline.fdncenter.org (accessed July 15, 2005).

42. King, *Operator,* 455, 470, 471.

43. Claudie Eller, "Company Town; The Geffen Camp Heh-Hehs All the Way to the Bank" *Los Angeles Times,* home edition, January 17, 1997.

44. Eller, "Company Town"; King, *Operator,* 536.

45. "David Geffen," *Forbes,* http://www.forbes.com (accessed August 19, 2005).

46. Ibid. MSNBC Newsweek Periscope, "Hollywood: DreamWorks Sale–Why the Dream Didn't Work," http://www.msnbc.com/id/10415568/site/newsweek (accessed April 17, 2006).

47. Actors' Equity Association, "Los Angeles 99-Seat Plan," http://www.actorsequity.org (accessed August 9, 2005).

48. Randall Arney, artistic director, Geffen Playhouse, interview by author, Brentwood, CA, August 3, 2005.

49. Arney interview, August 3, 2005.

50. "Geffen Playhouse in Westwood," *Los Angeles Times,* home edition, August 11, 1996.

51. Shirley, "Geffen Gives."

52. Arney interview, August 3, 2005.

53. Arney interview, August 3, 2005; Jessica Padilla, "New Geffen Gift Benefits Playhouse," *UCLA Today,* http://www.today.ucla.edu/2002/020625geffen.html (accessed May 2, 2005).

54. Padilla, "Geffen Gift."

55. Geffen Playhouse, "Geffen Playhouse Overview," http://www.geffenplayhouse.com (accessed May 2, 2005).

56. Arney interview, August 3, 2005.

57. Geffen Playhouse Web site.

58. Padilla, "Geffen Gift"; Shirley, "Geffen Gives."

59. Diane Haithman, "Working at Industrial Strength: Gil Cates, The Man Behind the Oscar Show, Finds All Those Hollywood Contacts can Occasionally Come in Handy in His Role as Producing Director of the Geffen Playhouse," *Los Angeles Times*, home edition, May 9, 1999, 6.

60. Margo Jefferson, "Will Theater in Los Angeles Fade to White?" *New York Times*, August 7, 2005.

61. The Geffen Playhouse, "Geffen Playhouse Overview."

62. Jennifer Edwards, director of grants and communication, Geffen Playhouse, interview by author, Brentwood, CA, August 11, 2005.

63. Debra Pasquerette, education director, Geffen Playhouse, interview by author, Brentwood, CA, August 11, 2005.

64. The Geffen Playhouse, "Geffen Playhouse Overview."

65. The Geffen Playhouse, "Geffen Playhouse Opens Their Doors to At-Risk Youths," http://www.createnow.org/geffen.htm (accessed May 2, 2005).

66. Pasquerette interview, August 11, 2005.

67. Arney interview, August 3, 2005.

68. Singular, *Rise and Rise*, 5.

69. Mitchell, "Free Man."

9

THE ART OF GOOD BUSINESS: PETER DONNELLY

Barry B. Witham

In May 2003, the Seattle Public Library unveiled its striking 355,000-square-foot Central Library designed by the famed Dutch architect Rem Koolhaus. As part of the opening ceremonies, it announced that the art and literature section of the collection would be named in honor of Peter Donnelly, longtime arts advocate and chief executive officer of one of the most dynamic fund-raising organizations in the Northwest. It was an appropriate tribute to Donnelly and the latest in a series of awards that recognized the critical role that he has played in securing and distributing corporate and private funds for arts organizations.

What made the tribute meaningful was that it did not honor Donnelly's philanthropy but his *leadership* and the widely held view that he had invested his adult life making Seattle a community in which the arts thrived and were prized. Unlike other "angels" in this volume, Donnelly was not the source of the philanthropy but rather the mediator. And like traditional angels who mediated between heaven and earth, he created a conduit between wealth and the arts. Terry Collings, director of the

Seattle Public Library Foundation, stressed that the naming campaign originated with Seattle arts donors who wanted to do something for Peter. "He gave so much to the area that they wanted to recognize the role that he had played[,] not just the dollars he had raised."[1] Six prominent families donated $1.5 million to celebrate the achievements of a man who began as a Ford Foundation theater intern and, over the course of forty years, pioneered a view that the arts flourish best when they are stripped of elitist notions and prized for what they are: good business.

Peter Donnelly. Courtesy of Peter Donnelly.

Donnelly grew up with the regional theater movement in the sixties, and it was in that context that he honed his skills and developed the strategies that would inform his management style: "There weren't many professional theatres in the early sixties, but the Ford Foundation saw the coming tide and knew that staff would have to be trained for the regional houses. They started matching young managers with theatres so we could train for a profession. Of course we had to make up a lot of it up as we went along."[2] He graduated from Boston University in 1960, worked as an assistant stage manager for Ellis Rabb's Association of Producing Artists (APA) company and with Robert Porterfield's celebrated Barter Theatre, where he met theater director Adrian Hall. In fact, he was planning to team up with Hall in Providence, Rhode Island, when the Ford Foundation notified him that they had approved his internship application and assigned him to the Seattle Repertory Theatre as a management trainee.

It was a prestigious opportunity, but Donnelly had never been to Seattle and knew very little about its theater. So in July 1964, he journeyed to the Northwest and interviewed successfully for the position. A month later, he was marketing season subscriptions and generating income for the infant Seattle Repertory Theatre, a company committed to rotating repertory under the direction of Stuart Vaughan. In spite of the enthusiasm generated by both a successful world's fair and its first ambitious season, however, the theater was in debt and already developing the fissures and strains that would characterize many emerging resident companies.

At the time Donnelly started, the theater was supervised by a board of directors—mostly successful business citizens—who were figuring out their own role in the management of a professional arts organization. Vaughan believed that his contract protected him from board interference in artistic matters, but sometimes the distinctions blurred, and he found himself increasingly at odds with Bagley Wright, founder of the theater and spokesman for the business side of the operation. Vaughan wanted a true rotating repertory. The board pointed out that modifying the number of changeovers could reduce costs. Vaughan did not wish to reappoint a certain actor, but the board argued that the actor had a large and positive following in the community. Vaughan believed that the board should concentrate on selling tickets and let him get on with directing the company.[3]

Donnelly's immediate boss was Bill Taylor, whom Vaughan had brought with him from New York and who had held a variety of theater jobs. Taylor also had connections to the Ford Foundation—he had helped administer its playwrights program—and had worked as a producer, director, and administrator in several theaters. He was enthusiastic about joining Vaughan in Seattle because he had been assured that he would be in charge of the management side, and he looked forward to building a thriving regional theater. Unfortunately, the lagging season subscription sales brought him into conflict with the board, and shortly after Donnelly's arrival, Bagley Wright moved to terminate Taylor's contract and replace him with a local businessman, Donald Foster. Vaughan agreed, even though Foster's background was in department store merchandising rather than the arts.

In spite of his junior status, Donnelly soon found himself involved in a lot of the decision making. Backed by the prestige of his association with the Ford Foundation, he was prized by both Bagley Wright and Donald Foster and became an active participant in the organization. Although he had lost the manager to whom he had been assigned, Donnelly flourished under Foster's direction. "He was brilliant in all the areas that I knew nothing about," recalled Donnelly, "especially marketing, community relations and finance."[4] Foster had a business degree from Stanford, and he had been an influential member of Century 21, the business corporation that had planned and produced the World's Fair in Seattle. But now the corporation wanted the theater to become a stand-alone venture managed by its own board of directors. The growing pains—as in many other regional cities—were difficult and often contentious. The theater did not have exclusive rights to the playhouse. They had to negotiate a special journeyman contract with Actors' Equity so that they could employ a handful of local actors. They had to obtain the mailing lists for their subscription drives and then persuade prominent women in the community to host fund-raising teas.

Donnelly worked on educating the board about how it could support the theater and also learned from them about community resources. "People understood that museums and symphonies could not survive without subsidy," he remembers, "but they had to learn that theatre needed it as well. Theatre definitely suffered in this regard because it was the only art form with a commercial counterpart."[5] He came to believe that theater boards had to be taught that raising money was not just one of their goals; it was their responsibility.

The board's tensions with Vaughan, however, continued to fester, and midway through his third season, he was fired and replaced the following year by Alan Fletcher. In an effort to explore a more effective calendar, Fletcher, Foster, and Donnelly modified the expensive repertory plan into a split season in which three plays alternated between November and February before the final three were introduced. They also expanded the resident company so they could do a wider variety of plays and inaugurated a second season, producing contemporary works like *The Blacks*, *Little Murders*, and *Krapp's Last Tape*. But, in spite of some excellent productions, it was difficult to build the subscription base. Expenses increased and the debt worsened. In July 1967, Foster was appointed executive director and Donnelly became general manager. At the start of their seventh season, they abandoned the repertory calendar completely and went to a six-play straight-run calendar. Still, they were unable to move the needle, and the board, faced with a deficit of $265,000, voted to replace Fletcher and reorganize the administration of the theater.

Donnelly continued to work closely with the board and was valued by its members. He believed that board members' expertise in matters of the community and their commitment to fund-raising were valuable resources for marketing and development. When he received an offer to become general manager at the American Conservatory Theatre in San Francisco, the board responded by renegotiating his contract and offered him the title and responsibilities of producing director. They hired Duncan Ross to replace Fletcher but dispensed with the traditional title of artistic director and made Ross managing director. The result was, in effect, to create a dual leadership and to reward Donnelly for the genuinely imaginative contributions that he had brought to the enterprise. Ross already lived in Seattle. He ran the Professional Acting Program at the University of Washington, and although trained in England, he was opposed to the repertory system, which he believed dissipated energy and focus. He also favored a more national focus in the acting company so that the theater could have higher visibility. He slashed the resident company to a half dozen players and filled the casts with open calls. Together, he and Donnelly began exploring a modified starring system bringing name talent to Seattle whom they could actively promote and market.

The results were extraordinary. Donnelly's sense of merging the business skills of the board with the glamour of a more aggressive starring system ignited audience curiosity and participation. Maureen O'Sullivan, Myrna Loy, Rita Gam, Hume Cronyn, Jessica Tandy, and others trekked to the Northwest. Eva Le Gallienne directed *A Doll's House*, George Abbott staged *Life With Father*, and Christopher Walken starred in *Hamlet*. When Richard Chamberlain—already widely known from television—evinced an interest in *Richard II*, Donnelly and Ross brought him to Seattle, where he played fifty-five sold-out performances and was celebrated in the national press.

The response was enormous. Season subscriptions climbed to twenty-two thousand by the mid-seventies and eventually exceeded subscriptions of both Seattle professional sport franchises. Donnelly increased the theater's visibility by promoting a second stage for experimental works, increased its summer park shows, added benefits and special occasions for season subscribers, and worked hard to support new theaters in the community. Rather than viewing an emergent ACT or Intiman as "competition," Donnelly believed that they enhanced the cultural value of the city, and he helped nurture them. Increasingly, he was viewed as someone who had both the expertise of the business world and a genuine love and appreciation of the arts. In the words of Bagley Wright, he was "not a difficult man in a profession full of difficult people."[6]

He was also ambitious, and one of his constant thoughts was how to replace the rather awkward and stodgy multipurpose auditorium that the theater had inherited from the 1962 World's Fair. From the theater's initial days on the grounds of the Seattle Center, it had been required by its lease agreement to share the facility with several other groups. Moreover, the theater operated out of a half dozen satellite locations, which made communication among scenery, wardrobe, rehearsal, and so on, extremely difficult. Drawing upon his connections in the community and supported by influential members of the board, Donnelly joined a campaign to upgrade the entire Seattle Center, which had not had any significant renovation since the World's Fair. He argued persuasively that the theater was coming of age, and that facilities that had been adequate for a fledgling institution were no longer viable for a mature program. In consultation with other members of the center, Donnelly promoted the passage of a $19 million bond issue, with $4.8 million dedicated to a state-of-the-art theater. His energy and enthusiasm were infectious, and, in 1977, Seattle passed the bond issue by the largest plurality in the history of the city.

Believing that the proscenium stage was the workhorse of theater, Donnelly and Ross sought a house that would combine the traditional proscenium arrangement with the intimacy of a number of modern theaters. They assembled an architectural team and visited American theaters including the pioneering Guthrie in Minneapolis. The drawings began to take shape: a vast scene shop, meeting rooms, a second space, and a lovely 856-seat proscenium auditorium. No seat—including those in the balcony—was further than sixty-five feet from the stage. Donnelly rallied the Seattle arts community by suggesting that the new theater be named to honor Bagley Wright, who had served as president of the board for seven years. Wright, with his wife Virginia, was an avid arts supporter and collector who had worked tirelessly in support of Seattle theater, and Donnelly felt that his contributions should be honored. "There was a lot of controversy in the early years," but in Donnelly's estimation, "Bagley was a hero in a number of the most important and difficult decisions."[7]

When the new theater opened in 1983, the public reception was enthusiastic. The premiere production—Michael Weller's *The Ballad of Soapy Smith*—signaled a commitment to new plays that would become a hallmark of the new artistic director, Dan Sullivan. Always concerned about the value of "good work," Donnelly encouraged Sullivan's skillful blending of classic and original plays, and when Herb Gardner's *I'm Not Rappaport*—which had premiered in Seattle—won the Tony Award in 1986, it was testimony to the national recognition of the theater.

The Bagley Wright Theatre also established Donnelly's reputation as one of the premier managers in the country. After the second season in the new space, the building was paid for, and Donnelly showed a $55,000 surplus and an endowment of more than $1 million. Community leaders began to seek his advice. He, in turn, aggressively pursued the community to contribute to the theater. Though he was long a member of national boards and councils, new honors and offers came his way. King County (Washington) recognized his achievements with a series of leadership awards, and his alma mater, Boston University, named him its Outstanding Fine Arts Alumnus.

Building a theater had taught him a great deal about raising money, and it was a skill that he pursued with considerable success. Like other managers who had shaped the regional theater movement, Donnelly sensed that the dollars needed to sustain a major theater were expanding from individual philanthropy to corporate support. In the future, he believed, it would be necessary to persuade the corporate sector that the arts were a good investment, both for its own self-interest and for the cultural life of the community.

In Seattle in the early eighties, corporate dollars were funneled through an organization called the Corporate Council for the Arts. Founded in 1960 as the United Arts Council, it initially provided annual grants to approximately ten institutions in the Puget Sound area. The money was raised from approximately 480 companies, including large corporations like Boeing, Pacific Northwest Bell, and Burlington Northern. Giving through the council did not prohibit companies from also making individual donations to particular groups, but it did provide a kind of annual base that arts organizations could rely on. Donnelly had been active in making the Rep's case to the council, because he believed that theater in general lagged behind symphonic music, ballet, and opera in terms of corporate support. While the Corporate Council was very successful, there was growing corporate discontent with both the impersonal nature of its leaders and the meager return that companies perceived for their dollars. This discontent would ultimately affect Peter Donnelly directly and signal an important shift in his career.

Dallas

By 1985, Donnelly's success in creating a vibrant theater scene in Seattle was resonating in a number of American communities. In Dallas, Adrian Hall had been hired to rejuvenate the Theater Center, and he needed a first-class managing director to run the organization, clear away some long-standing debt, and build a new theater. Donnelly had no intention of leaving Seattle, but he agreed to fly to Dallas and consult. After several trips, he discovered that he was being actively recruited. The center was complicated because it had offered academic training programs and had many holdovers from the days of Paul Baker, who had been a fixture there for some twenty years. Moreover, Hall would only be half-time, since he intended to retain his appointment in Providence. The problems were enormous, but so were the challenges. Eventually, the president of the Dallas center flew to Seattle and convinced Donnelly to accept the position.

Donnelly's arrival in Dallas unfortunately coincided with a downturn in the oil-based economy, which resulted in a postponement of the new building. "The theatre had a $1.2 million debt, a dispirited organization and only about 6,300 subscribers," remembers Donnelly.[8] But he thrived on challenges. He cut six weeks out of a very crowded season and reduced the budget by nearly $1 million. In addition, he set out to mend fences in the community. "It quickly became clear to me that people were somehow angry at the theatre, that the theatre was not connecting with the community."[9]

In spite of the oil depression, Donnelly was able to turn the corner. In three years, he cut the debt in half, energized the corporate campaigns, and produced three balanced budgets. In addition, he raised the season subscription list to ninety-five hundred, in what he described as one of the toughest economies in America. And he also made a wonderful discovery. "I learned that I really knew a lot."[10] He had built a theater in Seattle, put over twenty-six thousand subscribers in its seats, and found a way to raise personal and corporate dollars. But it was not until he tested himself outside the Northwest that he realized how much he had learned. He did not get to build a new theater in Dallas, but he was on the way toward it when a new challenge came his way.

In Seattle, the Corporate Council for the Arts was in trouble. Although it continued to raise substantial monies, there was a gathering perception that the organization was lethargic and in need of new leadership. Mary Bruno, writing in *The Weekly*, seemed to speak for a number of critics of the status quo: "Despite the value of the CCA concept, it isn't working in Seattle. *Everybody* knows it isn't working, and *everybody* knows that the reason it isn't working is the CCA itself. CCA has been twisting in the wind long enough. It's time for someone to cut the rope."[11] Among the numerous complaints was the view that big corporations and donors were not getting sufficient recognition for their contributions, and some were beginning to feel that they would be better off just making direct grants. Don North, of Burlington Northern, complained, "CCA is not proactive in their campaign for seeking money. It's more of a written than an eyeball campaign. There's very little personal contact, only a form letter. It's almost like a payroll deduction. You're just expected to do it."[12]

Pacific Northwest Bell was also unhappy and threatened to withdraw if things did not change: "We've had two major sponsorships this season with the Seattle Symphony Orchestra and those are examples of the way we are interested in getting more involved with the arts groups directly.

. . . It provides good recognition for us, and we are able to arrange special events, tickets and more interaction between the arts groups and PNB. It also is more effective to give direct support than to work through a third party."[13] The director of CCA, Robert Gustavson, feared that such shifts toward promotional giving would seriously affect the stability of the arts organizations and undermine the need for a guaranteed income stream. But sentiment was running away from the status quo, and in November 1987, Burlington Northern announced that it was also likely to withdraw from CCA.

Board members appealed to Gustavson to undertake a thorough review of the organization and determine whether accommodations could be made to halt the departure of these major donors. But Gustavson was reluctant. CCA was among the top five of its kind in the country. In its most recent fiscal year, it had raised and distributed $1.36 million. Gustavson knew that arts organizations counted on the council for operating funds—to pay the rent and light bill—and he feared that direct grants would provide no stability from year to year. The board disagreed. It argued that the problem was lethargy in the leadership, and it was time for a total review and reassessment of operations. In December, realizing that the new board intended to make significant operating and policy changes, Gustavson resigned.

Board president Steve Duzan and others began a series of meetings with local chief executive officers and arts directors to see if they wanted to continue the organization. All agreed about its value but articulated a number of flaws in the system. They also agreed that if Peter Donnelly could be coaxed back to Seattle, he would be the ideal choice to turn things around. Although his specific training had been in the theater, Donnelly was widely respected for his knowledge about music, art, dance, and architecture. His breadth of interests was formidable. He was respected by the arts community because he had "good taste" as well as a sense of how conflicts could be resolved without resorting to ugly confrontations.[14] And he had an enormous following in the business community. Jay Green, chief executive officer of U.S. Bank of Washington, commented, "We were extremely *lucky* to get Peter. He was an obvious first choice. . . . He understands the arts; he understands business."[15]

Donnelly was reluctant to leave Dallas without building the theater he had been promised, but it was clear that the economy could not support a new theater initiative, and the temptation to return to the Northwest was enormous. Friends were dispatched to woo him, and hours were spent examining CCA finances. He became convinced that his work with organizations like FEDAPT and Americans for the Arts, as well as other corporate connections that he had made in his travels for the Dallas Theater Center, would help him devise a plan to energize a new version of CCA. Plus, he still owned a home in Seattle. After almost three years to the day that he had left, Donnelly returned with a charge to raise money, not for just the theater but for *all* the arts in the Seattle-Tacoma metropolitan area.

From CCA to ArtsFund

In his testimony on behalf of the National Endowment for the Arts before the House Appropriations Committee in April 2000, Donnelly stressed what was becoming his mantra about the arts and their relationship to business, and what drove many of the decisions that he made upon returning to Seattle two years earlier. "The arts have dramatically contributed to the economic growth in our region. The activity of cultural organizations and patrons generates some $375 million in business sales annually and creates 16,000 jobs."[16] It was his firm conviction that the arts were critical for the life of a civilized community, and it was his mission to convince the community that they were also good for business.

The CCA board was firmly behind Donnelly, and he moved quickly to remake the organization. He secured an executive assistant and a director of communications and began making plans to move the offices to a more strategic location. Within a year's time, he had vacated the Spartan headquarters that had hosted CCA and occupied a spacious pro bono suite at the Pacific First Center, where he could literally rub shoulders with the financial heart of the community. Melinda Bargreen, music critic for the *Seattle Times*, described the transformation:

> When you ascend the escalator to the lobby of the elegant Pacific First Center, on your way to the Corporate Council for the Arts offices, the faint scent of first-floor Gucci leather follows you. Once in the fifth-floor offices, you peer past paintings, neon sculptures, and major glass pieces to the superb view from the windows, where most of Seattle's important downtown buildings appear to be jockeying for position. If the CCA president

> were to throw a few stones out of his panoramic window, he could connect instantly with the windows of several of the big bank executives, corporate CEOs and foundation directors who make up the high profile board of the Corporate Council. . . . If you are looking for a symbol of the change in the public profile of the CCA since its reorganization and Donnelly's arrival a little more than a year ago, the new office space does nicely. It puts CCA right up there with the big boys—and its *paid* for by the big boys.[17]

The visual transformation of the organization was important, but it was only symbolic of the more dynamic reconstruction that Donnelly was implementing. In order to dramatically increase the financial resources, he began a series of meetings with dozens of corporate executives, personalizing his campaign and making his case directly for business support for the arts. He had compiled a list of nearly three thousand businesses and, with his board president, began targeting ones who were critical. "It takes personal effort," said Josh Green. "Every week there are half a dozen calls on my calendar, where Peter and I go in person to brief CEOs on what's happening in the arts and how the CCA fits in. It's a lot harder to say no when someone pays a personal call."[18]

But the centerpiece for the revitalized Corporate Council was the annual luncheon at which arts leaders gathered with their corporate supporters to celebrate the year's achievements and to announce future plans. In a few short years, the luncheon became one of the highlights of the Seattle social season. Achievement awards in the arts were distributed, honoring people who had made significant contributions. Guest speakers with national reputations were invited to inspire continued business and individual support of the arts. After a decade of Donnelly's leadership, the luncheon in May 1999 at the Westin Hotel was attended by a thousand people, who learned that during that period CCA had more than doubled the dollar amount of annual grants and tripled the number of agencies served. It was on target to surpass the year's goal of $2.2 million and the permanent endowment had exceeded $4.5 million. But the biggest announcement was that the Kreielsheimer Foundation, which had donated $826,000 over the previous six years, was making a gift of a $2 million building as a permanent home for the Corporate Council. Rather than a tenant, it would now be a landlord, with its own corporate center and office rental space, which would ensure it a minimum of $100,000 annually.

Under Donnelly's leadership, CCA had continued the sustaining grants that were at the heart of the original organization and that continued to provide arts organizations with unrestricted dollars. These grants to organizations with a track record allow planning with the anticipation of a certain level of support. They have to apply annually and go through a review process, but the "intent is not to reduce." The bulk of the grants—approximately 80 percent—are in this category.

But Donnelly wanted to widen the landscape and open up the competition to other lesser-known or lesser-supported groups. As part of his recruitment agreement, a $1 million endowment was created in honor of council founder Ned Skinner, who had been a remarkable arts supporter and who was dying of cancer. This new fund allowed Donnelly to create discretionary grants for smaller or start-up companies. These now constitute approximately 20 percent of the awards and are avidly competed for by dozens of organizations. Altogether, CCA is currently funding approximately seventy groups in its two categories, an increase of fifty-eight since the restructuring of the enterprise.

Every successful grant applicant goes through a rigorous review, during which the arts directors are questioned by a panel of corporate executives who have agreed to devote their time to this important committee work. Donnelly is very proud of the allocation process and calls it one of his major achievements. He has convinced many corporate directors of giving at some of Seattle's most prestigious companies to read the applications and then spend six to seven full days interviewing the arts leaders. It is a thorough and rigorous process that ensures quality work and brings the two important constituencies of the CCA personally together again. Liz Crossman, who supervises giving for the Weyerhaeuser Corporation, says that it is an extremely thorough process and very typical of Donnelly's method of operation. "He's very smart and charismatic. And it's hard to say 'no' to him. But he stresses that arts bring business to our communities as well as provide for public debate. And he brings value to the investors."[19] Across the table from her, Susan Trapnell, the managing director of Seattle's ACT theater, stresses that Donnelly is very much concerned with "excellence" in awarding the discretionary grants and is also an excellent judge of character. "One of his great strengths is that he keeps his eye on the prize and he asks people to do what they are capable of doing."[20]

At the turn of the twenty-first century, it was clear that Donnelly's reputation had extended well beyond the Pacific Northwest, and a number of people were keeping their eyes on him. When William Ivey announced that he was stepping down as head of the National Endowment for the Arts in the summer of 2001, cultural handicappers immediately developed a short list of candidates that included Donnelly. While some believed that he would be hindered by his liberal (Seattle) background in a conservative administration, others believed that his business sense and background were exactly what the troubled agency needed. In July, the Washington-based American Arts Alliance, where Donnelly had served as a vice chair, submitted an official recommendation that named Donnelly, as well as three others, the most qualified to run the organization. Donnelly was surprised and pleased but insisted that it was something that he neither sought nor wanted and graciously declined. "I'm flattered to be considered but I am happy here. There is still a lot of work to be done. Why leave one of the best art communities in the country?"[21]

A bulk of the work that he was doing was transforming the CCA into a new organization known as ArtsFund. Seattle might be one of the best arts communities in the country, but by the end of the nineties, Donnelly believed that the level of corporate giving had reached a plateau, and he wanted to remake the organization so that its streams of income could be increased. Certainly, the gift of the Kreielsheimer building had been a major boost for the new organization, but it was further enhanced by a very imaginative and unique donation by one of Seattle's most prominent families.

Harriet Bullitt and her sister, Patsy Bullitt Collins, had inherited from their mother, Dorothy Bullitt, the KING broadcasting empire, which included one of the most successful FM classical music stations in the country. Concerned about broadcast economics, which were driving classical stations off the air, and the disposition of the station after their deaths, the Bullitt sisters sold the AM half of the station and then put KING-FM under the control of Classic Radio, a newly incorporated company. Profits from that company were then donated to a nonprofit company that the sisters named Beethoven. The object of these transactions was to ensure the continuation of a classic radio station *and* to put profits back into the arts in Seattle. Peter Donnelly, who eventually would serve as president of Classic King FM, was enthusiastic about the Bullitt's philanthropy because it affected him in two important ways. First, ArtsFund was designated—along with the Seattle Symphony and Seattle Opera—as one of three official recipients of Beethoven's annual dividends. Second, the station moved into the Kreielsheimer building and became a tenant of the ArtsFund. "Beethoven was the creation of two very smart women," remarked Donnelly. "I hope this tweaks the imagination of philanthropists everywhere, especially in the theatre or visual arts community."[22]

Donnelly believed that the example of people like the Bullitt sisters and Ned Skinner served as models to attract the younger wealthy, and even after the downturn of the economy and the aftermath of 9/11, he continued to campaign aggressively on behalf of the arts. "What is unique about Peter," says Trapnell, "is that his level of engagement with the arts has made Seattle, a relatively small city, into a very large art space. He's so well connected and active *beyond* ArtsFund. Plus, he follows through; he does what he says."[23] Arts companies retrenched in the new century; most tightened their belts and some failed. But at the ArtsFund annual lunch in May 2004, Donnelly was upbeat about the increases that he saw in individual gifting. And he was delighted that ArtsFund's campaigns like encouraging employee-giving programs were paying off handsomely. Weyerhaeuser, Puget Sound Energy, and KING Broadcasting were joined by nearly sixty other companies in establishing employee drives for the arts.

In October 2004, Donnelly announced that his friend Kayla Skinner had bequeathed $3.5 million over ten years to ArtsFund. The principal is to be held permanently intact, with income going to specific music, theater, and art organizations. The gift provided another boost to the endowment ArtsFund was trying to grow and also helped raise the expectations among potential donors. "This endowment continues Kayla's life work and passion for the arts," said Donnelly. "It also serves as an inspiration to the rest of us for the work that must follow."[24]

But it is one of his lesser-known projects that speaks so eloquently to Donnelly's impact on the arts. In November 2004, ArtsFund announced the results of a survey that it had commissioned to evaluate the impact of arts programs on the state economy. Funded by the Paul Allen Family Foundation, the survey analyzed the expenditures of 269 nonprofit arts organizations and their audiences for 2003 and demonstrated that they generated business activity of $1.05 billion, creating 28,626 jobs, with $465.16 million in labor income and $39.11 million in tax impacts.[25] The survey, which also had bad news in the sense of an increasing gap between earned income and contributed income, was the third one that ArtsFund had commissioned and definitely depicted a growing and healthy arts community. Although there was concern over narrowed operating margins and scant endowments, the landscape was clearly supportive of his central notion about the relationship between good art and good business. "What the study underscores," said Donnelly, "is that we have succeeded in building an arts life for this region impressive for both its diversity and its size. . . . Our challenge continues to be maintaining the operations we've built. Seeing the scale of impact arts make on our economy gives us all the more reason to do so."[26]

On December 7, 2004, Donnelly announced that he would step down as president and chief executive officer of ArtsFund. Although he has no plans to retire from an active engagement with the arts, he felt that it was a good time to pass on the leadership of the organization and "begin my next act." His legacy as a fund-raiser and angel is enormous. He leaves the organization with a $10 million endowment and impressive real estate holdings as well as a record of sustained support for seventy Northwest organizations. And, in time, his legacy will be enriched with a new understanding of the role that he played in America's regional theater. That movement, which decentralized professional theater in the United States and created new opportunities for thousands of artists, has been largely written as a history of its artistic directors. Eventually, a more sophisticated narrative will recognize a generation of managers who raised the money, massaged the boards, produced the plays and enabled the institutions of theater to access the institutions of philanthropy.

Notes

1. Donnelly, phone interview with the author, May 3, 2005.

2. Donnelly, interview with the author, May 18, 2005.

3. Vaughan has told his side of the story in *A Possible Theatre* (New York: McGraw-Hill, 1969). Conflicts between boards and artistic staff were often central in the emerging regional theater movement. In the late eighties, for example, Daniel Sullivan was approached by a member of the Seattle Rep board who wished to form a committee that would play a more active role in season planning and artistic matters. "We don't know, however, what to call our committee." "You would call that," Dan replied, "a search committee"

4. Donnelly, e-mail to the author, August 16, 2005.

5. Donnelly, e-mail to the author, July 27, 2005.

6. Bagley Wright, quoted in "Wrap-Up at the Rep," *Seattle Times*, July 18, 1985.

7. Donnelly interview, May 18, 2005.

8. Donnelly, quoted in "Donnelly Plans to Extend Arts Group," *Seattle Times*, January 31, 1989.

9. *Seattle Times*, January 31, 1989.

10. Donnelly interview, May 18, 2005.

11. Mary Bruno, "Another CCA Scare," *The Weekly*, November 18, 1987.

12. Don North, quoted in Bruno, 43.

13. "Telephone Co. May Pull Out of Arts Panel," *Seattle Times*, November 5, 1987.

14. My favorite Peter Donnelly story involves a production of Michael Frayn's *Make and Break* at the Seattle Rep in 1984. As dramaturg, I had arranged a program essay by a local finance professor that examined how contemporary business mergers and buyouts frequently sacrificed workers and how golden parachutes and other bonuses feathered the nests of executives and board members. It was a very good essay and perfectly illuminating of Frayn's play. Unfortunately, it was this issue of the season's programs that Peter had designated to thank all of our corporate donors! He winced but agreed that it served the production. We ran the piece.

15. Jay Green, quoted in Melinda Bargreen, "A View of Success," *Seattle Times*, March 4, 1990.

16. Peter Donnelly, "Testimony to the U.S. House of Representatives in Support of FY 2001 Appropriations for the NEA," Washington, D.C., April 6, 2000, http://www.artsusa.org (accessed July 6, 2004).

17. Bargreen, "A View of Success."

18. Ibid.

19. Liz Crossman, phone interview with the author, June 2, 2005.

20. Susan Trapnell, phone interview with the author, June 10, 2005.

21. "Donnelly Says No to NEA," *Seattle Post-Intelligencer*, July 18, 2001.

22. "Music to Their Ears," *Seattle Times*, August 17, 1997.

23. Trapnell interview, June 10, 2005.

24. *Seattle Times*, October 26, 2004.

25. *Seattle Times*, November 24, 2004.

26. Ibid.

PART TWO

INSTITUTIONAL ANGELS

10

THE FOUNDING OF THEATER ARTS PHILANTHROPY IN AMERICA: W. MCNEIL LOWRY AND THE FORD FOUNDATION, 1957–65

Sheila McNerney Anderson

During the eight years between 1957 and 1965, the Ford Foundation's Division of Humanities and the Arts generated one of the nation's first and most enduring policies for funding the performing arts, a policy that would ultimately give rise to the current generation of not-for-profit theaters. During this period, the foundation instilled its institutional values around sustainability, endurance, fiscal responsibility, and a new sense of cultural relevance in the pioneers of what is today known as the American regional theater movement. Before the foundation arrived on the scene, theater artists wishing to start a theater did not necessarily set up tax-exempt organizations with the purpose of creating institutions that would outlast the founding artist or whose identity would transcend its artistic leadership or its original mission. The funding policy that guided the foundation's grant actions in the performing arts would be replicated by other funding organizations that followed suit and persists even today. Chief architect of this policy was the division's director, W. McNeil Lowry, who oversaw the distribution of more than $320 million to performing arts organizations, artistic institutions, and individual artists during his tenure at the foundation. Lowry, as the foundation's principal arts policy maker, exerted significant influence over both the evolution of the resident professional theater sector and how it has been subsidized over the last five decades.

The Ford Foundation's funding of the arts, beginning in 1957, was unprecedented in the history of private philanthropy in the United States. Since the late nineteenth century, family foundations—those formed with the wealth of such families as the Carnegies, Rockefellers, and Pughs, for example—have been very active as subsidizing agents in a broad range of fields, from alleviating the effects of poverty, to exploring and applying advances in science and technology. Typically, however, those first foundations did not have an orientation toward arts and letters beyond their support of higher education and the occasional debt-relief grant. The Carnegie Foundation's commitment in 1925 to fund arts programming that emphasized education was representative of such giving. Its funding went to art history and appreciation courses, as well as teacher and museum personnel training. No funds, however, were earmarked for direct support of creative artists.[1] In 1932, the Rockefeller Foundation granted the Cleveland Play House $35,000[2] in matching funds so that it could pay off its $70,000 debt. The following decade, Rockefeller broadened its subsidy of artists, albeit indirectly, through grants to higher-education artist-in-residence programs. In light of these ad hoc subsidies, Abraham Flexner observed in his 1952 study, *Funds and Foundations*, "The thoughtful reader of these pages must have been struck by the crying inadequacy of the funds devoted to humanistic studies—to languages, literature, art, archaeology, philosophy, music, history."[3] Within five years of Flexner's observation, the Ford Foundation would drastically change the relationship between private philanthropy and the arts. When, in the post–World War II era, the Ford Foundation became the wealthiest and most influential of these foundations, the arts were finally elevated to a viable field of philanthropic activity.

The Ford Foundation was established in 1936 under very different circumstances from those of its peer institutions. In creating his trust, Henry Ford was less motivated by social consciousness or any paternalistic feelings toward the working person than by federal income tax laws, laws that were not on the books when Carnegie, Rockefeller, and Mrs. Russell Sage first began giving away their money. Henry and Edsel Ford were primarily concerned with the possibility that their heirs would have to sell the family's majority share in the Ford Motor Company in order to pay estate taxes after their passing. To prevent this loss of family control of the corporation, the couple jointly bequeathed 90 percent of (nonvoting) shares to a charitable trust that would provide their family foundation with a self-sustaining income for the years and decades to come.

Between 1936 and 1950, the Ford Foundation limited its philanthropy to the Detroit area, home to the bulk of the Ford Motor Company employees.[4] In 1947, after Henry Ford Sr. died, the foundation trustees began preparations to distribute the foundation's wealth nationally and even internationally. At the time, they anticipated disbursing grants in the amount of $50 million a year. After Ford Motor Company stock was offered on the public market, however, the foundation would spend as much as eleven times that in a single year.[5] The valuation of its holding created by the public offering resulted in a foundation budget an order of magnitude larger than anything Henry Ford or the first trustees ever anticipated. The foundation's board of trustees, for example, announced in 1955 that it would disburse $50 million in grants to private colleges alone. With its rapid accumulation of wealth, however, even such large outlays could not meet its IRS-mandated spending obligations at a time when Congress was debating changes to the tax-exempt status of private philanthropies. Furthermore, financial prudence dictated that the foundation diversify its assets as soon as possible. As a consequence, in January 1956, after complex negotiations with the Ford family and the Ford Motor Company, the foundation began selling off its shares in the automobile company. "The sale," according to Dwight MacDonald, author of *The Ford Foundation*, "which was the biggest single offering of common stock in Wall Street's history, consisted of about one-fifth of the Foundation's Ford stock and brought in some $643 million."[6] The public sale compelled the foundation to consider how it could consistently spend the percentage of its income mandated by tax laws.[7] Although not immediately or directly, these investment concerns led the foundation to consider seriously alternate fields of philanthropy and eventually resulted in the formation of the Division of Humanities and the Arts.

Nineteen fifty-seven was the first year that the Ford Foundation made a substantial commitment to funding the arts and humanities directly. The foundation considered the next five years to be a period of exploration into arts funding, with the theater used as a test case. Then, in 1962, the arts and humanities became one of five main areas of focus for the philanthropic organization. Over the next three years, its activities in theater became more directed and comprehensive. Nineteen sixty-five is a year that marks a number of changes at the Ford Foundation, in its interest in the theater, and in the funding opportunities for the arts. By then, the foundation had declared its "experiment" in the theater a success. Nineteen sixty-five was also the first year that Congress funded the National Endowment for the Arts, and the last year that W. McNeil Lowry was an immediate supervisor of activities at the Division of Humanities and the Arts, before being made a vice president at the Ford Foundation. For all of these reasons, in 1965, the foundation's work with resident professional theaters became less central to its activities and interest in the arts, although the foundation never stopped supporting resident professional theater through individual grants.

W. McNeil Lowry: Model Philanthropoid Turned Arts Czar

Chief architect of the foundation's grant programs and funding policies for the arts during this period was W. McNeil Lowry. To most artistic directors, managing directors, or development officers who worked with a not-for-profit arts organization during the 1960s and 1970s, Lowry was a familiar name, if not a personal friend. Known to many as "Mac," he helped convince the foundation trustees to lend their support to the arts and supervised the organization's activities in this arena, in one capacity or another, between 1957 and 1975, when he retired as a foundation vice president. During his tenure at the foundation, Lowry shaped arts policy and institutional development in the performing arts community in the United States more than any other single individual. He directed the foundation on how to disburse the money it had allocated for the arts, and he counseled the artists on how to spend their foundation grants. His oversight of the foundation's arts funding earned Lowry such monikers as "Mr. Money," "Mister Arts," and "a Czar in the Arts." Eulogizing Lowry in 1993, Peter Zeisler observed: "When the history of the performing arts in 20th-century America is written, a very long chapter will be devoted to the extraordinary accomplishments of W. McNeil Lowry."[8]

Left, W. McNeil Lowry; *center*, Brooks Atkinson; *right*, George Peterkia (Alley board president). Photo from an October 9, 1966, article in the *Houston Chronicle* about Jones Hall Commemorative Week in Houston at the Alley.
Courtesy of the University of Illinois Archives, W. McNeil Lowry Papers, 26/20/96, box 1.

W. McNeil Lowry was born in Columbus, Kansas, on February 17, 1913. Nothing in Lowry's educational pursuits or early career suggested that he would have an inclination toward arts advocacy, or that he would eventually devote himself to developing the performing arts. Nor is there evidence to suggest that he actively sought out such responsibilities. In 1934, he received his bachelor's degree from the University of Illinois, where he then went on to complete a Ph.D. in English in 1941. He served on the university's English department faculty from 1936 to 1942.[9] While on the faculty, in 1940, Lowry and some colleagues founded a literary journal, *Accent: A Quarterly of New Literature*. He later offered his experience with journalism to the war effort, writing for the Office of War Information in Washington, D.C., in his capacity as a navy lieutenant. In 1946, he pursued a career as a journalist with the *Dayton Daily News*, followed by a five-year stint as the chief of the Washington, D.C., bureau for James M Cox newspapers.

Lowry's introduction to the Ford Foundation came in 1948, when he was contacted by William McPeak, a staff secretary, whom he had first met in the Office of War Information. McPeak sought Lowry's advice about the viability of a large philanthropic program to fund the humanities. McPeak never explained why the foundation was interested in Lowry's opinion in particular. Lowry assumed it was because he had a background in the humanities at the University of Illinois and because he had established a literary journal.[10] Five years later, McPeak offered him a job in the Education Division of the Ford Foundation.

During his twenty-two-year tenure, Lowry served as a dedicated member of the staff and moved quickly through its ranks. He was first hired on as McPeak's assistant at the education program. One year later, he was an executive assistant in education, and less than two years after that, he was in charge of that program. When the foundation created the Division of Humanities and the Arts in 1957, Lowry was named director. In 1964, Lowry was promoted to vice president of Policy and Planning: Humanities and the Arts. He retired from the foundation in January 1975.

The position that Lowry came to hold at the foundation is known in the world of private philanthropy as a *philanthropoid*, a term apparently coined by Frederick P. Keppel while he was president of the Carnegie Corporation.[11] Offering a definition of a *philanthropoid* in 1956, Dwight MacDonald explains that it is "the middleman between the philanthropist and the philanthropee." These are the people who report to the trustees and have direct and regular contact with the grant recipients. They research and advise the foundations about potential new fields of philanthropy.

In the period when Lowry joined the foundation, philanthropoids were typically young men, friendly, humble, and "not at ease until [they were] on a first-name basis with a visitor."[12] The foundation, at that time, tended to hire academics or those who had government connections, or, preferably, both. When Lowry joined the foundation "the Ford philanthropoid [was] of a liberal turn politically, habituated to collective, nonprofit enterprise," according to MacDonald, "and inclined more toward internationalism than isolationism."[13] Lowry had all the attributes necessary to succeed at the foundation.

Pioneering Arts Policy

The Ford Foundation's Division of Humanities and the Arts, under Lowry's direction, was a pioneer in arts funding; in the 1950s, no precedents existed upon which it could base its grant actions. The federal government, by way of the National Endowment for the Arts (NEA), would not begin funding the arts until eight years after the foundation was. Furthermore, neither the Rockefeller panel report *The Performing Arts: Problems and Prospects* nor William J. Baumol and William G. Bowen's study *Performing Arts: The Economic Dilemma; A Study of Problems Common to Theater, Opera, Music and Dance* was published until the mid-1960s. Both were seminal studies of the material conditions of performing arts in the United States, and each made a case based on the cultural benefits to society for government and private support of not-for-profit arts institutions. Without the benefit of such studies, and necessitated by his responsibilities to guide the grant actions of the foundation, Lowry proceeded in 1957 to develop the first policy for arts funding along with a vision for the role of arts in America. When others in the private and the public sectors began to take an interest in the arts, Lowry's policy and philosophy were adopted and adapted. While he never articulated his policy in a single, cohesive, coherent document, Lowry left behind traces of it. In many respects, these fragments—taken together—serve to document the first policy on the arts in the United States.

The cornerstone of Lowry's policy was that arts should serve as a much-needed counterweight to the post–World War II domination of scientific and social scientific research.[14] Making his case in 1955 that the foundation should invest some of its vast endowment in arts and cultural institutions, Lowry pointed out to the trustees that "cultural institutions, by their very nature, provide opportunities for the investment of large sums of philanthropic money." He also suggested that the general public would consider supporting the arts as an acceptable way to spend private funds. "Finally," he observed, "public acceptance itself would today be heightened by awareness of the difficulties cultural institutions experience in obtaining large grants of private funds."[15] In other words, he argued that giving money to the arts would draw attention to the lack of money traditionally given to the arts. The foundation could create a new arena for philanthropy that extended beyond private foundations, following the now well-understood principle that money follows money.

Lowry believed that the Ford Foundation could make a significant impact on American culture. Wanting to identify a test case, he offered a number of suggestions in a 1955 report to the board of trustees, titled "Cultural Affairs Program." Notably, the first suggestion concerned noncommercial theater in the United States. Lowry developed his preference for the theater long before arriving at the foundation, apparently having been a theatergoer since childhood. And he openly expressed his preferences for certain types of theater. He wanted to see more of the classics, and he liked the plays of Thornton Wilder and Tennessee Williams. He hoped that foundation grants would contribute to the creation of a new body of American classics.

Lowry also had some well-formed notions about why the theater was in need of foundation support. In his report to the trustees, he pointed out that people in small cities outside of New York did not have access to theater beyond summer stock, nor did they have any opportunity to see professional productions of the classics. He therefore advocated for "a National Repertory Theatre of four to six dramatic companies" that would tour to cities with populations as small as twenty-five thousand. He informed the board that "a multi-company national repertory theater has been the objective of members of the profession for at least a generation," thereby planting in the minds of trustees the appealing idea that the foundation would be building upon their pioneering efforts. Apparently, the board found Lowry's case compelling. In 1957, the foundation established the Division of Humanities and the Arts and put Lowry in charge. Lowry now had at his disposal a limited but viable budget of $2 million, and the humanities and arts were finally elevated to the status of a "division" of the Ford Foundation. He and McPeak (who would continue to supervise Lowry in his role as head of the division) had been given a strong token of trust by the board and foundation president Henry T. Heald.

As the division initiated plans to use the theater as its first test case, it had no American model on which to base its program. So Lowry turned to Europe for inspiration. Shortly after the establishment of the division, Lowry toured France, the United Kingdom, Denmark, and Italy in order to educate himself about the means by which individuals, institutions, and government agencies were helping sustain and foster a cultural heritage in their respective countries. Lowry returned from the tour with an admiration for the European cultural model, a paradigm that placed high value on the arts and, most significant, arts institutions, and reinforced their central role with an unwavering and generous financial commitment.

Conveniently, the European approach that Lowry hoped to emulate in America was one that an institution such as the Ford Foundation could easily implement. It is no coincidence that when the foundation made its initial commitment to the arts, by establishing the division, its first plan of actions was to develop performing arts institutions.

Lowry's plans for arts funding did differ, however, from the European model in a fundamental way. Subsidies in the United States would come from the private rather than the public sector. The foundation developed its pilot program in the arts to maximize benefit for both the grant recipients and the grant maker, resulting in a highly symbiotic relationship. The foundation needed to educate itself about the state of the arts, and the artists needed resources and exposure. The staff members at the division became students of anyone who was associated with the resident theater and were determined to learn anything and everything about the needs and desires of artists nationwide. In order to do this, and at the same time fulfill the division's immediate mandate to help fund the arts, the staff attempted to include a research component into each grant action, forcing it to maximize every resource and opportunity in service of the theater program's overall objectives. For example, when the foundation gathered the directors and producers together (sometime in 1958 or 1959) to choose an acting company for the Cleveland Play House, it was not solely for the purpose of auditioning young actors. According to Lowry: "We then held over for two days these thirteen people representing very different and isolated experiences in the theater to confer with them and make them talk as we had done with each one of them individually before, but now in concert make them talk about other possible expenditures in theater under the exploratory program; a possible program for giving visibility to the works of young playwrights, which we did as a result of this two days of sessions."[16]

The foundation felt that each encounter with a professional artist should be a mutually beneficial exchange. Its request of the artists: "help us to help you." In this highly collaborative venture, the artists were eager to share their experiences with the Ford Foundation. Reportedly, Lowry and his staff were the first people outside of the arts community or the academy to solicit artists' and arts administrators' thoughts and opinions about the role of the arts in American culture. Furthermore, Lowry formed very personal and multifaceted relationships with many of the artists. In his correspondence with different artists, he emerges at times as father-confessor, touchstone, counselor, analyst, guide, mentor, cheerleader, and prophet.

Lowry and his staff were deliberate and self-reflective in their efforts on behalf of the resident theater. They understood that any success the foundation had with the grant programs in the theater would have broad implications. Lowry conceived of the division's importance not so much in terms of the financial assistance it offered the artists, but in terms of the information, insight, guidance, and exposure it provided to them. Lowry recalled in 1973 that one New York journalist, Thomas B. Hess, mocked the Ford Foundation for its jury process after it announced its first series of awards to individual painters and sculptors. Hess felt it was cumbersome, and unnecessary; that he would have come up with the same list without going through such a laborious process. Lowry explained, however, that

> they missed the point. The point was that the artists in every part of the country knew two things: first of all, they'd had a look at their work by somebody who cared; secondly, they knew—because we told them this much without any names—that every jury, regional or national, was dominated two-thirds by artists and if there was a third person who was a museum curator or director or connoisseur or critic, he was in the minority; they were being judged by their peers. And the fact that the Ford Foundation even cared that there might be artists who could win a national contest in Kansas City, or Dubuque, or somewhere, meant a lot psychologically to the artists.[17]

This approach enabled the foundation to select the participants of the division's programs while at the same time exposing the work of many artists to a jury of their peers. Everybody benefited.

> So here we were with a demonstration [grant program] aimed at testing the appetite for live theater in smaller towns and cities across the country, but reaching two other kinds of priorities in the program at the same time, and totally comprehensively learning—having our whole small staff out there—more and more about the theater, and principally the theater as a cultural resource rather than as commerce or entertainment. This is just one illustration of how we added to our field work in this exploratory

process, how we used grants and projects themselves both for their own intrinsic merit, and for our further education in the field, and how we also began to reduce the isolation of artists, artistic directors, artistic producers, by bringing them together.[18]

The close communication, and site visits from foundation staff contributed significantly to the shaping of grant programs. Season contracts for actors, for example, became a significant component of the foundation's pilot program with resident professional theater after Lowry visited the Alley Theatre in 1957. That visit convinced him that such contracts would provide greater stability for both the performers and the theaters themselves. At the time of his visit, artistic director Nina Vance was primarily using local actors, occasionally supplementing the talent pool with professional actors jobbed-in from New York. Without subsidy, neither the Alley nor any other resident professional theater, for that matter, could afford such contracts.

Lowry felt that what the Alley really needed was the resources to hire professional actors on a seasonal basis, "not to keep them off the bread line but to get the ensemble effect in production." Lowry later explained his understanding of why ensembles produce better theater: "when you chose your actors you chose at least ten or more with a whole season's repertoire in mind and in one play he might have an important role and in another play a walk-on, but they cast him right through the season. And they'd all work together with the same director and you'd get a higher state of the art from the ensemble, perhaps, if that happened."[19] The quality of the acting he observed on his European tour, where season contracts were standard, only served to reinforce this belief.

Lowry was aware, of course, that his was not a new idea, that "It had been done for years in Russia, in France, in England," but he also understood it to be a relatively new concept in the United States. He acknowledged that the Group Theatre and Eva Le Gallienne's Civic Repertory Theatre were antecedents to this model (although these two pioneering companies are characterized as "abortive experiments" in his Oral History). Lowry was convinced that "you'd get a higher state of the art" from a group of actors who spent a season working together with the same director. This belief led to the development of a grant project that subsidized seasonal contracts for a company of ten actors at three resident theaters: the Arena in Washington, D.C., under the artistic direction of Zelda Fichandler; the Alley in Houston, led by Nina Vance; and the Actor's Workshop in San Francisco, founded by Jules Irving and Herbert Blau.[20]

Lowry was a powerful agent for the artists in other respects as well. When he discovered that most of the theater artists who attended that first meeting with the foundation in 1959 were not acquainted with one another, he prioritized a grant action that would fund the development of improved communication. The organization, which would become known as the Theatre Communications Group, known today as TCG, was in the works as a foundation-administered program by 1961, but Lowry had started discussing such a program with artists as early as 1959.[21] According to its current mission, TCG still seeks to "to strengthen, nurture and promote the professional not-for-profit American theatre."[22]

One reason that most of these grantees did not know one another is that the foundation had chosen to work primarily with theaters and artists outside of New York, since one of its stated goals was to develop noncommercial theater in small and midsize cities across America. Historian Joseph Zeigler later speculated about the foundation's motives in focusing on smaller cities (smaller relative to New York). Referring to the Mummers Theater, he observed, "I suspect that the theatre's location on the vast prairies of America also appealed to Ford's sense of cultural justice; if this gargantuan feat could be accomplished in a spot so remote and isolated as Oklahoma City, then it could happen anywhere in this country."[23]

Apart from location, the human factor had a large bearing on which theaters were selected to participate in the demonstration program. Lowry always insisted that leadership was the most significant ingredient in the success of any theatrical enterprise, and particularly when that enterprise was an institution. Only a handful of artists around the country met Lowry's criteria for strong leadership. He engaged with those who displayed an entrepreneurial spirit. For example, Lowry involved Herbert Blau and Jules Irving of the Actor's Workshop in many aspects of the division's theater programs. He was impressed by their ingenuity, once remarking upon the fact that they used the resources from their employment at San Francisco State University as a means to bring stability to the Actor's Workshop—a theater company that was independent of the university. Nina Vance of the Alley Theatre, Zelda Fichandler of Arena Stage, and Mack Scism of Mummers Theatre were among those who worked closely with Lowry and the division during this period. Each of them had developed their own theaters based on innovative use of space and, in many cases, creative financing. Because Lowry had such faith in their abilities, he employed them as his first field consultants and continued to rely on their advice and observations over the years. He also used their theaters again and again for demonstration grants. These leaders shaped Lowry's values and aesthetic, and he oriented them toward professionalization and institutionalization. In many respects, they coauthored the country's first policy on the arts.

The Legacy

As early as 1965, Lowry authored a progress report to the trustees, titled, "The Resident Professional Theatre." This report serves as the most coherent and unified documentation of Lowry's intentions for the theater. In it, Lowry characterized the Theatre Communications Group as one of the most important grant programs in the theater. He explained to the trustees why TCG was continuing "to play an important and indeed somewhat unique role in the arts." Accounting for this distinction, he wrote, "This is chiefly because as yet no other central agency has had the opportunity to put itself in touch with so many artists and artistic directors and link them together toward common objectives. Increasingly the Foundation has been approached as a source of information about the arts and artistic problems and this role has continued meaning."[24]

The report also summarized the first two phases of the division's activities in the theater in a fashion consistent with Lowry's vision dating back to 1955. He pronounced that "between the establishment of the Ford Foundation Division of Humanities and the Arts in 1957 and the kick-off of the Guthrie Theatre in Minneapolis in February 1963, the Ford Foundation served as the focus of experiment and development for what the critics and drama reporters now call—but we do not—'the repertory theatre movement.'" He also insisted, "Money had less to do with this than the organized way in which the Ford Foundation went into staff work in the field visiting people and institutions and organizations and companies in the arts in more than a hundred communities in the United States, learning by talking with people, by taking . . . people in the theatre, from New York and from the rest of the country, locking them in a room for two days and listening to them talk without an agenda."[25] In other words, it was the human element rather than the financial one that made the difference. And that human element emanated out of Mac Lowry's personal style and commitment to the arts.

The last section of the report is devoted to measuring progress. Lowry feared that the theater companies the foundation had been supporting might be expanding too quickly. He acknowledged that operating expenses were continuing to rise, as were subscription sales. Unfortunately, these changing trends appeared to be placing the theaters under ever-increasing pressure. Despite evidence of new problems, Lowry displayed reserved optimism:

> The pot that we stirred is really boiling and the movement around the country by actors, directors and designers is far greater than it was. Whether it will ever be like the established repertory company in the United Kingdom or Germany is a question. Whether it can finally survive from its own resources or must be treated like opera and ballet and symphony (dependent upon a large annual maintenance drive and meeting an annual deficit) is being argued. I hope it can. Tyrone Guthrie's book says it can't. And I admit there are not very many adherents to my side of the question. But even now, for a number of actors, directors, playwrights, designers there is a new professional outlet, even—in a very few places—a new artistic one.[26]

The foundation was only toying with the idea of funding the arts when Dwight MacDonald observed in 1956 that the Ford Foundation had been no different from the Carnegie or Rockefeller foundations in its privileging of the sciences. He also characterized the field of arts and philanthropy as "risky, since the element of personal taste and imagination is the decisive one, and if the Foundation, by luck or good management, finds a twentieth-century Lorenzo de' Medici, or even a modern Dr. Johnson, to direct its art . . . the skeptics may be confounded. Or, again, they may not."[27] Appropriately, when Lowry retired from the foundation two decades later, Lincoln Kirstein, a major figure in twentieth-century American ballet, described the foundation's patronage of the arts during his tenure as "Medician" in scale.[28] The arts needed a Medici, and they found one in the person of W. McNeil Lowry.

Lowry was determined to see the foundation put its money to good use for the theater and the arts. He concentrated its resources on shaping arts policy and fostering cultural institutions throughout the country. In the same tribute to Lowry, Kirstein also observed, "With his retirement from the Ford Foundation a great epoch has ended, and, when such service [to the arts] is again rendered, it will hardly be through the talent and taste of a single person. Instead, government bureaux supported by panels of informed individuals, must, in concert or by consensus, come to decisions he was capable of making on his own."[29]

As a direct result of the division's grant programs, professional theater firmly rooted itself in the American cultural landscape. Today, Americans do not have to travel to New York if they want to see quality professional theater. Most do not have to leave their state, or even their city, to see a play produced by a not-for-profit professional theater. In fact, since the mid-1970s, more and more Broadway audiences have lined up to see productions that originated from resident professional theaters across the country. Located 2,850 miles from New York City, the Seattle Repertory Theatre has produced such world premieres as Herb Gardner's *I'm Not Rappaport* and Wendy Wasserstein's *The Sisters Rosensweig* and provided an artistic home for local playwright and national treasure August Wilson. To exert such influence so far from the city once considered the epicenter of American theater was inconceivable fifty years ago. This was the Ford Foundation's legacy under Lowry's leadership.

Notes

1. Waldemar A. Nielsen, *The Big Foundations* (New York: Columbia University Press, 1972), 38.

2. All monetary figures are presented as historical values, with no conversion to account for inflation.

3. Abraham Flexner, *Funds and Foundations: Their Policies Past and Present* (New York: Harper & Brothers Publishers, 1952), 129.

4. Robert H. Bremner, *American Philanthropy* (Chicago: University of Chicago Press, 1988), 179.

5. W. McNeil Lowry, Oral History Transcript (hereafter, "OHT"), January 14, 1972, 12–13, Ford Foundation Archives (hereafter, "FFA").

6. Dwight MacDonald, *The Ford Foundation: The Men and the Millions* (New York: Reynal, 1956), 4.

7. A primer on the history of tax legislation is warranted, at this point, because such legislation informed the behavior of the Ford Foundation as it made the transition from local to national and international philanthropy. Congress first exempted charitable organizations from federal tax on business income in

1894, but the precedent for such legislation can be traced back to precolonial England and beyond. Individual states soon followed suit, as the relevancy of such activities became more apparent. When a 1909 excise tax on corporations was levied, again, charitable organizations were explicitly exempt. The same was true when income tax was extended to individual earnings, with the Revenue Act of 1913. In 1917, Congress added a provision for income tax deduction, in an effort to encourage charitable donations. These laws obviously favored private trusts and promoted the formation of new foundations. The first effort to seriously tax the wealth of private trusts came in the form of the Revenue Act of 1950. By this point, foundations had to file information returns with the Internal Revenue Service and could lose their tax-exempt status if they accumulated too much wealth or used it for prohibited activities. Not until 1954, however, did Congress establish spending guidelines for trusts, such as the Ford Foundation, to ensure that they would spend all of their net income or some designated percentage of the value of their assets. The formula was complex and not standardized. It was determined by the type and amount of an individual foundation's assets and income.

8. Peter Zeisler, "They Broke the Mold," *American Theatre* 10 (1993): 5.

9. A comprehensive collection of the Wilson McNeil Lowry papers is held in the archives of the University of Illinois. An extensive collection of his papers, related to his work at the foundation, is held in the archives of the Ford Foundation.

10. W. McNeil Lowry, OHT, January 14, 1973, 5–6.

11. MacDonald, *Ford Foundation*, 96.

12. Ibid., 97.

13. Ibid., 98.

14. Lowry, OHT, January 14, 1973, 2.

15. Lowry, "Cultural Affairs Program," November 1955, 2, FFA Report #010783.

16. Lowry, OHT, May 17, 1973, 375.

17. Ibid., 382.

18. Ibid., 375.

19. Ibid., 391.

20. Ibid..

21. No other foundation-sponsored grant program expressed the values and objectives of the division's work in the theater better than that which culminated in the formation of the Theatre Communications Group (TCG). In general, this grant program aimed to improve communication between different theater institutions and their artistic leaders. Specifically, it sought to find ways in which the academic and community theater could help support and develop resident professional theater—including both existing organizations and those that wished to make the transition from amateur to professional or from commercial to not-for-profit. TCG started out as a Ford Foundation–administered program in 1961 and later became an independent tax-exempt organization.

22. Theatre Communications Group, "Mission Statement," http://www.tcg.org/frames/about/fs_about_mission.htm (accessed November 8, 2005).

23. Joseph Zeigler, *Regional Theatre: The Revolutionary Stage* (1973; New York: De Capo, 1977), 40.

24. Lowry, "Arts Program: Evaluation (1957–1961) and Statement of Current Objectives and Policies," FFA, 8.

25. Lowry, "The Resident Professional Theatre," July 1, 1965, 5, FFA Report #001107.

26. Lowry, "Resident Professional Theatre," 10.

27. MacDonald, *Ford Foundation*, 163.

28. Lincoln Kirstein, "W. McNeil Lowry" (privately printed, 1975), n.p.

29. Kirstein, n.p.

11

FUNDING "MAMA": THE MACARTHUR FOUNDATION AND ELLEN STEWART

Bruce Kirle

In 1986, the MacArthur Foundation honored Ellen Stewart, the "MaMa" of the La MaMa Experimental Theatre Company, with its "genius grant." The fellowship is unusual in that it recognizes individuals rather than organizations; moreover, candidates are nominated anonymously and selected by a committee representing a wide variety of disciplines. The rationale for this selection process counters that of traditional funding mechanisms, which honor a specific proposal within a specified field. Conversely, the MacArthur Foundation intends to reward those whose work crosses traditional disciplinary boundaries. In 2006, when theater is increasingly multicultural and cross-disciplinary and when performance technologies tend to be increasingly complex and characterized by mixed media, the foundation's rationale could well serve as a reference point for arts funding. In honoring Stewart, the foundation, in effect, authorized funds for a theatrical producer to continue her own work as theatrical angel, internationalizing American experimental theater by exporting her stable of writers, directors, and performers throughout the world and challenging the parochialism and insularity of American theater by importing her global theatrical family to perform at La MaMa's East Village complex in New York.

If Stewart is a maverick, so was John D. MacArthur, who, along with his wife, Catherine, created the foundation that bears his name in 1970. Owner of the Chicago-based Bankers Life and Casualty Company and a real estate entrepreneur, MacArthur selected a board to run the foundation but established no guidelines about how the money would be disbursed. Reportedly, MacArthur told the first trustees, including son Roderick and attorney William T. Kirby, "I made the money; now you fellows will have to decide what to do with it."[1]

John D. MacArthur.
Courtesy of the John D. and Catherine T. MacArthur Foundation.

The original motives for setting up the foundation are murky. According to grandson Rick, MacArthur may well have instructed Kirby to establish the foundation as a tax hedge. Indeed, the foundation sold Bankers Life and Casualty soon after MacArthur's death to avoid conflict-of-interest rules at the urging of Rod, an independent thinker who was often at odds with his father.[2] Even with the significant influence of Rod and Kirby in setting up the fellowship program, however, the ghost of MacArthur seems to hover over the recipients. Indeed, one might say that the fellowship program is the legacy of a life-insurance salesman, with a self-proclaimed epitaph: "I'm not a builder, I'm a saviour. When someone gets caught in a wringer they call me to bail them out."[3]

This is certainly the case for the 659 MacArthur Fellows from a variety of fields who received funding through the foundation between June 1981 and October 2003.[4] It is particularly true for Ellen Stewart. Plagued with financial worries throughout her forty-four-year career, Stewart, like MacArthur, is a self-reliant iconoclast who used the fellowship funds to promote her vision of theater as a universal language and playwrights as play makers who collaborate with others in a spirit of cultural pluralism and ethnic diversity. She is a poster girl for the trust that the foundation places in its recipients to use the funds to expand the traditional boundaries of their field.

One of the most successful salesmen in American history, John D. MacArthur was the youngest son of William Telfer MacArthur, a coal miner who heard his religious call as he watched his threshing machine go up in flames on his Pennsylvania farm. According to Ben Hecht, William "ordained himself as a minister on the spot, and [went] forth to recruit souls for the Lord."[5] William doted on the homeless and the destitute. Georgiana, his wife, would stretch one cabbage to fill twenty plates to accommodate the preacher's disciples. Hecht reports that she made lemonade in a chamber pot; it was the only container big enough to quench the thirst of her husband's stray parishioners.[6] William's attempts to instill Baptist values in his children apparently met with little success: "'The old Pollywog roared at us from morning to night,' claimed [Charles] MacArthur. 'He was constantly uncovering some new streak of wickedness in us. He would line us up at night, all still hungry as wolves, beseech God in a firm voice to forgive us, uncover our backs and whale the hell out of us. He kept a strap soaked in vinegar to make it a finer instrument of the Lord."[7] Apparently, John was impervious to his father's attempts at discipline. Known as a prankster, he failed his courses and dropped out of school after the eighth grade.

Eventually hired by his oldest brother, Alfred, who owned Central Standard Life Insurance, John claimed to have sold $1 million worth of life insurance policies in 1917.[8] For reasons that are unclear, he left the insurance business to follow in the footsteps of his two journalist brothers: Telfer, who owned Pioneer Press, a chain of suburban newspapers, and Charles, who later became the award-winning journalist, screenwriter, and playwright of *The Front Page* (1928) and husband of noted actress Helen Hayes. John worked briefly as a copyboy and cub reporter for the *Chicago Herald and Examiner* after World War I. In 1919, however, he resumed his insurance career and married Louise Ingalls in 1919. They had two children, Rod and Virginia.

By 1927, MacArthur had become sales vice president of State Life Insurance of Illinois. Preferring to work for himself, he enlisted Alfred's help in purchasing a small, floundering insurance company, Marquette Life, of Jerseyville, Illinois. MacArthur moved the company to Chicago and sold insurance policies door-to-door during the Depression. The stock market collapse on October 25, 1929, nearly bankrupted the life insurance industry, but MacArthur refused to admit defeat: "I had shot my mouth off to my brothers about making a big success . . . so I couldn't throw in the sponge when things got tough."[9] Whereas the big companies could not afford to collect premiums of less than $5, MacArthur accosted potential customers on the streets of Chicago and sold them term policies for anything he could get, including their lunch money: "I was in a somewhat better position than the bigger, established firms because I had just made a fresh start and didn't have too many dead horses to bury. I didn't have any assets, but I didn't have any liabilities either, and the liabilities were destroying the big firms."[10]

Seven years after acquiring Marquette, MacArthur borrowed the money in 1935 to buy Bankers Life and Casualty for $2,500. He almost went bankrupt when four death claims were filed in the first month that he owned the company. Although his assets shrank to less than $100, he eventually turned the Depression to his favor, as Bankers Life assumed the market share relinquished by failed companies. In 1938, MacArthur divorced his wife and, within a year, married his secretary and bookkeeper, Catherine

Hyland, who was to become involved in the management of her husband's companies for four decades. That same year, he sent out thousands of flyers and began marketing life insurance via mail. During the 1940s, MacArthur sold hundreds of thousands of low-cost policies. With the economic postwar boom, customers began to buy more expensive coverage. By the 1950s, Bankers Life had become an empire and MacArthur its sole owner. His corporate policy championed privately held assets: "Go public? . . . What for? This way I've got nobody to quarrel with. My life is a million times easier."[11] By July 1958, he employed a sales staff of more than five thousand and serviced three million clients with $5.5 billion in policies.[12] MacArthur held onto his privately owned empire until the foundation sold Bankers Life after his death.

Despite his wealth, MacArthur frequently dodged questions about his net worth: "Anybody who knows what he's worth isn't worth very much."[13] Indeed, in his *New York Times* obituary, it was noted that the magnitude of his estate was unknown. His will revealed that he left $700 million to the John D. and Catherine T. MacArthur Foundation. An unspecified additional sum was bequeathed for a retirement research foundation. Eventually, foundation money was allotted to the Human and Community Development Fund for Affordable Housing, Education Reform, and Mental Health, as well as the Global Security and Sustainability Fund for World Peace, Population Reduction, Conservation, and Human Rights. Additional funds have aided National Public Radio and arts and cultural organizations in Chicago. The remainder of MacArthur's estate, variously reputed to be anywhere from $2 million to $80 million, was split among his wife (half) and his two children (one-quarter each).[14]

MacArthur embraced an eccentric lifestyle. He lived with his wife and two poodles in a duplex overlooking the parking lot of the Colonnades, a small hotel that he owned in Palm Beach. He ran his insurance companies, banks, hotels, and real estate operations from his breakfast table in the hotel's crowded coffee shop. Trading quips with his waitress, MacArthur claimed in 1976, "I like to talk to people, to exchange ideas."[15] Driving a battered, four-year old Cadillac, MacArthur smoked over fifty cigarettes a day, which he lit with a plastic, throwaway lighter, and reportedly consumed an average of twenty cups of coffee daily.[16] He frequently wore a rumpled shirt and baggy wash-and-wear slacks, flew economy class, and often stood at the hotel's reception desk to greet guests, particularly when the hotel was short staffed. He refused to hire maids, butlers, chauffeurs, or bodyguards and freely granted interviews to reporters, making him one of America's most accessible billionaires.[17]

Surprisingly, MacArthur became editor and publisher of *Theatre Arts Magazine* in the 1950s. Although his enthusiasm for the prestigious publication could conceivably have been the result of the influence of his brother Charles and sister-in-law Helen Hayes, a financially shaky arts magazine was hardly the kind of enterprise one would expect to interest a pragmatic billionaire. Even odder was his involvement in the notorious Murph the Surf case; it was MacArthur who ransomed the DeLong star ruby, which had been stolen from New York's Museum of Natural History. His relationship with his children was stormy. In 1973, his grandson Greg Cordova-MacArthur disappeared on a hitchhiking trip to Mexico. MacArthur refused to help his daughter in the search. When interviewed about the boy's disappearance in 1977, a year before his death, MacArthur claimed he could not remember his name: "I have so many grandchildren."[18]

An interview with Rick MacArthur reveals much about his grandfather's personality, the contention between John and Rod, and, inadvertently, the similarity in values between father and son. Author of *Second Front: Censorship and Propaganda in the Gulf War* and *The Selling of Free Trade (NAFTA, Washington and the Subversion of American Democracy)*, Rick offers an insight into John's iconoclastic personality: "My grandfather instilled a spirit of independence. He didn't belong to clubs; he went his own way. He was conventionally right wing, but he didn't give money to politicians. He may have backed a tax assessor in Palm Beach County, might have tried to bribe him . . . but it was strictly business. His ideological thoughts were primitive. His interest in politics didn't go beyond what it took to buy influence for his vast businesses."[19] The friction between John and Rod obviously affected Rick's attitude toward his grandfather. As a child, he realized that MacArthur would sooner leave money to his aviary of parakeets than to his family.[20] The bulk of the fortune was indeed bequeathed to the foundation, of which Rod was a trustee.

According to Rick, enormous tension existed between his grandfather's cronies on the foundation board and Rod. Finally, Rod persuaded the trustees to add liberal academics to encourage an ideological balance: "It was a regular horse trading board. 'You back my project and I'll back yours.'"[21]

He threatened to sue the trustees for self-dealing and violating fiduciary laws. Rick remembers that "these conventional Midwestern businessmen were horrified by the bad publicity coming out of the lawsuit."[22]

In the midst of the legal battle, Rod was diagnosed with pancreatic cancer. The lawsuit was dropped when he died at age sixty-three in 1984. According to Rick, "They never forgave us, and we never forgave them."[23] Despite bitterness toward his grandfather and his cronies on the foundation board, Rick concedes that his own self-reliance was formed by knowing he would not inherit the bulk of his grandfather's fortune. Moreover, he owes a personal debt of thanks to foundation funding. Working as a reporter in Chicago, like his grandfather before him, he learned that *Harper's* was going out of business in 1980: "I called my dad from the city room at the *Sun-Times*. I said, 'Dad, *Harper's* magazine just announced that it's folding. Do you think the foundation could bail it out?'" His father agreed to try. "So, we lobbied, and two weeks later, they voted to save it."[24] In 1983, Rick became publisher of a solvent *Harper's*.

F. Champion Ward, one of the original trustees, offers an insider's view on the beginnings of the "genius grant." Ward had previously worked on designing the Ford Foundation; like MacArthur, Ford had not specified how his funds were to be spent. In her essay in this volume, Sheila McNerney Anderson discusses more fully the origin of the Ford Foundation. According to Ward, the first trustees sought advice from a variety of experts on how to distribute MacArthur's fortune. Rod championed a letter received from G. E. Burch, chairperson of Tulane University's Department of Medicine, who complained that research scientists were constricted by strings attached to their grants.[25] Burch believed that granting agencies needed to reward researchers and practitioners interested in advancing knowledge for the sake of knowledge: "Recipients should be left alone without the annoyances and distractions imposed by grant applications, reviewing committees, and pressure to publish."[26] Burch's article inspired Rod to develop the five guidelines of what would eventually become the basis of the MacArthur Fellows Program:

> (a) Identify creative individuals with extraordinary promise for significant accomplishment; (b) Select these individuals from across a broad range of fields and professions; (c) Give them enough money to live decently, so that they would not be required to take other work; (d) Pay out this

> money over a long enough time period to allow them the freedom to set their own agenda; and (e) Leave them alone to work on whatever they might choose, without any strings attached to the use of the funds or any reporting requirement.[27]

Backed by Kirby, his father's lawyer and a fellow trustee, Rod fought to support creative individuals without calling them to account, a position of which "his fiercely self-reliant father would have approved."[28] Actually, Rod fought for lifetime support of recipients of MacArthur Fellowships and argued that the entire income of the foundation be spent to support these worthy individuals. In hindsight, Ward takes responsibility for the five-year duration of the award. Rod's lifetime scheme was bolder, but Ward succumbed to the "habitual prudence of conventional philanthropy."[29] Rod felt that one Einstein would justify lifetime funding, and Ward is now inclined to agree.

Ward advocated relying on approximately one hundred anonymous nominators, who select candidates (preferably without initially informing them) and send the individual files to another anonymous selection committee consisting of representatives from a variety of disciplines. Part of the reasoning behind the anonymity of nominees and selectors is to prevent participants in the selection process from being burdened with unsolicited requests from potential candidates. Anonymity also encourages frankness about those considered for the award, since no information is disseminated beyond the selection committee. Although several hundred individuals may be nominated, not all are considered in the same year. Typically, twenty to thirty recipients are selected annually.

Although it is often referred to as the "genius grant," the foundation eschews this label, which connotes intellectual superiority. Recipients have other qualities perhaps even more impressive: the imagination to transcend traditional disciplinary boundaries, the ability to synthesize a variety of approaches to their field, and the persistence to pursue their vision despite the risks involved. Fellows, who may be chosen from virtually any field, ideally are those whose work does not fall within conventional categories established by other funding agencies, which tend to be organized by discipline and peer review. Currently, the stipend is $500,000, paid quarterly over a five-year period.[30] The philosophy is that recipients best know how to use the funds to maximize their potential;

thus, the award is given with no strings so as to provide those honored with maximum freedom and flexibility. In another essay in this volume, Jeffrey Eric Jenkins describes a different philosophy behind the Harold and Mimi Steinberg Charitable Trust.

After the first MacArthur selections were announced in 1981, Ward was asked to suggest ways to redefine the process. He interviewed fellows, assuring them that they had the right to confidentiality since the award promised nonaccountability. According to Ward, "Once reassured, they were glad to talk."[31] Most had made intelligent use of their grants; however, over time, Ward notes, the MacArthur Fellowships were criticized for a variety of reasons, perhaps the most serious being that since the nominators and selectors were anonymous, they could be suspected of favoritism or chicanery. The rotation of nominators and selectors eliminated possible objections that the selections were random and unfair and tended to underplay potential accusations of partiality.

Over the years, the success of the program has been difficult to measure. Rod had originally argued against any formal evaluation, such as having recipients write diaries. The tension between allowing the program to flourish with mystery and succumbing to measurable outcomes has always been controversial. Many fellows have volunteered information about how the program has changed their lives. Several have revealed how their money has been spent. Some pursued present obligations; some made financial arrangements so they could juggle their normal activities with periods of total freedom.

For instance, Mary Zimmerman, a 1998 recipient, is a Chicago-based director who specializes in theatricalizing such epic tales as Homer's *The Odyssey* (2001) and Ovid's *Metamorphosis* (2002) with stunning visual imagery, not unlike dance theater. She teaches in the Performance Art Program at Northwestern University, and her work has been seen in such Chicago venues as the Lookingglass and Goodman theaters, as well as on Broadway. Like other theater recipients, Zimmerman tends to challenge conventional disciplinary borders. She relies heavily on design, movement, and music, as well as on text, which she often creates herself. The award has enabled her to travel and research her productions: "I went to Egypt on my own for an opera called *Akhenaten*, and I went to Italy for *Galileo* and to Japan for *Silk* and to India . . . . I learned so much from my travels, saw so much that I would never have thought to look for in term's of design and music in particular."[32] She has also used the funds to augment her own budgets.

For Zimmerman, the award allows the recipient to feel more confident about his or her own work and helps in ways that are not always readily apparent, such as looking for grants or pitching a play. Because the MacArthur grant includes people from every profession, and "so many admirable people who do good for others . . . it legitimizes one in a sort of irrefutable way."[33] Zimmerman speculates that the award enables recipients to continue working on what they would have worked on anyway, but with the added benefit of attracting money and opportunity in ways they are probably unaware of. The fellowship, she hypothesizes, allows recipients to just become more themselves.

One could well argue that the MacArthur Fellowship enabled Ellen Stewart, whose vision of theater transcends national boundaries, to continue being herself. She decided to use the MacArthur funds to firm her home base in New York by founding La MaMa Umbria, a nonprofit cultural center and artists' residence just outside Spoleto, Italy, in 1990. Although it was not necessary to account for her use of the funds, Stewart gratefully acknowledges that she used the MacArthur grant as seed money to establish her artists' center. Each summer, the La MaMa Directors' Symposium at Umbria features an international faculty of master teachers, who give workshops to practicing actors, directors, dancers, performers, and choreographers. In this way, Stewart's international family grows annually.

Stewart opened her New York theater in 1961, three years after Joe Cino, the "Papa" of Off-Off Broadway, founded the historic Caffe Cino in Greenwich Village's Cornelia Street.[34] From the start, Stewart's desire for community was representative of the 1960s avant-garde:

> In common parlance, a community is usually understood as built out of families. But while community, and even a brand of domesticity was often a desired value in the Sixties avant-garde, this notion was radically different from that of the bourgeois community, for here—foreshadowing the countercultural utopian communes of the later Sixties—"togetherness" was sought outside of family life, in groups coalescing around common work or common play. . . . This alternative communalism linked the assertion of community to the politics of egalitarianism and liberation.[35]

Dedicated to the playwright and all aspects of the theatre, La MaMa was a close-knit family and Stewart a loving mother who selectively chose her children. She would often put her hand on a script after talking with the writer. If the vibes were good, she would produce the play. If the vibes were not good, she would not consider producing it, even if it was a potential Pulitzer Prize winner. Once she adopted a "chickie," however, the playwright could count on her support and sustenance: "Ellen Stewart cooked soup to feed her actors and playwrights. Her salary went into the communal kitty. She understood the importance of her playwrights. She rang a cowbell at the beginning of each performance and welcomed the audience to the theatre with her now famous, 'Welcome to La Mama; dedicated to the playwrights [sic] and all aspects of the theatre.' They were her life and she was their mother."[36] Like Caffe Cino, La MaMa was "an offbeat version of a family business, run by an antifamily."[37] Here was an ex–fashion designer from Saks Fifth Avenue, a rather glamorous, 1960s counterculture version of Josephine Baker, dressed in flamboyant scarves and paisleys, who made sure that her adopted children ate at least one hot meal a day—usually hot dogs and lentil soup—and who insisted on their freedom not only to make mistakes but also to forge creative alliances among writers, composers, directors, and designers.

Over the years, Stewart has chosen a formidable group of "chickies." She has produced over 1,900 plays by writers including Sam Shepard, Lanford Wilson, Julie Bovasso, Tom Eyen, Maria Irene Fornes, Paul Foster, Israel Horovitz, Adrienne Kennedy, Leonard Melfi, Rochelle Owens, Robert Patrick, Megan Terry, Jean-Claude van Itallie, and Mario Fratti; directors such as Tom O'Horgan, Joe Chaikin, Andrei Serban, and Jerzy Grotowski; and countless composers, actors, musicians, puppeteers, and play makers whom she has hosted from more than seventy countries. Moreover, La MaMa's resident troupes have performed throughout the world.

Oddly, Stewart is the first to admit that her original passion was music rather than theater. She has not only directed but also composed the scores for productions internationally and seems proudest of her musical achievements.[38] According to the La MaMa Web site, "Not only is the work we do experimental because of new directions in writing, but also because of the exciting collaborations that we foster, especially musical ones. To date we have presented over 1000 original scores on our stages. Creative risk-taking, experimentation, and challenging artistic boundaries have always been the focus of the work created and performed at La MaMa."[39]

I met Stewart in 1968, when I composed several scores for Tom Eyen and his Theatre-of-the-Eye Repertory Company. We performed in a first-floor space next to the old Electric Circus on St. Mark's Place. Within a year, she had secured a permanent home for La MaMa at 74A East Fourth Street in the East Village. Eyen and I wrote the first production for the new theater, *Caution: A Love Story*, a musical that somehow managed to combine the story of the Duke and Duchess of Windsor with a band of gypsies, who explained the myriad sexual possibilities of the *Kama Sutra*. Perhaps my strongest memory of Stewart in those days is her standing proudly at the entrance to her new building, which at that time had no floor and no stairs. To get to her living quarters, she put spikes on the walls and hung ropes. Interviewing her thirty-six years later for this essay, I found Stewart living in the same space, a five-flight walk-up on the top floor of her theater. She was as proud and excited about the future of La MaMa as ever. When I contacted her by phone, Stewart was getting ready for an interview about a new project involving Native American theater, which she has long championed. Our conversation was occasionally interrupted as she spoke in Italian to one of her coterie; gave directives about setting up cameras in the La MaMa archives, an incredible resource for those who wish to research the history of Off-Off Broadway; fielded a television crew; and put me on the phone with a Korean, a Columbian, and an Israeli, all of whom were participating in various projects.

For me, Stewart's artistic legacy at La MaMa in the late 1960s and early 1970s involved a remarkable spirit of collaboration, which I have never rediscovered anywhere else in quite the same way. Even before meeting Stewart, I remember watching author Jean-Claude van Itallie and Joe Chaikin rehearse the Open Theatre production of *America Hurrah!* (1966) and being stunned by the lack of compartmentalization so typical of commercial theater. At La MaMa, director, playwright, and actor were unafraid to decompartmentalize and play with one another's roles in contributing to the rehearsal process. The same was true when I worked with Eyen and the Theatre-of-the-Eye. Everyone involved in the production was free to initiate ideas without fear of overstepping their boundaries or trouncing on egos. When I asked Stewart how she managed to foster this kind of interchange, she replied that she refuses to put restrictions on her artists: "When Tom [Eyen] rehearsed *The White Whore and the Bit Player* in the basement, I only said I don't want to see anything going in and out—front or back!"[40] Other than that warning, Stewart gave Eyen total artistic control.

Although Stewart's original motivation for bringing her playwrights to Europe was to get their work reviewed and their plays published, she also realized that being in Europe and interacting with different cultures changed the aesthetics of her writers, directors, and actors. After the first European tour in 1965, Stewart noticed that her playwrights "began fixing up their apartments, hanging nice things on the wall."[41] Between the first tour in 1965 and 1986, the year in which Stewart was awarded the MacArthur Foundation grant, she exported American experimental theater throughout Europe, Asia, and South America. She also imported her increasingly international theatrical family to the United States. It was she, in conjunction with Ted Hoffman of New York University, who brought Jerzy Grotowski and Andrei Serban to America. Her commitment to Eastern European theater has been particularly noteworthy. During the war in the Balkans, her company played outdoors in Belgrade amid American bombings and death threats. Her activities during the war in Yugoslavia were rewarded when Serbian theater artists chose her, despite being an American, to represent their country in the Theatre Joy Festival, an honor of which she is justifiably proud.

Stewart had maintained an apartment in Spoleto since the early 1970s. With hindsight, her decision to establish an artists' center in Umbria was canny. Not only could she forge contacts and alliances through the annual Spoleto Festival, she was a train ride away from other potential European operations. When she decided to found Umbria, she anticipated financial help from the United States and from Italy. Surprisingly, both countries rejected her pleas for funding. The United States had no interest in backing a project in Umbria; American philanthropic sources told her to initiate the project in Idaho, Iowa, Ohio, or Montana. Even then an isolationist philosophy toward arts funding was pervasive in America. Stewart was also turned down by the Italian government, which was reluctant to fund an American.[42]

Stewart credits the MacArthur Foundation's $300,000 stipend with providing her with the seed money to establish Umbria. She stumbled upon a seven-hundred-year-old convent that was in ruins and used the grant to purchase the property. Friends thought that she was crazy. She had invested the stipend in what was little more than a pile of rubble, and she did not have the money for adequate renovation and construction. Operating on the theory that money needed is money available, Stewart slowly began to gather the resources to transform the property in Umbria into an international arts center. She won a National Endowment for the Arts prize that fed $215,000 into the project. Her playwrights, actors, and La Mama family—many of whom were struck down by AIDS in the late 1980s and early 1990s—gave her additional funding to pursue her dream. Tom Eyen left her $100,000, Leland Moss left another $300,000, Theatre of the Eye actor Bill Duffy left her $40,000, and the Tokyo Kid Brothers gave her $10,000.[43] By 1990, she was able to open her nonprofit cultural center and artists' residence, which would promote cultural exchange and international understanding.

La MaMa Umbria is about two hours from Rome, just off the Via Flaminia, the road from Spoleto to Assisi. The highlight of the center is the annual three-week International Directors' Symposium. A resident group of twenty-seven directors, six or more master teachers, coordinators, and guest artists share ideas, exchange cultural traditions, and celebrate their own diversity. Master teachers, selected by Stewart in coordination with David Diamond and Mia Yoo, conduct workshops during the day, while students often initiate workshops at night. All are expected to engage with one another's work. The roster of master teachers for summer 2005 was typically diverse: Anne Bogart (United States), director of the SITI Company, which she formed with Tadashi Suzuki in 1992; Andrea Paciotto (Italy), a director and media artist who works in Amsterdam; Jan Klug (Germany), a composer and programmer; Jun Tanaka (Japan), a specialist in Japanese traditional marionette theater; Joanne Akalaitis (United States), celebrated international director and cofounder of Mabou Mines with Philip Glass; Alido Neslo (Suriname) and Nilo Berrocal Vargas (Peru), specialists in epic theater and master storytelling; and Ivica Bulan (Croatia), former director of the Croatian National Theatre in Split and current artistic director of the World Theatre Festival in Zagreb, who incorporates film, video, and photographs to create political theater. With master teachers sharing such a diversity of cultures and specializations, symposium participants are exposed to the myriad possibilities of live theater.[44]

"Student" participants tend to be mostly midcareer American directors, often affiliated with a university.[45] Participants in the 2005 summer symposium represented thirteen states and China. In this way, the Umbria experience ripples across the United States. Often, those participating from the academy find subvention money from their home universities. The admission fee for participants is approximately $2,850, which includes all workshops, housing, and meals. Staffing is minimal: "After all," says Stewart, "This is La MaMa."[46] There is, however, a cook, Elisa, who prepares meals on a five-hundred-year-old wood oven. Forty people, speaking a variety of languages, eat together twice a day. The feeling of community through this shared experience is not unlike Adriane Mnouchkine's Théâtre de Soleil or, for that matter, La MaMa in the 1960s, when Stewart used to fix hot dogs for her writers, directors, and actors.

Umbria has come a long way from the rubble that Stewart purchased with the funds from the MacArthur Foundation. The Directors' Symposium is an outgrowth of her belief in a global, theatrical family that complements and strengthens the work she has encouraged for over forty years at her New York base. The foundation gave her the opportunity to expand this vision. Would she have pursued it without the genius grant? For Stewart, funding has always been crucial. Interviewed in the Sunday *New York Times* in 1969, before the opening of the current theater at 74A East Fourth Street, she was candid about her needs: "'What does La Mama need most?' I [the interviewer] asked. 'Money,' she said. '$25,000. We need, we need, we need! Stage equipment, a lighting board, more money for air-conditioning and heat. We need $5,000 to complete our poetry room. We need money to paint the place. Grants are getting harder to come by. I should have asked the foundations for more money to begin with, but I didn't. The agony of it is people always believe Ellen Stewart will come through. I suppose I will.'"[47]

Somehow, despite years of struggling to survive, Stewart has always come through for her "chickies." After a debilitating illness, she managed to direct her new adaptation of *Perseus* in May 2005 at the New York La MaMa Annex. Jason Zinoman of the *New York Times* praised Stewart's determination to continue presenting challenging work that pushes the conventional boundaries of theater: "La MaMa, like Ms. Stewart, often seems unaffected by changing times. The dusty downtown theatre, which started out in a basement in 1961, still produces international artists and classic work in an era when fewer theatres are willing to take the risk. But while the Brooklyn Academy of Music or St. Ann's Warehouse apply a glamorous sheen to challenging productions, La MaMa retains the mood . . . of the old, pregentrified East Village. It is decidedly not hip—and proud of it."[48]

On opening night, she appeared during the curtain calls, joyfully navigating her wheelchair (in which she was temporarily confined) in circles as she and the rest of the cast proudly acknowledged the enthusiasm of the audience. Despite financial setbacks and physical illness, Stewart is as fiercely self-reliant as John D. MacArthur was. If MacArthur bailed out his insurance clients, Stewart has helped sustain her "chickies" throughout her career. Thirty-six years ago, shortly before the opening of 74A East Fourth Street, she was recuperating from another illness. While she was in the hospital, some members of the La MaMa troupe had begun squabbling: "We can take anything," said actress Julie Bovasso at the time, "no food, very little sleep and poor rehearsal conditions, but we need to know she's around."[49] Thirty-six years later, we still do.

Notes

1. Quoted in F. Champion Ward, "The Birth of the MacArthur Fellows Program." *Foundation News and Commentary*, 42 (September/October 2001):5, 38.

2. Justine Blau, "Rick MacArthur '78: Maverick Journalist," *Columbia College Today*, http://www. college.columbia.edu/cct/may03/cover.php, 3 (accessed October 9, 2005).

3. Quoted in Dena Klexman, "John D. MacArthur, Billionaire, Dies," *New York Times*, January 7, 1978.

4. John D. and Catherine T. MacArthur Foundation, "The MacArthur Fellows Program," http://www.macfdn.org/programs/fel/announce.htm, 10 (accessed September 8, 2004).

5. Ben Hecht, *Charlie: The Improbable Life and Times of Charles MacArthur* (New York: Harper, 1957), 24.

6. Hecht, *Charlie*, 25.

7. Quoted in Hecht, *Charlie*, 26.

8. *Dictionary of American Biography: Supplement Ten, 1976–1980*, ed. Kenneth T. Jackson, Karen E. Markoe, and Arnold Markoe (New York: Charles Scribner's Sons, 1995), 477.

9. Quoted in *Dictionary of American Biography*, 477.

10. Quoted in Klexman, "John D. MacArthur."

11. Quoted in *Dictionary of American Biography*, 478.

12. *Dictionary of American Biography*, 478.

13. Quoted in Klexman, 1.

14. See Blau, "Rick MacArthur," 2; Klexman, "John D. MacArthur"; *Dictionary of American Biography*, 476

15. Quoted in Andrew Jaffee, "The Richest Men in America," *Newsweek*, August 2, 1976, 34.

16. Jaffee, "Richest Men," 35.

17. Klexman, "John D. MacArthur."

18. Quoted in Klexman, "John D. MacArthur."

19. Blau, "Rick MacArthur," 2.

20. Rick's assertion is not entirely accurate. Depending on conflicting accounts, Rod was left somewhere between $500,000 and $20,000,000. True, the foundation acquired the bulk of the MacArthur fortune. See Blau, "Rick MacArthur"; Klexman, "John D. MacArthur"; Ward, "Birth of MacArthur Fellows"; *Dictionary*.

21. Quoted in Blau, "Rick MacArthur, "2.

22. Ibid., 3.

23. Ibid.

24. Ibid., 4.

25. Ward, "Birth of MacArthur Fellows," 1.

26. Quoted in MacArthur Foundation, "The MacArthur Fellows Program: Frequently Asked Questions," http://www.macfdn.org/programs/fel/faq.htm, 9 (accessed September 8, 2004).

27. MacArthur Foundation, "The MacArthur Fellows Program: Frequently Asked Questions," http://www.macfdn.org/programs/fel/faq.htm, 10 (accessed September 8, 2004).

28. Ward, "Birth of MacArthur Fellows," 2.

29. Ibid., 5.

30. According to Stewart, her stipend was $300,000 in 1986. Ellen Stewart, interview with author, May 18, 2005.

31. Ward, "Birth of MacArthur Fellows," 3.

32. Mary Zimmerman, interview with author, May 8, 2005.

33. Zimmerman interview, May 8, 2005.

34. Of all the Off-Off-Broadway theaters active in the 1960s, La MaMa is the sole survivor, having operated continuously since 1961. For more information on the Caffé Cino, see Wendell C. Stone, *Caffe Cino; The Birthplace of Off-Off Broadway* (Carbondale: Southern Illinois University Press, 2005).

35. Sally Banes, *Greenwich Village 1963: Avant-Garde Performance and the Effervescent Body* (Durham, NC: Duke University Press, 1993), 36.

36. Albert Poland and Bruce Mailman, *The Off-Off Broadway Book* (Indianapolis: Bobbs-Merrill, 1972), xxxii. Actually, Stewart's famous line of welcome to her audiences referred to the "playwright" rather than to "playwrights." For more on La MaMa and the Off-Off-Broadway movement, see Stephen J. Bottoms, *Playing*

Underground: A Critical History of the 1960s Off-Off Broadway Movement (Ann Arbor: University of Michigan Press, 1994); David A. Crespy, *Off-Off Broadway Explosion: How Provocative Playwrights of the 1960s Ignited a new American Theatre* (New York: Backstage, 2003).

37. Banes, *Greenwich Village*, 50.

38. Stewart interview, May 18, 2005.

39. La MaMa, "About the La MaMa Experimental Theatre Club," http://www.lamama.og/about.html, 1 (accessed September 9, 2004).

40. Ellen Stewart, interview with the author, November 18, 2004.

41. Stewart interview, November 18, 2004.

42. Ellen Stewart, interview with the author, May 30, 2005.

43. Stewart interview, November 18, 2004.

44. For a personal perspective on the Second Annual International Symposium for Directors, see Rebecca Engle, "Space and Synchronicity," http://www.lamama.org/Umbria%20Folder/AmTheaMagArticle.htm (accessed November 13, 2005), reprinted from *American Theatre* 19 (January 2002): 32–34, 106.

45. See Engle, "Space and Synchronicity."

46. Stewart interview, November 18, 2004.

47. Quoted in Patricia Bosworth, "Mother Is at Home at La Mama," *New York Times*, March 30, 1969.

48. Jason Zinoman, "Keeping the Ancient in an Ancient Greek Saga." *New York Times*, May 4, 2005, http://theater2.nytimes.com/2005/05/04/theater/reviews/04pers.html?ex=1130907600&en (accessed October 31, 2005).

49. Quoted in Bosworth, "Home at La Mama."

12

A COMMUNITY OF ANGELS FOR ACTORS THEATRE OF LOUISVILLE

Jeffrey Ullom

The opening night of a new theater season always provides a reason to celebrate, and the August 18, 2005, performance of *Love, Janis* at Actors Theatre of Louisville was no exception. Board members, theater staff, and longtime supporters of the local institution gathered in the voluminous lobby of the 637-seat Pamela Brown Auditorium with high expectations for the evening—after all, the Pamela Brown is the space that presented audiences with some of Actors Theatre's most famous productions including the premieres of *Dinner with Friends* and *Crimes of the Heart*. This night, the opening of Actors Theatre's forty-second season, would be memorable for reasons other than the upcoming production. Before the Joplin retrospective, community leaders and theater professionals convened for a brief ceremony in the lobby to recognize the accomplishments of one theater staff member. Although the evening's events highlighted one man's service to the theater, the brief celebration also served as reason to commemorate the many achievements of Actors Theatre as a whole, from its contentious beginnings to its steady growth under former producing director Jon Jory and finally to becoming the host of the nation's preeminent new-play festival. Also helping commemorate Actors Theatre's achievements that August night were its major donors—or angels—several patrons and civic leaders who also helped guide the theater to success, giving their time and money to help ensure stability for the once-struggling institution.

The principle that guides and unites these angels is a credo of "community first," a belief among the donors and patrons that their support and endeavors should not be for self-glorification or publicity but, instead, for the Louisville community's benefit. Often labeled the "old money" of Louisville, the donors and patrons embody a smaller community, yet they act in the interest of the entire city. These civic leaders—who also founded and helmed Louisville's major foundations and corporations—are responsible for helping Actors Theatre maintain its stability throughout its forty-two-year history, providing funds and support for both the theater and the arts community at large. Although Actors Theatre faces the same challenges as other theaters in attaining its fund-raising goals, the Louisville theater relies heavily upon the generosity of these donors, more than other theaters of a similar size in cities with a population equivalent to that of the Kentucky city.[1] For example, according to 1984's *Theatre Profiles* (the last year in which the Theatre Communication Group publication provided figures for a company's operating expenses, earned income, and grants and contributions), Actors Theatre reported $3.2 million in operating expenses, with its grants and contributions providing $1.38 million toward the operating costs, accounting for 42.6 percent of its income. Other regional theaters were much less dependent upon the generosity of local corporations, foundations, and donors—Atlanta's Alliance Theatre reported 33.4 percent deriving from grants, while Indiana Repertory Theatre (Indianapolis) and Milwaukee Repertory Theatre reported figures of 35.9 percent and 32.1 percent, respectively.

As a result, Actors Theatre takes great care to involve corporate donors in its business affairs, inviting chief executive officers and other representatives of the corporations to serve on its board of directors.[2] With its business partners serving a vital role for the theater through both leadership and financial support, Actors Theatre operates with the mentality of a smaller community theater rather than one of the nation's leading regional theaters, where the bottom line and a foundation's preferences for nonoffensive works dictate the season and where self-promotion drives corporate giving. Much like a community theater, these angels not only donate money to fund productions but also share a vision for the prosperity of the arts in Louisville. The examination of each angel's contribution to Actors Theatre also highlights how the theater's leaders work tirelessly with these angels to ensure a bright future for both the theater and all arts organizations in the community.

To theater professionals across the country, the name Actors Theatre of Louisville is synonymous with the Humana Festival of New American Plays. Considered the premiere new-play festival in the United States since its inception in 1976, the festival has presented over three hundred productions, including multiple Pulitzer, Drama Desk, and Obie award winners. As noted in the theater's publicity materials, the festival is made possible by "a generous grant" from the Humana Foundation to Actors Theatre for the expressed purposes of supporting the annual event. With its initial donation of $100,000 in 1979, the long-standing relationship between Humana (later the Humana Foundation, established in 1981) and Actors Theatre demonstrates how Actors Theatre successfully encouraged angels in the forms of foundations.

The relationship between Actors Theatre and the Humana Foundation developed from a personal relationship and from a mutual desire to contribute to the Louisville community. The Humana Corporation—described as "one of the nation's largest publicly traded health benefits companies with more than seven million members" in its health-care plans—became a public corporation in 1968, and the Humana Foundation, the philanthropic arm of the corporation, was established thirteen years later in order to identify, fund, and nurture "projects and organizations in three fields: domestic and international health, education, and civic and cultural development in communities where the company has a meaningful presence."[3]

When both Humana and Actors Theatre were in their early years, Jory and executive director Alexander "Sandy" Speer frequently held business lunches at the same small, downtown restaurant as David Jones and Wendell Cherry, the two founders of Humana. Over time, a relationship developed between the men as they discussed a variety of ways that both Actors Theatre and Humana could publicize their businesses to the Louisville community. The "Humana Boys" (as they were labeled by old-money Louisville) were described as ambitious in their attempts to make a name for themselves in the community. Cherry, also the co-owner of the Kentucky Colonels basketball team, and Jones, a former lawyer and accountant, spread their wealth throughout the city, helping construct the Kentucky Center for the Arts (a large performance complex down the street from Actors Theatre) and hiring world-renowned architects to design and build their headquarters in downtown Louisville.[4]

By 1979, after only three years, the Festival of New American Plays had produced such critical hits as *Getting Out*, *The Gin Game*, and *Crimes of the Heart*, providing a burgeoning reputation for the new-play festival. As the festival grew in national prominence, Jory and Speer realized that they needed to discover new sources of revenue to sustain the increasingly popular annual event.[5] The business relationship between Humana and Actors Theatre began when Jory first contacted Humana about becoming the festival's corporate sponsor. According to an essay published by the corporation that celebrates the festival's twenty-fifth anniversary, Jory "sent a mission statement to Humana co-founders David A. Jones, Sr. and Wendell Cherry. Jones recalls that Jory's statement glowed with lucidity and fire. ATL's clear vision, along with Humana's desire to nourish the arts in Louisville, propelled the two organizations to work together."[6] While Actors Theatre needed financial support for its festival, Humana needed support of another kind. Jory solicited funds from Humana because he perceived the Louisville-based corporation as a business looking to increase its standing in the community. To that end, he promoted the growing festival as an opportunity for the young corporation to firmly establish its reputation in the Louisville community.[7] In other words, Jory garnered financial support from a Louisville-based corporation whose reputation was not established firmly in the Louisville community.

David Jones, in a letter published for the celebration of the Tenth Annual Humana Festival of New American Plays in 1986, described the mutual benefits of the relationship: "The two go hand in hand: both young, yet both determined to establish and maintain a tradition of providing only the highest quality to the public. The mission of Humana, to provide an unexcelled level of quality in the delivery of affordable health services, is one we undertake with enthusiasm. Just as launching a theater festival has brought out the creative talents of this resident company, so our mission inspires us to serve those who depend on us for their physical well being."[8] Since Jory and Jones both described Humana as a young corporation, it is no surprise that the Louisville health insurance company desired to build stronger ties with the Louisville community. Proclaiming that funding "artistic expression enhances people's lives by promoting creativity, learning, and open-mindedness," the generosity of Jones and Cherry established them as leading philanthropists and civic heroes, providing them the publicity and social clout that they desired.[9]

After funding the annual event for five years on an annual basis, Actors Theatre and Humana made history in 1981 with the decision to rename the festival in exchange for greater financial support. According to Speer, "[Actors Theatre] asked for either a two or three year commitment initially, but we felt that the money wasn't enough in retrospect, and we went back and asked to renegotiate." As part of the renegotiations, Actors Theatre officially offered to name the festival in the corporation's honor. "We went back and asked them for a lot more money," Speer explained, "and then we offered the name." The Humana Foundation's support of the festival has led to the largest philanthropic donation to a single institution in the history of American theater, giving over $12 million to Actors Theatre for the festival.[10]

Obviously, the Humana Foundation's generous gift to Actors Theatre helped support the continuation of the festival for many years. As Speer explained, "The key to the marvel of their support—which is still true today but even more so during the early years—was the three-year commitment because it allowed the planning time that we needed. We could foresee that there would be a Humana Festival two years from now."[11] Perhaps more remarkable is the Humana Foundation's hands-off approach to the festival and its content. "We wouldn't for a moment think about interfering with [any] artistic decisions," Wendell Cherry once asserted. "Of course, some would argue they'd never bite the hand that feed [*sic*] them, so they'd never pick anything [that criticized hospitals]. But I can assure you that's not in our thinking at all."[12] The trust exhibited between the two organizations is the key to their long partnership, as both institutions benefited greatly from the union. Although Jory once admitted that he would have sought out another corporate donor if he was turned down by Cherry and Jones, no other company in Louisville at the time possessed the same qualities that Jory and Speer deemed advantageous: a young company in need of exposure yet in possession of enough wealth to donate substantially to the festival. No one will ever know how the festival might have fared if not for the Humana Foundation's contributions—as Jory simply stated, without the Humana Foundation, "There wouldn't be this festival."[13]

Ironically, the Humana Foundation's support had a larger impact on a national level in terms of publicity for the Humana corporation than it had on the Louisville community. When asked how other Louisville corporations reacted to the amount of press that the Humana Foundation receives for the annual event, Christen McDonough Boone, director of development for Actors Theatre, explained, "It's very interesting because the Humana Festival is probably more well-recognized nationally and internationally than even locally."[14] In order to achieve its desired goal of community involvement, the Humana Foundation also gave substantially to other arts organizations in the community—including the Kentucky Opera Association and the J. B. Speed Art Museum—resulting in the foundation winning the Business in the Arts Award from the Business Committee for the Arts and *Forbes* magazine.[15] More important, the consistent support by the Humana Foundation for the festival allowed theater professionals around the country to witness a successful model for developing and producing new work, and the prominence of the festival on a national level inspired many theater practitioners to try their hand at new-play workshops in their own communities.

In addition to Humana, the theater receives support from a variety of local foundations, corporations, and individual donors. According to Roanne H. Victor, former president of the board of directors, although the staff works tirelessly to raise money for the theater's annual $8 million budget, Actors Theatre has an easier time of fund-raising than other Louisville arts groups because of its national reputation.[16] The challenge for Actors Theatre (as well as all Louisville arts groups) is to elicit foundation and corporate money—angels who will provide substantial support—in a town where few corporations are headquartered. One board member, when asked to discuss corporate growth in the city over the past thirty years, described Louisville as "a dead city."[17] Indeed, numerous large corporations moved out of Louisville in the 1980s and 1990s, and many of Louisville's largest businesses, especially the large banks like PNC and Fifth-Third, are owned by out-of-town companies. While Actors Theatre has nurtured relationships with many of these companies (such as Philadelphia's Right Management Consultants in 2005), the theater fortunately receives substantial donations from a variety of other resources.[18]

Throughout Actors Theatre's history, numerous angels in the form of other corporations and individuals also provided consistent support. These benefactors have not enjoyed the level of national publicity akin to that of the Humana Foundation for its support, but they quietly helped Actors Theatre expand its role in the community while providing critical support for its regular season. Although these groups may not be considered foundations in the traditional sense—an institution supported by an endowment gift—the actions and donations of these individuals and corporations served as "foundations," influencing the endeavors and financial stability of Actors Theatre for the future.

Similar to a foundation in its giving practices, the Brown-Forman Corporation became an angel because of its leaders' personal relationships with Actors Theatre personnel and their desire to help the Louisville community. In 1870, a young salesman named George Garvin Brown, who "had the then-novel idea of selling top-grade whiskey in sealed glass bottles," founded the Brown-Forman Corporation, and "out of his idea grew a company that in fiscal 2004 had sales of $2.5 billion, of which $1.9 billion was accounted for by sales of wines and spirits."[19] Although the corporation does not have a separate foundation like Humana Inc., the Louisville-based business operates in a similar fashion by accepting applications for the many generous grants it provides on a yearly basis. While the Humana Foundation's donations primarily benefit the festival and help Actors Theatre maintain its visibility on a national level, Brown-Forman's generous gifts serve the Louisville theater's year-round activities, helping raise the theater's profile in the Louisville community.

The angel for Actors Theatre has been Owsley Brown II, the former chief executive officer and current chair of the Brown-Forman board of directors who helped guide the theater through two major construction projects: the renovation of an old bank building into Actors Theatre's current home in 1972 (when he also served as a fund-drive chairman) and a major expansion project in 1994. Brown worked his way up the hierarchy of his family's company, beginning as an assistant treasurer in 1968 and accepting a variety of jobs over the next eighteen years during his ascension through the ranks.[20] During his time with Brown-Forman, Owsley Brown II and other members of his family gave generously to many local groups and projects, including city landscaping developments, building restoration projects, museums, higher-learning institutions, and arts organizations. When asked about Brown-Forman's charitable contributions to the arts, one family member stated, "One of the strongest things that make the area a vibrant one, and one in which our employees live and thrive, is in the arts. And if you can help provide a quality of life, a sense of pride in the community, as a company we are going to be better off."[21]

Through Brown-Forman and through their personal gifts, members of the Brown family gave to the local opera, the ballet, and the orchestra, but Owsley Brown II became a significant donor to Actors Theatre, sponsoring the main-stage series for many years. When Actors Theatre announced its latest fund-raising project on October 26, 2005, the Next Generation of Excellence Campaign, the Brown family made the "lead gift to the campaign" (Owsley Brown II is the campaign trustee), and Brown-Forman led corporate gifts with its $1.3 million donation.[22] Furthermore, in the early years of the festival and in an effort to publicize Louisville's hospitality, Brown hosted many Humana Festival parties at his home for out-of-town guests. In its support of the regular season of Actors Theatre, the Brown-Forman Corporation subsidizes a variety of fund-raising activities. For example, Brown-Forman sponsors wine tastings on opening Friday-night performances, and it frequently concocts specialty drinks to coincide with particular productions. One of the most unique contributions from Owsley Brown II came in the form of a birthday present to his mother, Sara Brown. In 1998, the main lobby of the Actors Theatre complex was renovated to restore the original coloring and grandeur of the facility, featuring plush blues and greens, gold trim, and new lighting fixtures. The gorgeous lobby was named in honor of Brown's mother as a birthday present, but, as is typical with most of the generous monies given by the Brown family and its corporation, the gift benefited a larger community as well.[23] For example, Brown-Forman's interest in community involvement led to the foundation of the now-defunct Classics in Context Festival, an effort by Actors Theatre to diversify its offerings and attract new audience members by exploring literary masterworks in the context of their political, social, and aesthetic climates.

The Classics in Context Festival attracted "scholars, theatre-lovers, and theatre professionals who enjoyed mixing and mingling while exploring the history, biography, philosophy, and aesthetics of the annual topic."[24] Conceived in 1985, the Brown-Forman Classics in Context Festival presented productions, lectures, films, and discussions on the work of Pirandello,

Molière, Thornton Wilder, the Victorians, and the romantics, to name a few. The generous gift from Brown-Forman allowed Actors Theatre to interact with other arts organizations in the Louisville community, as these groups contributed relevant works of art in conjunction with the year's chosen theme or artist. Although this newer festival eventually failed due to rising costs and administrative difficulties, the support that Actors Theatre received for its artistic endeavors encouraged Jory and the theater to further diversify its productions and audience by creating a third festival, Flying Solo and Friends—an annual collection of celebrated solo performers that helped the theater attract audience members oftentimes outside the mainstream (such as gay and lesbian and African American). Brown-Forman's contributions to Actors Theatre have not only helped underwrite the main-stage season but also allowed the theater to position itself as the leading arts organization in Louisville, spearheading community-wide events for the city of Louisville to compliment its nationally recognized Humana Festival. The donations from both the Humana Foundation and Brown-Forman have been critical to Actors Theatre's success. As one board member put it, "There would be no Actors [Theatre of Louisville] if not for Brown-Forman and the Humana Foundation."[25]

While Actors Theatre's partnership with Humana derived from personal associations and the theater's relationship with Owsley Brown formed through his serving as a board member, another substantial relationship between a local foundation and the theater traces back to the contentious formation of the local theater. In May 1962, Louisville-native Richard Block founded Theatre Louisville and began the slow, laborious process of fund-raising and glad-handing in order to establish a solid financial basis upon which to mount productions. Also in 1962, the late Ewel Cornett, a classmate of Block's in high school, returned to Kentucky to establish Actors Incorporated with the goal of producing shows immediately and (hopefully) eliciting funds from patrons. These two groups merged to form Actors Theatre of Louisville in 1964, forcing the two competing boards to work together with Block and Cornett as coproducers. When Cornett and Block had both departed by 1969, the past board presidents interviewed potential replacements, recommending Jon Jory to become producing director. Jory, however, expressed concerns about the Actors Theatre position, namely the large debt that the young theater had amassed (approximately $38,000). The board of directors agreed upon a controversial solution when The *Courier-Journal* and *Louisville Times* Foundation offered to pay a large portion of the debt if the board members would pay the remaining $25,000.

The key players in these three landmark events—the founding of a theater in Louisville, the hiring of Jory, and the achievement of financial health for the theater—are the members of the Bingham family, one of Louisville's generous philanthropic families. The Bingham family established its media dynasty in 1918, when Robert Bingham purchased the two Louisville newspapers, the *Courier-Journal* (morning) and the *Louisville Times* (afternoon). After adding television and radio stations to its business, the Bingham family often drew comparisons with the Kennedy family, especially with the wealthy media empire and their family's unfortunate familiarity with heartbreak. After suffering through the death of two sons within a two-year period, family disagreements erupted about the direction of the family business when Barry Bingham Jr. served as editor of the *Courier-Journal*, resulting in the 1986 sale of the paper to the Gannet Corporation.[26]

The Bingham family loved the theater, and both Barry Sr. and his wife, Mary, acted in plays in college and in Louisville. Further exemplifying her interest in theater, Mary attended play-reading groups in town and also invested in the Broadway production of Marsha Norman's *'night, Mother*. Barry Bingham Jr., like his father, supported a wide array of charities and arts groups in Louisville. For his part, Barry Jr. oversaw the corporate giving as the family's lucrative newspapers contributed to local charities through its 5 percent "tithing" policy to the corporation's foundation.[27] Before Block returned to Kentucky to establish Theatre Louisville, he contacted Barry Jr. and proposed his idea for creating a theater in Louisville. Barry Jr. funded Block's early endeavors and helped him arrange meetings with other civic leaders to discuss his proposals. Both Theatre Louisville and Actors Inc. had their own boards and groups of supporters, and the Bingham family was squarely behind Block's theater. When the two groups merged, Barry Jr. became the second president of the board in Actors Theatre history (Dann Byck, the leader of the Actors Inc. group, was the first). When Block resigned after his troubled leadership, the past presidents of the board formed the selection committee for Block's replacement, meaning that Bingham was one of the leaders to recommend the hiring of Jon Jory.[28] Fortunately, the Binghams' charitable donations through The *Courier-Journal* and *Louisville Times* Foundation resolved Actors Theatre's debt, and, once the massive deficit was erased, Jory agreed to become the theater's producing director.

Even more significant than their early gift via The *Courier-Journal* and *Louisville Times* Foundation are the Bingham family's financial contributions to Actors Theatre through their personal funds, providing two significant donations that helped influence the fiscal endeavors and artistic presentations of the theater. In May 1989, the Mary and Barry Bingham Sr. Fund provided the theater with a large endowment for the purpose of producing a biennial Shakespeare production. Known as Bingham Signature Shakespeare productions, the sizable interest taken from the $1.3 million endowment provided enough money to support the productions. This generous gift allows Actors Theatre to adapt its financial planning by allocating more funds to other productions (resulting in larger casts) or by hiring notable artists to work for Actors Theatre, best exemplified in 1996, when Ming Cho Lee designed the Bingham Signature Shakespeare production of *The Comedy of Errors*. The Bingham endowment, in essence, gives Actors Theatre the capability to explore a variety of opportunities, allowing the theater to expand its artistic endeavors while providing great literary works to the Louisville community (and the many education outreach programs that accompany the biennial Shakespeare production).[29]

The Binghams' second donation involved Barry Bingham Jr. and his wife, Edith. The $12.5 million renovation and expansion project in 1994 led to new administrative offices, an adjacent parking structure, a new performance space (the Bingham Theatre, a 318-seat arena theater), expansive lobbies, and renovations for the existing two performance spaces. Unfortunately, Actors Theatre struggled to repay the debt as planned, crippling the theater with deficits and increasing pressure to mount more popular fare in order to increase revenue. According to Roanne H. Victor, the overruns in construction resulted in a larger debt than anticipated, yet the attempts to recover the money were not as successful as hoped: "We were digging a bigger hole. Everything we tried ended up costing more money than expected."[30] To the rescue came the Binghams, who spearheaded an effort in 1999 to raise funds to cover the remaining debt, nearly $4 million. Donated "anonymously by Barry and Edith Bingham and others," the sizable gift established a foundation for the future fiscal health of the institution and allowed Jory to announce his resignation in

January of the following year, knowing that he would not be leaving the theater with massive debt.[31] When asked what the Bingham gift allowed Actors Theatre to do financially that it otherwise would not have been able to do, director of development Christen McDonough Boone employed the same analogy as Victor: "[It has allowed us to] live. If not, we would still be paying off that [debt], and we would be in a very dark hole. . . . And so that allowed us to capitalize on the expansion as opposed to try to dig out of it, and that was [the Binghams'] legacy, that gift."[32]

The one commonality among the many angels for Actors Theatre was the figure who united and attracted such loyalty to the Louisville theater—the man who was honored in the lobby of the Pamela Brown Auditorium on August 18, 2005.[33] Following Jory's departure in 2000, Alexander "Sandy" Speer became the face of Actors Theatre simply because he was the most senior employee, beginning his employment as a part-time house manager and moving his way up through house management and the box office to become the business manager and eventually executive director in 1972. During his long tenure, he supervised two major construction projects, guided numerous fund-raising campaigns, and worked tirelessly to develop and cultivate relationships with the theater's business partners. Throughout Actors Theatre's history, the one pivotal participant has been Speer—he was with Jory when they met with Humana's leaders, and he worked with the Binghams, Owsley Brown II, and all the board presidents in order to guide the theater through forty seasons of productions. His consistent commitment to the development of Actors Theatre and Louisville at large often was cited as one of the reasons businesses and organizations contributed to Actors Theatre. In an interview shortly before Speer announced his retirement, Boone praised his dedication to helping the arts thrive in Louisville: "The community leaders see Sandy Speer at the key to that success in terms of financial viability and stability over the years. He is really an instrument in this community. His job is with the theatre, but he is instrumental in support for the arts. He was the founder of our Arts and Cultural Attractions Council, which is an organization of over a hundred organizations. He had left that to try to identify additional support from the government, so he's really seen as the 'dean' of the arts world here in Louisville."[34]

Although Speer avoided the limelight in comparison to Jory and current artistic director Marc Masterson, he was as influential in the development and continued success of Actors Theatre as Jon Jory, having laid the foundation for all of Actors Theatre's business relationships. Through his financial planning and advice, Actors Theatre grew to unexpected heights, both artistically and administratively, as his wisdom and guidance provided Jory with the opportunity to explore and produce a wide range of artistic endeavors, including the Humana Festival, the Classics in Context Festival, the Flying Solo and Friends Festivals, and the regular season of high-quality works.

Nurtured over many decades, Speer devoted time and energy to developing relationships with civic leaders as a means of doing business and soliciting donors. According to Boone,

The board of directors for Actors Theatre of Louisville holding a meeting in the theater's downstairs restaurant in the late 1980s. The two men seated on the left are Alexander Speer (*far left*) and Barry Bingham Jr.
Courtesy of Actors Theatre of Louisville.

> It's about personal investment in the theatre. It's about involving people as much as possible so that they have that investment and commitment. Sandy started out working with out Board of Directors. Those people have become our key advocates, and when you have forty years of board members, you continue to have strong relationships because you've actually cultivated those relationships over forty years. You have forty years of forty board members—that's a thousand people out in the community who have a personal commitment to the theatre.[35]

Actors Theatre still relies heavily on its personal relationships in the business sector to translate into financial support. As Roanne H. Victor claimed, "If every community had a Humana [Foundation] and a Brown-Forman, there'd be no problems." Acknowledging that financial support does not necessarily translate into audience attendance, she added, "But they can't support the world, either." As far as Actors Theatre is concerned, the focus is not the money, but the people who help sustain the arts. "Essentially, it's all about people," Boone explained, "and where their pocket of money is [located] is less important."[36]

One possible concern for Actors Theatre and other Louisville arts organizations is the future—more specifically, who will be the future angels and leaders for the institution once the Browns, Binghams, Victors, and the like pass on or retire? How will Speer's retirement in 2006 affect the theater's ability to attract support from the Louisville community? Any concerns about the Humana Foundation pulling its support of the festival were quickly allayed when Humana designated $1.95 million for another three years (through 2007). Also helping calm worries, many local businesses (most notably Brown-Forman) have been passed down to family members who understand and support the long-standing partnership with Actors Theatre, but others will certainly pass into the hands of outsiders, forcing Actors Theatre to rebuild relationships (or reeducate them to the value of its work). Roanne H. Victor believes that Actors Theatre will continue to thrive because "the relationships between all the [arts] organizations are strong" and adding new representatives to the board helps maintain their involvement. Boone agreed, adding that Speer's work established alliances with Actors Theatre as opposed to personal relationships, ensuring that the professional associations will continue. Still, Boone admitted, "His shoes are going to be hard to fill regardless."[37]

While many arts organizations often underestimate the value of personal (as opposed to financial) contributions and, instead, focus too much on the cultivation of money, Actors Theatre serves as a model for garnering support in an environment of limited financial resources, forced to develop from and thrive upon personal relationships. While the financial contributions of the Binghams and Browns certainly helped the theater in its infancy, the many contributors to Actors Theatre did so out of devotion to the community and as a result of their personal involvement with those in charge of the Actors Theatre. While the many angels helped Actors Theatre thrive as an institution, the Humana Foundation provided the Louisville theater with its international reputation via its support of the new-play festival. With its continued donations, the annual play festival grew to become "one of those hoops that all American playwrights at some point *must* jump through," according to Tony Kushner.[38] Because of the Humana Foundation's contributions, Actors Theatre provided the American canon with more than three hundred plays by more than two hundred playwrights, including three Pulitzer Prize winners, five winners of the Susan Smith Blackburn Prize, six American Theatre Critics Award winners, and four Obie Award winners. According to the Actors Theatre Web site, "Over 90 million Americans have seen additional productions of the many plays originated in the Humana Festival, not including film audiences who have seen Humana plays adapted for the screen."[39] Without the Humana Foundation's financial contributions or the support of its other angels, Actors Theatre and its Humana Festival could not have provided hundreds of playwrights with an opportunity to develop their works, hindering the growth of American theater during the past thirty years.

Notes

1. Roanne H. Victor, telephone interview with the author, June 14, 2005.

2. *Theatre Profiles* (New York: Theatre Communications Group, 1984), 6:6, 13, 107, 134.

3. Ben Z. Hershberg, "Focus Shifting for New Humana President," *Courier-Journal*, March 17, 1991; Humana, "Humana: Company Information," http://www.humana.com/visitors/compinfo.asp (accessed June 27, 2005); Humana Foundation, "The Humana Foundation/Our Giving," http://www.humanafoundation.org/giving.asp#Part1 (accessed September 9, 2005). At the time Humana went public, the company was known as Extendicare (Ibid.).

4. Marie Brenner, *House of Dreams* (New York: Random House, 1988), 308, 338, 351–52; James Cook, "'We're the Low-Cost Producer,'" *Forbes*, December 25, 1989, 65–66.

5. Victor interview, June 14, 2005; Alexander "Sandy" Speer, interview with the author, Louisville, KY, August 20, 1999. The festival grew quickly, and after the first festival, when only two plays were produced, the second collection offered six productions.

6. "A Standing Ovation from Humana," in *Humana Festival of New American Plays: 25 Years at Actors Theatre of Louisville*, ed. Michael Bigelow Dixon and Andrew Carter Crocker, 13–14 (Louisville: Actors Theatre of Louisville, 2000).

7. Jon Jory, interview with the author, Louisville, KY, July 6, 1999.

8. David A. Jones, "Humana Letter," program for the Tenth Annual Humana Festival of New American Plays (Louisville: Actors Theatre of Louisville, 1986), 5.

9. "Standing Ovation," 13–14; Brenner, *House of Dreams*, 308, 352.

10. Jan Sjostrom, "Festival of Plays a Gold Mine for Regional Theatre," *Palm Beach Daily News*, March 30, 2001.

11. Speer interview, August 20, 1999.

12. Wendell Cherry, interview by Alan Judd, in "Humana Takes the Lead in Helping Keep the Arts in Business," *Courier-Journal*, May 10, 1985.

13. Jon Jory, interview by Alan Judd, in "Humana Takes the Lead."

14. Christen McDonough Boone, telephone interview with the author, May 4, 2005.

15. '"Humana Inc. Receives Honor for Arts Support," *Business First* (Louisville), October 16, 1995.

16. Judith Egerton, "Louisville's Award-Winning A.T.L. Finds Itself in the Red," *Courier-Journal*, October 21, 2001; Victor interview, June 14, 2005.

17. Victor interview, June 14, 2005.

18. Egerton, "A.T.L. Finds Itself in the Red."

19. Brown-Forman Corporation, "Key Facts about Brown-Forman," http://www.brown-forman.com/content/facts.htm (accessed June 28, 2005).

20. Religions for Peace, "Religions for Peace—International Council of Trustees," http://www.wcrp.org/RforP/trustees_content.html#owsleybrown (accessed September 13, 2005).

21. Owsley Brown Frazier, quoted in Adler Andrew, "Donors and Dollars," *Courier Journal*, May 2, 1999.

22. Actors Theatre, "Actors Theatre Announces Today Its 'Next Generation of Excellence Campaign,'" October 26, 2005, http://www.actorstheatre.org/press_capital.htm (accessed November 1, 2005).

23. Victor interview, June 14, 2005; Brown-Forman Corporation, "Actors Theatre of Louisville—Special Value Subscriptions," http://www.brown-forman.com/content/facts.htm (accessed June 29, 2005); Actors Theatre, "Actors

Theatre of Louisville—History," http://www.actorstheatre.org/about_history.htm (accessed June 28, 2005).

24. Michael Bigelow Dixon, interview with the author, Louisville, KY, July 13, 1999.

25. Jory interview, July 6, 1999; Victor interview, June 14, 2005.

26. Kristina Goetz, "News Family Relieved, One of Its Own Is Safe," *Cincinnati Enquirer*, April 2, 2003, http://www.enquirer.com/editions/2003/04/02/loc_kybingham.html (accessed June 12, 2005).

27. Brenner, *House of Dreams*,51–52, 337; Alex S. Jones, "The Fall of the House of Bingham," *New York Times*, January 19, 1986.

28. Lucretia Baldwin Ward, "Actors Theatre of Louisville: An Oral History of the Early Years, 1964–1969" (master's thesis, University of Louisville, 1993), 5–6, 100; Barry Bingham Jr., tape-recorded interview by Lucretia Baldwin Ward, September 30, 1987, University of Louisville Library.

29. Actors Theatre, "Actors Theatre of Louisville—History"; Judith Egerton, "Louisville Arts: Reputation at Risk," *Courier-Journal*, October 22, 2001.

30. William Mootz, "Much Ado about Something," *Courier-Journal*, September 24, 1994; Victor interview, June 14, 2005.

31. Egerton, "A.T.L. Finds Itself in the Red"; Victor interview, June 14, 2005.

32. Boone interview, May 4, 2005.

33. Sara Shallenberger Brown and Pamela Brown are not related.

34. Trish Pugh Jones, interview with the author, May 12, 2004; Boone interview, May 4, 2005.

35. Boone interview, May 4, 2005.

36. Victor interview, June 14, 2005; Boone interview, May 4, 2005.

37. Victor interview, June 14, 2005; Boone interview, May 4, 2005.

38. Tony Kushner, quoted in Dan Hulbert, "River Town Theatre Fest Stages Stuff of Dreams," *Atlanta Constitution*, April 3, 1994.

39. Actors Theatre, "Actors Theatre of Louisville—Humana Festival Fun Facts," http://www.actorstheatre.org/humana_facts.htm (accessed October 20, 2005).

13

RAISING THE CURTAIN: ROCKEFELLER SUPPORT FOR THE AMERICAN THEATER

Stephen D. Berwind

Rockefeller—for most of the twentieth century, the name represented the great family fortune, a kind of riches beyond measure. John D. Rockefeller, a man who began life modestly, but over the course of his lifetime became the richest man in the country, built this great business and personal fortune primarily by recognizing the potential of the oil business at its earliest stage. If in the early twenty-first century newer and larger fortunes with names such as Gates and Walton surpassed the Rockefeller fortune, the Rockefeller name and legacy continue because of the many public benefits provided by the philanthropy of both the family and the family's foundation. An examination of the history of the creation of the foundation, and specifically its support for theater, reveals the role that the Rockefeller Foundation plays in filling the chronic income gap that plagues all arts organizations.

In 1909, John D. Rockefeller, then the richest individual in America, created the deeds of trust that set aside a major portion of his fortune for the creation of a philanthropic foundation. In 1910, Rockefeller suggested that the trustees apply to the U.S. Congress for a corporate charter.[1] Rockefeller had successfully applied for such a charter when he created another charitable foundation, the General Education Board, in 1901. During the first two decades of the twentieth century, Rockefeller's philanthropy created a series of foundations: the Rockefeller Institute for Medical Research (later Rockefeller University), in 1901; the General Education Board; the Rockefeller Sanitary Commission, in 1909; the Rockefeller Foundation, in 1913; and the Laura Spelman Rockefeller Memorial Foundation, in 1918. His gifts totaled $446,719,371.22—a true, down to the penny, Rockefeller reckoning.[2]

Rockefeller's fortune grew quickly during the first decade of the twentieth century, but his personal reputation sank in inverse proportion to his economic fortune. President McKinley closely allied his administration with businessmen such as Rockefeller who had helped elect him. Following McKinley's assassination in 1901, the new president, Theodore Roosevelt, espoused progressive politics much less sympathetic to rich industrialists. During his administration, he gradually moved to rein in the money and power concentrated in the hands of what he called the "malefactors of great wealth."[3] Both public and press regarded John D. Rockefeller and his business interests centered in the Standard Oil Trust with a mixture of skepticism, hostility, and envy, in part because of essays by crusading journalist Ida Tarbell, first serialized in *McClure's* in 1902 and later published in 1904 as a book. This muckraking journalism exposed the ruthless business tactics Rockefeller used in assembling the trust. By 1905, Rockefeller faced seven major lawsuits, filed in part because of Tarbell's allegations. Progressive senator Robert Lafollette, of Wisconsin, called Rockefeller "the greatest criminal of the age."[4] In 1907, Judge Kenesaw Mountain Landis ruled against Rockefeller and Standard Oil in the first of these cases to be adjudicated and levied a $29 million fine on the company. Even though appellate decisions greatly reduced the fine, attitudes toward wealth changed in the country's political climate between 1901 and 1909.

Anti-Rockefeller progressives stymied the request to incorporate the foundation in Congress, despite the efforts of Rhode Island Senator Nelson Aldrich to find compromise language for the articles of incorporation that was acceptable to all parties. Aldrich, related to the Rockefeller family by the marriage of his daughter Laura to John D. Rockefeller Jr., worked strenuously to negotiate conditions for the trust that would gain congressional approval. While negotiations on incorporation continued through 1911, Rockefeller received another apparent setback when the United States Supreme Court ordered the breakup of Standard Oil Trust. Ironically, the dissolution of the trust made Rockefeller even richer. He still owned a controlling interest in the new component companies, and traders on Wall Street quickly recognized that the value of the new oil companies created in the breakup exceeded that of the old trust.[5]

Despite three years of effort, Senator Aldrich could not get the foundation charter through Congress. President William Howard Taft saw the move to incorporate the foundation as a bill to "incorporate Mr. Rockefeller." He and his attorney general, George W. Wickersham, opposed the approval of this corporate charter because they did not trust Rockefeller to actually act for the general good.[6] Theodore Roosevelt expressed the public attitude toward the robber barons of the late nineteenth and early twentieth century: "Of course no amount of charities in spending such fortunes can compensate in any way for the misconduct in acquiring them." Labor leader Samuel Gompers suggested, "The one thing that the world would gracefully accept from Mr. Rockefeller now would be the establishment of a great endowment of research and education to help other people see in time how they can keep from being like him."[7]

Finally, in 1913, Rockefeller admitted that Congress would never approve his charter and had the request withdrawn. However, since creation of a charitable foundation did not require incorporation under a congressional charter, Rockefeller cancelled the first deeds of trust and created new ones. This time, he turned to the New York state legislature, which created the Rockefeller Foundation that same year with this lofty stated purpose: "To promote the well-being of mankind throughout the world." The charter of the Rockefeller foundation wisely provided elasticity to the trustees in deciding the direction of its giving. That flexibility has enabled it to adapt to the rapidly changing conditions that characterized the twentieth-century United States.[8]

Andrew Carnegie's essay "The Gospel of Wealth," which appeared in the *North American Review* in 1889, helped mold Rockefeller's thinking about philanthropy. Carnegie's thesis can be summarized as "The man who dies rich, dies disgraced."[9] Rockefeller read the article and wrote

Carnegie congratulating him on his ideas. The next year, in 1890, Rockefeller hired the Baptist minister Frederick T. Gates to help coordinate his philanthropy. Gates's evangelical zeal encouraged Rockefeller to be a more effective philanthropist. Gates proved decisive in the creation of the four foundations created by Rockefeller during the first two decades of the twentieth century.[10] Gates advised Rockefeller that the best course for him was to "make final distribution of this great fortune in the form of permanent corporate philanthropies for the good of mankind."[11] When Gates stepped down from leadership of the foundation in 1928, he addressed the trustees, "When you die and come to approach the judgment of the almighty God, what do you think he will demand of you? Do you for an instant presume to believe that he will inquire about your petty failures and trivial virtues? No. He will ask just one question, 'What did you do as a trustee of the Rockefeller Foundation.'"[12] The Rockefeller Foundation clearly took its mandate to promote the well-being of mankind seriously.

Rockefeller was no neophyte to philanthropy when he hired Gates. His record of charitable giving extended back to his first job as a clerk in Cleveland in 1855. He had donated 6 percent of his income of $6 per month to his church and church-related charities in his first year of employment after school. Rockefeller's meticulously kept ledger of income and expenses that started with that first job provides a vivid guide to the careful management of money that characterized his life.

As his income grew, so did his charitable giving. The exhortations throughout the New Testament to provide for the poor, reinforced by his Baptist faith, influenced his giving, and by 1905, his total gifts to the Baptist Church approached $100 million.[13] Rockefeller Foundation historian Raymond P. Fosdick wrote, "In his early giving, as later in life, he freely crossed lines of creed, nationality and color."[14] This broad-minded giving can be evidenced in the major gifts he made to the historically African American Spelman College in Atlanta and his central role in creating the University of Chicago as well as the extensive grants to programs in China and Latin America. The Rockefeller Foundation maintains this tradition today. Gates warned Rockefeller, "Your fortune is rolling up, rolling up like an avalanche. You must keep up with it. You must distribute it faster than it grows! If you do not, it will crush you and your children and your children's children."[15] As Raymond P. Fosdick writes in his history of the foundation, Gates shared Rockefeller's "passion to accomplish some great and far reaching benefits for mankind through careful distribution of charitable giving."[16]

The Rockefeller Foundation developed over its first two decades as the embodiment of an informal three-way partnership: John D. Rockefeller, who made and donated the money that provided the base for the foundation; his son John D. Rockefeller Jr., who molded the organization and established a pattern for running the foundation; and Reverend Frederick T. Gates, who became a principal business and philanthropic advisor to John D. Rockefeller and provided practical advice on creating a foundation drawn from his experience managing charities for the Baptist Church.

An early set of guidelines for the foundation excluded both individual charity and relief and gifts to institutions that were purely local. It encouraged gifts that participated in a larger pattern of community support and with guidelines that regarded funding any group in perpetuity as unwise. This principle in the foundation's giving policy (still adhered to in 2006) meant that the Rockefeller Foundation would never function as a source of continued annual support for any theater company looking to fill its budgetary gap with contributed income. Aware of public animosity toward the family and its business interests, the early giving by the foundation demonstrated a conservative policy that desired to avoid public controversy until the foundation's beneficence gradually altered public opinion in favor of the family and foundation. Public health and scientific research dominated early giving.[17] Donations in these areas, unlikely to prove controversial, avoided the kind of lightning-rod status experienced by the Rockefellers during the first decade of the twentieth century.

The decision to hire Ivy Lee as the public relations adviser for family, foundation, and corporate interests also reflected a concerted effort, mostly instigated by John D. Rockefeller Jr. (Junior), to change the image of the Rockefeller family and its interests.[18] Junior realized that to front Rockefeller businesses would undercut the public's perception of his position with the foundation. He chose charity over business and resigned his corporate board seats.[19] Through his work with the foundations, Junior came out from the shadow of his father and emerged as the primary architect for the foundation. During the foundation's meetings with brilliant men from all fields, he listened and learned much from them while also forging a strong personal identity.[20]

Junior carefully assembled an exceptionally effective professional staff to evaluate grant requests. Like his father, he recognized the difficult challenge of giving money away successfully. Fosdick reiterated this point in his history of the Rockefeller Foundation: "Effective philanthropy, especially in the main intellectual fields is by no means a simple and artless affair which anyone with good intentions can handle. Rather it is a highly specialized, arduous and complex business."[21] The Rockefeller Foundation envisioned itself as a public trust, and its philanthropic strategy was strongly affected by public interest rather than private philanthropy.[22] The Rockefeller family's extensive private philanthropies, such as the Museum of Modern Art, the Cloisters, and Colonial Williamsburg, received funding independently from that disbursed by the foundation.

In 1928, Gates's retirement enabled Junior to consolidate his dominance of the foundation. The public's more favorable view of the family and its interests allowed Junior to lead a major reorganization of the Rockefeller Foundation. As part of the reorganization, the foundation assumed responsibility for humanities grants from the General Education and International Education boards. The Rockefeller Foundation also absorbed the Laura Spelman Rockefeller Foundation.[23] Edward Capps, first director after the reorganization and a classicist, expanded the range of recipients beyond science, agriculture, and medicine by supporting grants in the areas of archeology and classical studies as well as important bibliographical work, such as the *Dictionary of American Biography*, *Dictionary of American English*, and the *Linguistic Atlas of New England*.[24] The early history of the Rockefeller Foundation reveals no funding of theater projects or the arts and humanities in general. Although treasurer Jerome D. Greene listed the "fine arts" as an area to be supported in minutes from a 1913 meeting, many years would elapse before such grants were made. Grants in the social sciences preceded those in the arts.[25]

During the 1930s, the foundation continued broadening its areas of support in order to position the Rockefeller Foundation as a less elitist and classicist organization.[26] As Fosdick, then the head of the foundation, writes in his history, the "Trustees decided in addition to maintaining certain older interests, to strike out experimentally in new fields and in a formal resolution authorized the officers to develop projects in the general areas of libraries and museums, drama, radio and moving pictures; the collection and interpretation of native cultural materials, and improvement of international communication through the development of language teaching especially in terms of Latin America and the Far East."[27] The foundation nonetheless moved into these new areas slowly and carefully. Fosdick explained the approach, "In undertaking a new line of work it is better to begin in a small way and progress through trial and error to larger ends."[28] Following the pattern first enunciated in 1913, modesty characterized (and continues to characterize) the role of the Rockefeller Foundation. It seeks to keep the focus on the recipients and not on the foundation itself.

The foundation's *Review of the Humanities 1934–1939* reflects evidence of these changes. David Stevens, head of the humanities program wrote, "Acted drama evokes active sharing in experience to a greater degree than any other form of expressive art, making each spectator in his own way a participant in the realities of the illusion."[29] From this time forward, the Rockefeller Foundation slowly emerged as an important part of the mosaic of funding in America's theatrical history.

Initially, the foundation utilized the framework provided by universities and supported the establishment and expansion of drama departments. To support American theater, the foundation wanted to ensure that a training network for theater artists existed. Important community theaters that were established as part of the Little Theater Movement also received support as the foundation strove to create a framework outside the commercial New York stage for innovation in theater to flourish. Examples of such grants listed in the 1934–39 review include money for the University of Iowa to complete a theater of advanced design. Yale School of Drama received support for research in the technology of stage lighting and for the creation of an extensive photographic collection preserving evidence of important theatrical set designs. The University of North Carolina's efforts in creating regional playwriting voices gained support, and the Lost Colony outdoor drama on Roanoke Island also received funding. An additional example of such support encouraged a partnership between the Cleveland Playhouse and Case Western Reserve University in Cleveland.[30]

Aware that writers often provide the impetus in the creation of a theatrical event, the Rockefeller Foundation, working in tandem with the National Theatre Conference and the Author's League of America, provided fellowships for young writers, the most famous recipient of which was Tennessee Williams.[31]

The full impact of the Rockefeller Foundation on theater did not become apparent until after the Second World War, when the foundation moved more boldly into supporting theater artists after two decades of small, conservative grants. As Fosdick had advocated earlier, "begin in a small way and progress through trial and error to larger ends." By working through an existing framework of institutions (as suggested in the 1913 guidelines), the foundation also remained true to another guiding principle of John D. Rockefeller, that "his money should make for strength rather than weakness, [and] develop in the beneficiary a spirit of independence and self-reliance."[32] The Rockefeller Foundation developed into a funding source that encouraged individual projects and provided early support for innovative programs. It does not provide regular annual support to any arts organization.

To highlight its efforts in the arts, the Rockefeller Foundation published a photograph-rich monograph, titled *A Special Report on the Rockefeller Foundation's Program in Cultural Development.* In the accompanying text, the foundation explained its decision to support the regional theater movement because it encouraged additional venues for arts to develop.[33] It provided funding for Washington, D.C.'s Arena Stage and the Guthrie Theatre in Minneapolis.[34] The foundation singled out the Guthrie Theatre for its support of young playwrights. Three of the four young writers mentioned in this report developed into accepted members of the theater establishment: Terrence McNally, Adrienne Kennedy, and Irene Maria Fornes. The Rockefeller Foundation's historical record of identifying important talent in every area it funded continued to be valid in its theater funding.

The report reveals the foundation's important role in fostering the often-innovative Off-Off-Broadway movement through support of the American Place Theatre, then in residence at St. Clement's Church, and a joint project between artistic director Wynn Handman and St. Clement's vicar Sidney Lanier. The foundation supported the American Place–St. Clement's management because it worked with established writers of literature, such as Philip Roth, Robert Lowell, and Robert Penn Warren, and then encouraged these writers to work in theater by offering them a theatrical home.[35] Similarly, the foundation provided support for Kenneth Nelson, a published novelist and author of *The Brig*, first produced by the Living Theatre.[36]

The distinguished list of grantees includes many organizations that continue to make important contributions to the American theater as of 2005: Actors Studio, Actors Theatre of Louisville, American Place Theatre, Arena Stage, Kenneth Brown, Carnegie Tech/Pittsburgh Playhouse, Drama Inc., Milwaukee Repertory Theatre, Frank Gagliano, critic Henry Hewes, Adrienne Kennedy, Kennedy Center, Lincoln Center, University of Minnesota, Guthrie Theatre, National Repertory Theatre Foundation, Pittsburgh Playhouse, Seattle Rep, Stanford University, Theatre Incorporated, the *Tulane Drama Review*, and Minneapolis's Walker Arts Center.[37]

This document also reveals the multimillion-dollar grants made to the capital campaigns for the creation of the Lincoln Center and the Kennedy Center. The Rockefeller Foundation rarely provided capital support, although the flexibility of its corporate charter permitted occasional exceptions. The creation of these two important performance venues did much to raise the importance of arts organizations in the public consciousness. Thus, the foundation's grants upheld its tradition of providing support when a substantial network of supporters existed.

Another publication that touts the Rockefeller Foundation's support for the arts, *President's Ten Year Review and Annual Report 1971*, provides another vivid record of the broad range of support for theater. "For the Arts the past decade was the liveliest in the nation's history. The sixties gave us happenings, multi-media and light shows; pop, kinetic, minimal art and a return to the human figure; electronic music, chance music and rock; Off Off Broadway, black theatre and street theatre; the 16 mm film maker, public television and experimental video."[38] The foundation boasted of its role in supporting programs in music, theater, and dance beginning in 1962 and identified its role in fostering this period of intense creativity and experimentation.[39]

The language of this report reveals clearly the foundation's efforts to remain flexible in order to facilitate the identification of innovative artists. This idea of letting the artists lead found an echo in a December 2005 interview between Joan Shigekawa, staff member in charge of the Multi-Arts Production (MAP) program, and the author. The Rockefeller Foundation continues to demonstrate both continuity and flexibility in its grant-making process. The foundation's Web site in late 2005 promotes this same artist-centered approach to grant making in its description of its principal theater program: The MAP Fund "supports innovative new works in all disciplines and traditions of the living performing arts."[40]

In 1971, the foundation wrote, "From the various options offered by artists and organizations claiming priority for support, the Foundation noted three prevalent themes: the desire to make the arts increasingly available for all; the desire for greater participation and involvement; and the desire of creative artists to experiment with forms, styles, techniques."[41] On the Rockefeller Foundation's Web site in 2005, the description of its current programs demonstrates the continuity in goals and flexibility in achieving them: "Our aim is to assist artists who are exploring the dynamics of live-performance within our changing society, thus reflecting our culture's innovation and growing diversity. In keeping with the mandate of its founding organization, The Rockefeller Foundation, MAP seeks especially to support work that brings insight to the issue of cultural difference, be that in class, gender, generation, ethnicity, or tradition."[42] The grants to organizations and artists such as Lee Breuer and Mabou Mines, the Ontological Hysteric Theatre and Richard Foreman, and the Wooster Group and Elizabeth Lecompte demonstrate that the foundation's support for some of the most important artists of the American avant-garde remains strong.

In the 1971 report, the foundation identified the support of creative environments hospitable to the arts on college campuses as an important initiative. Among the schools singled out for support were Stanford, North Carolina School for the Arts, and University of California, Los Angeles (UCLA). The present Web site presents an elaboration of that idea that also reflects the foundation's continued efforts help make the performing arts accessible to all citizens. "The Urban Institute's Arts and Culture Indicators in Community Building Project (ACIP) was launched in 1996, with support from the Rockefeller Foundation, to address some basic questions: How are arts, culture and creativity defined, presented, and valued at the neighborhood level? What should be measured and why? What kinds of information should be collected?" The reports generated by these questions are available online for "communities to use, debate and critique as they move to incorporate arts, culture and creativity as assets in building vibrant communities."[43]

In the 1971 report, the foundation identified another program that sought to support nurturing environments for artists by supporting a group of theatrical entrepreneurs who "create a place where the arts can happen."[44] These entrepreneurs included an impressive roster of theater impresarios, such as Joseph Papp (Public Theatre), Gordon Davidson (Mark Taper Forum), Arthur Ballet (Office for Advanced Drama Research), Ellen Stewart (Café La MaMa), Wynn Handman (American Place Theatre), George White (Eugene O'Neill Center), and Harvey Lichtenstein (Brooklyn Academy of Music). Additional recent grants to the Wexner Center for the Arts; ART in Boston; and the McCarter Theatre, in Princeton, New Jersey, indicate the ongoing support for groups that provide environments that support creation of new work by theater artists.

The board minutes for the meeting in 1988 when the Rockefeller Foundation created the MAP (Multicultural Arts Project) program are still under embargo, but staff member Joan Shigekawa, who was not a member of the staff then, stated: "The original name of the MAP Fund was the 'Multicultural Arts Project' and the first MAP Fund guidelines described the program as follows, 'The . . . Map Fund is specifically directed towards performing arts and will offer assistance to projects or productions that promote the understanding of diverse cultural heritages through innovative new works that comment on, and perhaps even change, the way we see the world.'"[45]

The list of recent annual grantees of the MAP program reveals that no group received annual funding.[46] The description of the recipients provides an interesting look at the ways some artists are seeking to break down the boundaries of genre, while others work and create within more traditional formats such as written play texts. Shigekawa said, "The work often challenges the pre-existing categories because a theatre piece may have a large video component or a dance work may include the spoken word. Sometimes it is a challenge to decide exactly which panel should evaluate a given proposal. The guidelines change from year to year to encompass the innovative ways that artists are expanding their work. The composition of the panels that evaluate the applications also changes every year to ensure that no single aesthetic point of view is dominant."[47]

The MAP Fund is a highly competitive annual program, funding less than 8 percent of the approximately 460 applications it receives per year. The MAP Web site states, "In 2004, the MAP Fund provided $1 million in grants ranging from approximately $15,000 to $50,000, supporting up to 40 projects by US-based nonprofit organizations undertaking the commissioning, development and/or production of new work in theater, music composition, dance, puppetry, opera and interdisciplinary performance."[48]

Shigekawa shared her understanding of the origins of the MAP program, which was originally created to be a multicultural complement to existing programs that supported the arts nationally. As support for individual artists under programs such as the National Endowment for the Arts has diminished, MAP has become more significant and wide ranging. The underlying philosophy that animates the foundation's funding decision is to support the creative voice of the originating artist.[49] Shigekawa asserts, "MAP is interested in building and maintaining a theatre culture in the United States and by a theatre culture, we mean one that produces new plays. We seek to advance the individual voice in theatre."[50]

Three recent grantees of the Rockefeller Foundation shared their experiences with receiving their grants and realizing their production. Each story has its own set of issues. Shigekawa contends that there is no "typical" recipient of a MAP grant, but there are things common to the stories of Brian Freeman, Phil Soltanoff, and Naomi Iizuka. All of them praise the foundation for the personal interest they felt on the part of staff members and the willingness of the foundation to respond flexibly when productions did not always appear on the original time schedule. Soltanoff and Freeman both felt that the grant from the Rockefeller Foundation provided validation to their positions as artists. The stories they tell provide a good picture of their experiences as grantees of the foundation.

Brian Freeman first attained national prominence as a member of the group Pomo Afro Homos, and it was as a member of that group that he first came to the attention of the foundation. The grant he received for the play that became known as *Civil Sex*, about the civil-rights leader Bayard Rustin, supported a five-year process of creating the project, which bounced between theaters before being produced first in 1997 at the Woolly Mammoth in Washington, D.C., followed by an official opening at Thick Description in San Francisco. In July 2004, *Civil Sex* was published as part of an anthology of recent plays titled *The Fire This Time*.

Freeman explains, "The proposal was originally made in late 1991 [and] early 1992. Pomo Afro Homos [had recently] opened a show that was very hot, very of the moment in a Queer-artists-of-color/Queer Nation kind of way."[51] The challenge of working as a touring performer and writing a new play proved difficult for Freeman. The original grant to Theatre

Rhinoceros ended up covering other expenses, so Freeman returned to the Rockefeller Foundation for a second request for the project. Even the second grant had to be moved from a second umbrella group, Brava, to the eventual producer, Thick Description. Freeman said, "The grant was great to get and tough to keep."[52] "Definitely in 1991 for them to fund an out, gay, and black artist was pushing the edge,"[53] he continued. Freeman pointed out that the number of projects that combine gay and black issues is quite small, whether in theater or film.[54]

Freeman claims that the struggle to hold onto the grant ended up helping the project. "To move a grant two times was painful. We missed deadlines. The second time the Foundation stepped in they were a little cranky with us as to why the project had not happened. The Foundation did some additional checking about us with the Public Theatre and Thick Description. They [Rockefeller Foundation] struggled internally about whether to stick with us. They ended up staying very engaged with the project."[55] Winning the Will Glickman Award for Best New Play in the San Francisco Bay Area demonstrates the production's success. In 1999, Freeman received the CalArts Alpert Award in Theater. Freeman sums up the experience, "The grant provided a nice chunk of money to some artists who were marginalized and that enabled us to try different things."[56]

Philip Soltanoff's production company, mad dog, is based at a small alternative space, called five myles, that he shares with the puppeteer Hanna Tierney in the Crown Heights section of Brooklyn. He develops his productions through work at multiple venues. In the summer, his fifteen-year association with the Act One program at the Williamstown Theatre Festival provides an opportunity for further development. He unsuccessfully applied for Rockefeller Foundation MAP grants in 2001 and 2002, before receiving a $20,000 grant in 2003.

Soltanoff almost decided not to apply the third time because of the previous rejections. He believes that he secured funding from the Rockefeller largely because of the superior production values in the artist's sample he submitted in 2003, which was a project he had directed in France, a country where experimental theater artists receive substantially more financial support than in the United States. His experience with the foundation has been very positive, and he believes that they take a genuine and ongoing interest in the artists they support.

Soltanoff developed the project *Lemnation*, a mixed video and live performer project inspired by the writing of Stanislaw Lem, over two seasons at Williamstown. The second year of development benefited from the Rockefeller Foundation grant and culminated in performances at the Massachusetts Museum of Contemporary Art (MASS MoCA) in August 2004. Although Moira Brennan from the Rockefeller Foundation attended the Massachusetts workshop and signaled support, plans to bring the production to New York have been stymied by the lack of an appropriate performance venue. The production may be revived in Europe before its New York opening because of the difficulties and expenses connected to production in New York.

Soltanoff represents a not-uncommon, small-scale avant-garde artist, and, as such, he finds obtaining the funding for his work the major challenge. Recently, the focus of his career has shifted to Europe because of the greater funding opportunities there. His first collaboration with the Toulouse, France–based Compagnie 111, *Plan B*, moved to the New Victory Theatre in New York in 2004. His most recent collaboration with Compagnie 111, *More or Less Infinity*, received a $25,000 grant from the Rockefeller Foundation and was to be presented at the Skirball Center at New York University in November 2005, but technical problems related to the scenery have put that production on hold also. Soltanoff confessed, "I find myself working more in Europe because the access to resources is easier there. In New York, real estate has a profound impact on your life. In Lyons, France, we gave ten performances in a 1,100-seat theatre and we sold out every performance. Probably more people saw my work there than in twenty-five years of performing in alternative spaces in New York."[57]

Playwright Naomi Iizuka regards collaboration as integral to her process as a playwright. When considering how to find a road into a play such as *Hamlet*, she simultaneously wished to explore ways of making the writing process less solitary. Her process included collaboration with San Francisco's oldest alternative-arts organization, Intersection for the Arts, and resident theater company Campo Santo, including executive director Deborah Cullinan, program director Sean San Jose, and director Jonathon Moscone (also artistic director of California Shakespeare Theater). She began by posing this question, "How do you approach iconic works from a contemporary vantage point that is grounded in personal experience?"[58]

A $20,000 grant from the Rockefeller Foundation in 2001 helped start a workshop process among the artists and members of the Bay Area community at Intersection for the Arts. The initial workshop was followed by a year and a half of writing, augmented by smaller workshops with spoken-word poets and community members. The collaborators decided to set *The Hamlet: Blood on the Brain* in Oakland during the crack wars of the late 1980s, a time of great violence. The writing process with its alternation of workshops and writing is reminiscent of the development process used by the Joint Stock company in the 1970s. Iizuka used similar processes in developing plays about the meatpacking industry in Louisville, Kentucky, and the Mission District of San Francisco. *The Hamlet* was produced in October 2006 at Intersection for the Arts, with Moscone as director. Repercussions of this project extend beyond the production. Inspired by the work, the California Shakespeare Theater created an initiative focused on communities that typically do not see themselves portrayed on stage—in this case, that of the California Shakespeare Theater. The theater wants to create a long-term process of grassroots community conversations, the type of which Intersection creates regularly and has done previously with Iizuka. The Rockefeller Foundation has also supported this project through workshops for another Shakespearean adaptation at California Shakespeare in the summer of 2005. Naomi Iizuka can develop a play through such a labor-intensive working process that requires time and resources because of support from groups such as Rockefeller Foundation and others such as the Irvine Foundation.[59]

The Rockefeller Foundation is certainly not the largest foundation supporting production of live theater in terms of the dollar value of its grants. What makes it so important is its willingness to take chances on emerging artists while loyally supporting established artists whose work continues to expand and shift traditional ideas of theater. The foundation funds, in part, individual projects and does not wish to assume the role of annual funding organization for any group. These two principles taken together enable it to embrace one important role of supporting noncommercial theater projects while avoiding the other need for annual support to fill the gap between expenses and earned income. No organization can or should try to be everything to everyone. In the absence of substantial government support for the arts, such as exists in Europe, the role of foundations such as the Rockefeller will continue to be vital in providing opportunities for new work and new voices to emerge. Certainly, American theater culture would be significantly poorer without the Rockefeller Foundation.

Notes

1. Peter Collier and David Horowitz, *The Rockefellers: An American Dynasty* (New York: Holt, Rinehart and Winston, 1976), 15.
2. Ibid., 100.
3. Ibid., 3, 4.
4. Ibid., 4.
5. Ibid., 64.
6. Raymond Blaine Fosdick, *The Story of the Rockefeller Foundation* (New York: Harper, 1952), 17, 18.
7. Collier and Horowitz, *Rockefellers*, 64.
8. Fosdick, *Rockefeller Foundation*, 290.
9. Ibid., 5.
10. Ibid., 1.
11. Collier and Horowitz, *Rockefellers*, 63.
12. Fosdick, *Rockefeller Foundation*, 65.
13. Ibid., 4.
14. Ibid., 5.
15. Collier and Horowitz, *Rockefellers*, 65. Quoted in Allan Nevins, *John D. Rockefeller; The Heroic Age of American Enterprise* (New York: C. Scribner's and Sons), 2:291.
16. Fosdick, *Rockefeller Foundation*, 2, 3.
17. Ibid., 23, 27.
18. Ibid., 27.
19. Ibid., 108.
20. Ibid., 106.
21. Ibid., 292.
22. Ibid., 289.
23. Ibid., 239.
24. Ibid., 240–41.
25. Ibid., 238.
26. Ibid., 241.
27. Ibid., 242.
28. Ibid., 295.
29. Ibid., 253.
30. Ibid., 254.
31. Ibid., 256.
32. Collier and Horowitz, *Rockefellers*, 6.
33. Richard Schickel, *The Arts: The Creative Individual and the Community: A Growing Collaboration* (New York: Rockefeller Foundation, 1965), 4.
34. Rockefeller Foundation, *Arts*, 30, 42.
35. Ibid., 36.
36. Ibid., 51.
37. Ibid., 54, 55.

38. Rockefeller Foundation, *Presidents Ten-year Review & Annual Report* (New York: The Rockefeller Foundation, 1971), 66, 67.

39. Ibid., 66.

40. Rockefeller Foundation, "MAP Fund," http://www.mapfund.org (accessed August 17, 2006).

41. Rockefeller Foundation, *Ten-year Review*, 67.

42. Rockefeller Foundation, "MAP program," http://www.mapfund.org/about.html (accessed January 10, 2006).

43. Rockefeller Foundation, "Arts + Culture," http://www.rockfound.org/ArtsAndCulture/Announcement/10 (accessed January 10, 2006).

44. Rockefeller Foundation, *Ten-year Review*, 77.

45. Joan Shigekawa (principal staff member for performing arts, Rockefeller Foundation), in discussion with the author, December 2005.

46. All recipients since 1999 are listed at http://www.mapfund.org/sps/swish.cgi?search_phrase.grant_year=2005&confirm=1&is_2005=1 (accessed January 11, 2006).

47. Shigekawa interview, December 2005.

48. Creative Capital, "MAP program," http://www.creative-capital.org/programs/mapfund.html. Since 1999, the Rockefeller Foundation has entered into a partnership with Creative Capital in New York that has evolved into something of a partnership in the administration of the MAP program. Creative Capital is a group that directly supports individual artists in a variety of ways. Creative Capital is national in scope, with programs in professional development that seek to help artists develop the skills to survive in a highly competitive marketplace. The Rockefeller Foundation mission is to support given structures that support artists, and it chose Creative Capital to administer the MAP program because it enabled the Rockefeller Foundation to maintain a long-term goal of retaining a small, permanent staff so that more of its money is available for grants.

49. Shigekawa interview, December 2005.

50. Ibid.

51. Brian Freeman (grantee of Rockefeller Foundation), in discussion with the author, October 2005.

52. Freeman interview, October 2005.

53. Ibid.

54. Ibid. The Marlon Riggs film *Tongues Untied* is perhaps the most widely known of these projects. Freeman was also a part of that project.

55. Freeman interview, October 2005.

56. Ibid.

57. Phil Soltanoff (grantee of Rockefeller Foundation), in discussion with the author, November 2005.

58. Naomi Iizuka (grantee of Rockefeller Foundation), in discussion with author, January 2006.

59. Ibid.

14

FUNDING THE THEATRICAL FUTURE: THE HAROLD AND MIMI STEINBERG CHARITABLE TRUST

Jeffrey Eric Jenkins

"In the Beginning"

Nestled near the end of the January 15, 1993, arts section of the *New York Times* was a three-inch news item marking the emergence of a major force for the development of new American plays. The announcement that the Harold and Mimi Steinberg Charitable Trust had given \$1 million to the American Repertory Theatre (ART) in Cambridge, Massachusetts, "for the production of new American plays," was tucked beneath a book review and beside that weekend's notice of closing art exhibitions. According to ART's artistic director at the time, Robert Brustein, it was believed to be the largest single grant to support the production of new American work—yet the story was buried on page twenty-six of the section. In a subtle irony, the major theater news of that date included an enthusiastic Frank Rich review of Eugene O'Neill's *Anna Christie*, in a revival directed by David Leveaux. In his review, Rich noted that "British directors, far more than our own . . . dust off neglected American plays and startle audiences with their discoveries." In the newspaper's theater column, "On Stage, and Off," reporter Bruce Weber used his space to recount the comings and goings of creative personnel in high-profile productions—one involving a juicy feud between Neil Simon and Gene Saks. The prominence given a starry revival of an American classic and internecine theater gossip—both sops to the theatrical past—might reasonably have made the Steinberg Charitable Trust's directors wonder what it took to be noticed by the "paper of record."[1]

Even if the *Times* seemed to take small notice of the trust, the impact on the New York theater community was immediate. Barry Grove, executive producer of Manhattan Theatre Club, said,

> I had seen an announcement in the papers of a grant going to ART from this foundation, but I didn't know what it was. I thought I had known all of the funders of the arts and our antennae went up when we heard there was this new organization out there—and we approached them. . . . Lynne Meadow and I went to meet with the full group of trustees and made a presentation. With many foundations there is a paid staff that keeps you at arm's length from the trustees. What was wonderfully exciting and refreshing about this group is that there we were actually in a room talking to the principals.[2]

That presentation must have gone well, because the trust announced in late September 1993 that Manhattan Theatre Club would receive $1 million in a five-year grant similar to the one for American Repertory Theatre. This time the trust's largesse was treated prominently in Weber's Friday *Times* theater column, along with the news that the New York Shakespeare Festival—then under the direction of George C. Wolfe—had received its own $1 million grant from the trust.[3]

Since those first $1 million grants, the Harold and Mimi Steinberg Charitable Trust has emerged as one of the most energetic supporters of new-play production and developing playwriting talent in the United States. In addition, though, the trust also funds outreach programs that allow companies such as Manhattan Theatre Club (MTC) to work with city schools, and the trust has been consistent in its support, renewing MTC's grant twice.[4] If, as Emerson suggests, "a foolish consistency is the hobgoblin of little minds," then it might easily be argued—especially for advocates of new plays—that a *wise* consistency is the hallmark of expansive minds.

André Bishop, artistic director of Lincoln Center Theater, which will have received Steinberg grants totaling nearly $3 million by 2009, said that it has "become harder and harder to raise money for the one thing that the theater is supposed to be doing—which is new productions." Bishop likened the difficulty in fund-raising for new works to running a hospital where "it is easier to raise money for improving the food in the cafeteria than it is for syringes, bandages, and doctor training." When it comes to the work of the Steinberg Charitable Trust, Bishop said, "it is beyond a benefit [to the theater]. Given the world we live in, we would be really sunk without them."[5] A fairly random sampling of the productions cited by Bishop as relying on Steinberg funds includes an impressive array of work: *The Sisters Rosensweig*, by Wendy Wasserstein; *A Fair Country*, by Jon Robin Baitz; *Pride's Crossing*, by Tina Howe; *Contact*, by John Weidman and Susan Stroman; *The Carpetbagger's Children*, by Horton Foote; and *The Light in the Piazza*, by Craig Lucas and Adam Guettel.

Bishop's producing partner, Bernard Gersten, understandably views this crucial funding from a slightly different perspective. Since the trust began working with Lincoln Center Theater in 1992, its funding has underpinned thirty projects, all—except the acclaimed 1995 production of *The Heiress*—"in support of new American plays and musicals." Of those productions, about twenty were staged in the smaller (and less expensive) Mitzi Newhouse Theater, "at a cost of about $1 million each," said Gersten. The other ten productions funded with Steinberg money were done in the 1,080-seat Vivian Beaumont Theater, which operates under a modified Broadway contract, "at an average cost of $2.5 million" per production. Using Gersten's figures, it is clear that at Lincoln Center Theater, new-play production alone has cost somewhere in the neighborhood of $45 million since 1992. Although the Steinberg grants total only approximately 7 percent of the production money, Gersten heartily agrees with Bishop that the funding is significant in today's cultural marketplace: "Rarely do we get money that is dedicated to new production. It's always an effort to get somebody to underwrite new work because there's a certain danger in new work—a perceived danger. The Steinberg Trust has been wonderful. It's been extraordinary."[6]

The retired artistic director of American Repertory Theatre, Robert Brustein, still an active creative consultant at ART, concurred with Gersten's assessment: "The Trust made possible our production of new American plays, and renewed our commitment to that cause. . . . The board has been particularly wise in its gifts to other theaters who produce new plays, and has also contributed to capital funds for building new spaces for that purpose. It may be the most sagacious theater foundation in the country."[7]

As Brustein suggested, the trust has been involved in capital projects beyond (but related to) its focus on new plays. The foundation made a substantial donation to the Roundabout Theatre Company in New York City, which helped the company secure and renovate the former American Place Theatre, now known as the Harold and Miriam Steinberg Center for Theatre. This new complex, housing an Off-Broadway theater and a planned black-box theater, is devoted to the development and production of new plays.

The Harold and Miriam Steinberg Center for Theatre in New York City, formerly known as the American Place Theatre. The theater was renamed by the Roundabout Theatre Company on February 26, 2004, in honor of a major gift from the Harold and Mimi Steinberg Charitable Trust.
Courtesy of Roundabout Theatre Company/Paul Goode.

During the marquee-lighting ceremony for the Steinberg Center, on February 26, 2004, Roundabout artistic director Todd Haimes recalled for an invited group how the commitment of the Steinberg Charitable Trust crystallized for him in 1998. By that summer, the trust had funded new-play development in Roundabout's Laura Pels Theatre for three years, and the company was riding a crest of artistic and financial success. At the Tony Awards in June, Roundabout received awards for best revival in both musical (*Cabaret*) and play (*A View from the Bridge*) categories. Four performers from the shows were also honored, bringing the nonprofit company's Tony total to an impressive six awards for only one season. As the musical settled that summer into a projected (and lucrative) long run, disaster struck on July 21, 1998, when an elevator tower collapsed on a construction site adjacent to the theater housing *Cabaret*, killing a woman and causing the surrounding streets to be closed for a month. While the show remained closed, Roundabout continued to pay its cast, crew, and theater rent at a reported rate of $140,000 per week—which did not take into account $1.5 million in lost ticket sales.[8] Then, as Haimes told the story during the marquee-lighting ceremony, a letter came in the mail.

In a joint telephone interview with executive director Julia C. Levy, Haimes recounted the tale. "They had read about [the accident] in the paper," he said. Levy continued the story: "I don't think we had said anything to them. It was August, after all. A check arrived with a letter from Bill Zabel saying they were making this contribution to the theater to be used for general purposes. It blew us away. I swear to God, I cried. It was more than the money, it was the emotional significance of the support behind it."[9] Haimes, though, also sees the trust's influence resonating far beyond the needed emotional and financial lift of that difficult summer in 1998. The Steinberg Charitable Trust "really made possible the renovation of the Steinberg Center. If they had not given us this grant, I don't know if we would have had an off-Broadway theater."[10]

The first production in the Harold and Miriam Steinberg Center for Theatre was the New York premiere of Lynn Nottage's *Intimate Apparel* (April 11, 2004), which went on to win the New York Critics' Circle Award for best play. The Critics' Circle declined to honor a musical or foreign play in 2004, making Nottage's work the first to be the group's sole new-play honoree since Edward Albee's *Three Tall Women* in 1994.[11] Earlier in the season, there had been a pleasant Steinbergian convergence when *Intimate*

Apparel, which had been long scheduled to play in the Steinberg Center, won the Steinberg New Play Award—given by the American Theatre Critics Association to a play produced outside New York City—a few weeks before the New York opening.[12] It was not, however, the first instance in which the Steinberg New Play Award carried a felicitous timing. The year before, playwright Nilo Cruz's *Anna in the Tropics* received the 2003 Steinberg New Play Award from the American Theatre Critics Association in a Louisville ceremony less than forty-eight hours before it was announced that the play would receive the Pulitzer Prize in drama.[13]

The relationship between the trust and the American Theatre Critics Association began in 1999, when the two groups entered discussions aimed at providing better funding for the critics' group's prestigious new-play prizes. The national critics' association had begun its play awards in 1977, with citations honoring at least one play that premiered somewhere in the growing network of regional theaters beyond New York City. By 1986, the organization began to obtain funding from major newspaper publishers that underwrote a $1,000 cash prize for a top honoree and two citations for honorable mention. When the trust and the theater critics came to terms, it led to the creation of the American Theatre Critics/Steinberg New Play Award and Citations, first given in 2000.[14] For the theater critics' association, the new funding meant that its prestigious prizes now had greater immediate financial impact—$15,000 for the award and $5,000 for each of two citations—than even the Pulitzer Prize. In 2006, the trust increased its funding, so the award is now worth $25,000 and the two citations earn $7,500 each. The prizes are now referred to as the Harold and Mimi Steinberg/ATCA New Play Award and Citations.[15]

At the first ceremony honoring the Steinberg New Play Award and Citation recipients in 2000, trust director James D. Steinberg said, "In the beginning was the word, and that is what we are here to honor tonight. My father and mother loved the theater and were especially passionate about new works, which is why the Trust is so pleased to be a part of this great tradition."[16]

Steinberg's Theatrical Passion

Harold Steinberg formed the trust as part of his estate planning in 1986, with attorney William D. Zabel, to honor the memory of his wife Miriam—known as Mimi—and to focus his substantial accumulated assets on the development and promotion of his one great passion: theater. As Zabel said, "He wanted to create an entity that would be able to fund new American plays because he loved the theater, he thought there wasn't enough done for it, and it's always in danger of decline and disinterest." Steinberg named as his trustee successors Zabel, Seth Weingarten, and Charles Benenson.[17] After Steinberg's death in 1991—Miriam Steinberg died in 1973—the trustees added the Steinbergs' adult children as directors in 1992. It was in 1992 that the trust first gave substantial grants to theater, which led, as noted above, to the first $1 million grants in 1993.[18]

Although the genesis of Steinberg's passion for the theater is a mystery even to some who knew him well, the former trumpet player turned real estate entrepreneur had a family network of connections in the theater. Before her marriage to Harold Steinberg, Miriam's last name was Smoleroff—she was the daughter of Mitchell Smoleroff, a New York realtor in the early twentieth century. Among Miriam Smoleroff's cousins were two significant figures in mid-twentieth-century Broadway theater: Sidney Kingsley and Jack Small. Kingsley, the Pulitzer Prize–winning author of *Men in White* and eight other Broadway plays, was the son of Sophie Smoleroff Kirshner. Small, the son of Mendel Smoleroff, began his career as personal manager to his cousin Kingsley, before becoming a general manager, producer, and seventeen-year employee of the Shubert Organization. In 1944, Small codirected (with Robert H. Gordon) *Allah Be Praised!* a musical comedy that lasted a mere twenty performances—one of the show's backers was Miriam Steinberg.[19]

As Harold Steinberg acquired and developed properties around New York, he also acquired a deeper understanding and appreciation for the theater. Bernard Gersten, who had approached Steinberg for funding at the behest of Lincoln Center president Nathan Leventhal in 1987–88, found a kindred spirit on meeting the entrepreneur:

> The thing that bound us more than anything else was that he used to hang around with the Shuberts. . . . He knew Mr. Lee and Mr. J. J., and he knew their general manager, Jack Small. . . . It happens that I knew Jack because I had been stage manager of a show some years before that Jack had general managed. . . . I visited [Steinberg] fairly frequently, but to my recollection never wound up with any kind of money from him at all. I kept urging him to come and see the work that we were doing—and this went on for about two or three years.[20]

Robert Brustein told a similar story of knowing Steinberg socially through their mutual friend, Zabel. It was not until after Steinberg's death, however, that the American Repertory Theatre was given a Steinberg grant.[21]

Seth Weingarten, a retired Southern California neurosurgeon and one of the original trustees, said that Steinberg "was a very kind, generous person" whose passion for the theater occasionally took him to London with a friend in the aviation business. "It seemed to be quite exotic that he and Dan Fraad would fly to London to see plays," Weingarten said. "This was in the 1960s, when it was still a little hard to fly to Europe."[22] Steinberg's adventurous theatrical spirit has also inspired Weingarten's own perspective: "It's been educational for me to see the truth of what Harold said about creative people in the theater. I've learned so much about the need for money—and that we can help artists present their work to a larger public. . . . When I thought of the theater years ago, I only thought of plays that were on Broadway and very successful—and the actors and producers were sort of household names. Because of Harold I've come into contact with off-Broadway, off-off Broadway, and small theaters around the country."[23] Despite Steinberg's connections to and interest in the Broadway theater establishment, the guiding spirit of his bequest is to support theater at every level, as Weingarten put it, "not just the Manhattan Theatre Clubs, but also the smaller organizations."

The Steinberg progeny seem to have inherited their parents' passion for theater and the desire to help foster it at all levels. Michael A. Steinberg, a New York–based assets manager and the Steinbergs' eldest, said, "I think it's really to the smaller institutions that we can make a bigger difference. Those that don't have the resources or access that the larger institutions do" are of particular importance to the trust.[24] Michael Steinberg's sister, Carole A. Krumland, lives in the San Francisco Bay Area and serves on the board of the Berkeley Repertory Theatre. Although she did not mention her mother's investment in the 1944 musical, Krumland noted that her father also "was an angel for commercial theater. Not a lot, but he was involved in a few shows like *The Subject Was Roses*." Krumland said that she does what she can to support theater because she "can't imagine not having art in my life." Asked about the affect that the trust has had on theater in this country, she said, "it's hard to tell what's the greatest impact. Hopefully, it's on the smaller theaters that really need us."[25] Colorado-based nature photographer James D. Steinberg agreed strongly with his siblings, "it makes a difference when you give [a company] $100,000 out of a $27 million budget. But it's not nearly as significant as giving $25,000 to [a company] that has a $1 million budget."[26] James Steinberg, who holds a doctor of arts in English literature, considered other elements of the trust's mission:

> From day one we supported a lot of companies that do new work and, as we have gotten into this over the years, we've realized that there really isn't a lot of new-play development support around the country. We're now commissioning at two of the major festivals every year, the Humana Festival of New American Plays and South Coast Rep's Pacific Playwrights' Festival. . . . We also support a few theaters such as the Pearl Theatre Company and the Jean Cocteau Repertory, which do no new works, as well as companies such as Atlantic or Roundabout—both of which are a mix nowadays. Generally, the idea is to support whatever the majority of the board feels is good work—with an emphasis on new-play development.[27]

Ultimately, though, one of the great strengths of the foundation—which emerges in conversations with artists and with the Steinberg trustees—is that of its flexibility. As trustee Zabel said, "We're a nimble foundation. If we see there's a special need for help or just extra money, we'll give it. We'll call a telephone conference meeting and do whatever is necessary." Whether the special need is due to a construction accident, to bomb threats related to a Terrence McNally premiere, or to the economic fallout in the wake of the 2001 terrorist attacks, this private trust can react in ways that organizations with more extensive bureaucracies often cannot.[28]

Virginia P. Louloudes, executive director of the Alliance of Resident Theatres/New York, found herself in an extraordinarily difficult position in the aftermath of the September 11, 2001, terrorist attacks. ART/New York, as it is more colloquially known, is a service organization for nearly four hundred constituents in New York nonprofit theater. Louloudes and others interested in the downtown theater scene spearheaded a variety of efforts aimed at keeping theaters afloat at a time when much of downtown—particularly below Fourteenth Street—was quite literally a disaster area. Small theaters, which often survive in a hand-to-mouth existence, were on the verge of closing permanently, while medium-sized companies faced mounting financial crises.[29] Louloudes told of meeting James Steinberg after the panel "Theater in a Time of Crisis": "Jim said to me,

'We really should find a way to help you.'" In addition to providing much-needed funds to ease financial burdens for small theaters in the weeks and months following the attacks, the trust also worked with ART/New York to enhance its program for developing the theater leaders of tomorrow through the Harold and Mimi Steinberg Theater Leadership Institute.[30] "They are," Louloudes said, speaking of the trustees, "in so many ways a grantee's idea of ideal funders. They've made the longest commitment anyone has ever made to this leadership program." She also marveled at the speed with which the group worked—that nimble quality to which Zabel referred. Louloudes was notified four hours after her presentation that ART/New York would receive Steinberg funding. Nimble, indeed.

Artists Respond to Support

The Pulitzer Prize–winning playwright Paula Vogel believes that "everybody is an expert in theater. It's not a matter of school or knowledge, it's a matter of the heart." Noted in the theater community for her openness to the opinions of others, Vogel told Michael Steinberg—not long after meeting him—that, as far as she was concerned, "what you observe about my plays, to me, is equal to what a critic will tell me. You tell me what you feel is working and what's not working." The playwright explained how the relationship evolved:

> We started this tradition in which I invited Michael and Joan [his wife], to the first preview of all of my plays—and they came. It was such a remarkable act of generosity that, with their busy lives, they came out to Bay Street Theatre and saw the first preview of *Desdemona*. He saw the first preview of *How I Learned to Drive* and came early to *The Long Christmas Ride Home*. And then I would ask him: "What's working, what's not working?" . . . He would notice the most amazing small details. For example, he noticed a lighting cue in one of the scenes in *How I Learned to Drive*. And he was right, it was too dark. He said, "I know you need the intimacy of this moment between Peck and Li'l Bit, but I can't see it." I went to Mark [Brokaw] and said, "Can we boost that lighting cue? I understand we want the intimacy and the mood, but we're not seeing their faces." It was the small things like that.[31]

When Vogel and director Oskar Eustis committed to creating a consortium between Brown University and Trinity Repertory Company—she heads the playwriting program at Brown and he was artistic director of Trinity before joining New York's Public Theater in 2005—they turned to the Steinberg Charitable Trust, which underwrote a pilot program and made the consortium a reality. "There was a one-act by a twenty-year-old undergraduate named Sarah Ruhl in that pilot festival of new plays—the Steinberg Festival," Vogel said. "The play was the first act of *Passion Play*," which received a September 2005 production at the Arena Stage in Washington, D.C. Vogel referred to the play as a "huge epic" and drew parallels between it and Tony Kushner's *Angels in America*. Although it took twelve years for Ruhl to finish her play, Vogel said it was the Steinberg pilot grant that gave the young playwright a sense of what she might be able to create. She called the Steinberg funds "seed money" that has resulted, in Ruhl's case, "in a young woman writing for the American theater." Speaking of the other Steinberg siblings, Vogel said, "it's remarkable the way they embrace education and theater—and know that they go hand-in-hand." She continued: "This may sound strange, but the truth about great philanthropists is that it's not about the money. It's about the connection. It's about the generosity of spirit and letting younger artists know that what they do matters—and that takes a *personal* giving. A giving of spirit that I think Michael, Joan, Jim, and Karolynn [Lestrud] offer. In fact, the whole board gives personally of themselves to the theater. That, to me, is why they're angels."[32]

Director Eustis noted that his relationship with the Steinberg Charitable Trust went back to his time as associate artistic director of the Mark Taper Forum, which now functions under the umbrella of the Center Theatre Group in Los Angeles. "That's where I first met Michael Steinberg and Seth Weingarten who, of course, lives in L. A. and has been a particularly wonderful champion of new work and young writers all along."[33] In discussing his relationship with the Steinbergs, Eustis said, "Seth, Jim, and Michael are all people that I've interacted with at the Taper, then at Trinity, and now here at the Public. They have, I would say, a unique appreciation of new-play development. I can't think of any other family foundation that has made such a long-term and consistent commitment to the development of new writing for the American theater."[34]

When Eustis and Vogel were working on the consortium plan—which created a working relationship between Trinity Rep and Brown for degree-granting programs at the M.F.A. and Ph.D. levels in playwriting, directing, acting, and theater studies—Eustis said, "I had a great conversation with Michael early in the development of the consortium. He said, 'It is absolutely clear that you have a big idea and that you don't know what it is yet. So why don't we start with the festival and see what happens.' He was exactly right."[35] As he spoke about the importance of the Steinberg Charitable Trust to the American theater, Eustis's comments echoed those of others who appreciate the trust's broad, national commitment:

> We are obviously in an era when most foundation support has shifted away from the arts in general and, specifically, from new-play development. There are very few programs or foundations left that have a primary interest in new writing for the theater. Therefore, we have increasing difficulty finding support for new programs . . . that aren't marketing opportunities for corporations. . . . I've worked in three different theaters, in three completely different communities, in three different parts of the country, and the Steinberg has supported every one of them. That's amazing.[36]

Eustis's former boss at the Mark Taper Forum, Gordon Davidson, retired at the end of 2004, after thirty-eight years at the company's helm. He told of receiving the first grant from the Steinberg Charitable Trust in 1994, for the Taper's production of Eduardo Machado's epic tetralogy, *Floating Islands*. Throughout the 1990s, the trust provided hundreds of thousands of dollars for new-play production at the Taper, including the New Theater for Now Festival and programs for young people. In Davidson's last season, the trust made a five-year pledge of $50,000 per year that has become part of the Gordon Davidson Endowment Fund for Artistic Excellence. "I was a bit overwhelmed," Davidson said, by the generosity of the gift. "You're so grateful when any money comes your way," he continued, "that something like this is tremendous." Davidson also reiterated what others had said about the importance of the trust's consistency and the way the funder makes a contribution "and then lets you run with it."[37]

Considering the risks attendant to new-play development and how they affect funding in today's philanthropic climate, Berkeley Repertory Theatre artistic director Tony Taccone said, "There's not a huge payback in the sense that you're automatically going to see every new play gather a huge audience or go on to Broadway." What the trust supports, in Taccone's view, is process. "They're funding a way for people to continue to research, investigate, experiment," he said. "It takes a particular kind of person or group of people to value process as opposed to product." Taccone's experience with the trust is that it "embraces and encourages our sense of experimentation with both the form and content" of Berkeley Rep's work. "I think it's risky stuff and you need people with vision," he said, "who understand the creative process and support it." Finally, though, Taccone said he believed that "the Steinbergs represent the age of quiet and dignified philanthropy. . . . I don't get the feeling that they want their 'brand' on every available eyelid. . . . I think the style with which they conduct themselves is almost as important as the money."[38]

Funding the Future

The Harold and Mimi Steinberg Charitable Trust clearly is treasured by the theater community it funds not only in New York but across the nation. It would be naive not to acknowledge that most people—not only theater artists who struggle for funds—are likely to think well of those who provide financial resources. There is, however, something truly distinctive in the way that the Steinberg trustees pursue their mission. It is not merely the money; it is what Paula Vogel referred to as the personal commitment: the giving by the individual trustees of their time, effort, and considerable passion to ensure the future of the American theater.

When Michael Steinberg was interviewed for this piece, he gave no indication of his personal involvement in the development of works by Vogel. He answered questions briefly and provided helpful reference to others who might have information about the trust. It was the same with his sister, Carole Krumland, whose interest, it is obvious, is her lifelong passion for the theater, which dates back to frequent attendance with her parents as a child and young woman. That same self-effacement continues in James Steinberg, whose scholarly background in literature surely informs his aesthetic and his advocacy. For the Steinberg offspring, though, it is not about themselves; it is all about the work: what should be funded and how. The enthusiasm of the directors, however, is not limited to the Steinberg descendants. The trustees who were there at the beginning, William Zabel and Seth Weingarten, have in their own ways had specific and profound influence on the theater in New York and Los Angeles as well as around the country.

In 2003 alone, the most recent year for which public records are available, the Steinberg family foundation distributed more than $4 million.

Of that amount, nearly 90 percent was given in direct grants to arts organizations, with the balance donated to educational institutions and health-care research.[39] Trustee Zabel said, "This is an ongoing legacy built on real estate and money that should be able to continue for the indefinite future." Although the trust has a term limited to the year 2036—which, as Zabel said, "seems a long way off"—the trustees could probably fund "another Steinberg Foundation and keep it going."[40]

The 1993 *New York Times* piece by Bruce Weber reported that the trust was "considering awards to theater artists akin to the MacArthur Foundation grants, the so-called genius awards."[41] Bruce Kirle describes the MacArthur Foundation's point of view in another chapter in this volume. The trust has wisely eschewed this path to date, which has meant funds that otherwise might be concentrated in the hands of a few have operated as the seed money that playwright Vogel values so much. This approach seems to reflect Harold Steinberg's original wishes, because, as trustee Weingarten said, "he felt that a lot of times somebody who has a lot of talent, for one reason or another, doesn't get recognized. Not necessarily an eighteen-year-old or a twenty-year-old; maybe a forty-five-year-old."[42] Lincoln Center's André Bishop lauded that part of the trust's broad-based approach, saying it is "not one of these foundations that is just into what's new, what's hot, what's the buzz. They understand that if we are producing the eighth play of Wendy Wasserstein's . . . that is as important as discovering the wonderful new writer."[43] If nothing else, the breadth of the Steinberg trust's approach—as well as its deep commitment in certain areas—has set it on a path to positively influence the growth of the American theater for at least the next two generations.

Despite changes that may be on the American theater's horizon, Harold Steinberg's legacy has inspired a surge in the development and production of new plays that marks the trust as forward thinking and courageous. It is always safer to fund, say, the millionth revival of *Hamlet* than it is to support a play about a Catholic priest who may or may not have abused boys in his charge. While Shakespeare's Danish prince generally holds a certain fascination, a self-righteous nun's struggle with her own perception of possible offenses by a young priest takes us into emotional, spiritual, and intellectual realms that are powerfully human—and present collateral risks to artists, theaters, and their funders. When John Patrick Shanley's *Doubt* premiered at Manhattan Theatre Club—the author's third play to be funded by a Steinberg grant to MTC—there was no guarantee that its prickly questions about faith, certitude, and godliness would go on to win the Pulitzer Prize and a Tony Award for best play.[44] That it succeeded is a matter for celebration by everyone involved. Once those celebrations are over, though, writers return to their work, the theater moves on, and the Steinberg Charitable Trust makes it possible to ask, What's next?

Notes

1. "Boston-Area Theater Wins $1 Million Grant," *New York Times*, January 15, 1993; Frank Rich, "A Fierce View of Tragic Lives," *New York Times*, January 15, 1993; Bruce Weber, "On Stage, and Off," *New York Times*, January 15, 1993. In a *Boston Globe* article of the same date, reporter John Koch stated that the grant had been committed by the trust in spring 1992 (John Koch, "Grant Means Power, Plays for ART," *Boston Globe*, January 15, 1993).

2. Barry Grove, telephone interview with the author, September 12, 2005.

3. Weber, "On Stage, and Off."

4. Grove interview, September 12, 2005.

5. André Bishop, telephone interview with the author, December 14, 2005.

6. Bernard Gersten, telephone interview with the author, December 14, 2005.

7. Robert Brustein, e-mail interview with the author, September 17, 2005.

8. Peter Applebome, "Collapse in Times Sq. Hurts Fortunes of Four Hit Shows," *New York Times*, July 24, 1998; David Kirby, "Life May Soon Be No *Cabaret* at Kit Kat Klub," *New York Times*, August 9, 1998; Terry Pristin, "City to Reopen 43d Street, 4 Weeks After Collapse," *New York Times*, August 18, 1998.

9. Todd Haimes and Julia C. Levy, telephone interview with the author, August 5, 2005. Bill Zabel is William D. Zabel, Esq., a partner in the law firm Schulte Roth & Zabel, which manages the trust.

10. Ibid.

11. Jeffrey Eric Jenkins, ed., *The Best Plays Theater Yearbook 2003–2004*, (Pompton Plains, NJ: Limelight Editions, 2005), 387–88.

12. Christopher Rawson, "Spring Brings New Plays," *Pittsburgh Post-Gazette*, sooner edition, April 7, 2004.

13. Bruce Weber, "Tapping Cuban Roots for American Drama," *New York Times*, April 9, 2003, late edition, E1.

14. Jenkins, *Best Plays*, 396–97.

15. In the interest of full disclosure, it is worth noting that the author was chair of the American Theatre Critics Association when the awards program with the trust was presented and approved. He is also series editor of *The Best Plays Theater Yearbook*, to which the trust has displayed consistent generosity.

16. James D. Steinberg, remarks at American Theatre Critics Association awards ceremony, Actors Theatre of Louisville, Louisville, KY, April 1, 2000.

17. William D. Zabel, telephone interview with the author, September 30, 2005. Benenson, a commercial real estate executive died February 22, 2004 (Landon Thomas Jr., "Charles Benenson, Developer and Philanthropist, Dies at 91," *New York Times*, February 24, 2004).

18. Zabel interview, September 30, 2005. Harold Steinberg's full name was Elihu Harold Steinberg, and Miriam Steinberg's name before marriage was Miriam Rose Smoleroff. Her mother was a member of the Rose family, a noted family in New York real estate and philanthropy.

19. Obituary of Mitchell Smoleroff, *New York Times*, October 15, 1938; Obituary of Pauline Smoleroff, *New York Times*, January 10, 1941; "Jack Small, Aide of Shubert Chain," *New York Times*, April 30, 1962; Lewis Nichols, "The Play," *New York Times*, April 21, 1944; "*Allah Be Praised!* to Close Saturday," *New York Times*, May 4, 1944; Sam Zolotow, "19 of 31 Matinees Play to Standees," *New York Times*, February 23, 1944.

20. Gersten interview, December 14, 2005.

21. Brustein interview, September 17, 2005.

22. Seth Weingarten, telephone interview with the author, September 22, 2005. Daniel Fraad Jr. was chief executive of Allied Maintenance Corporation, which cleaned and fueled jet airplanes at many airports. The company had a monopoly on the business at John F. Kennedy International Airport (Landt Dennis, "N.Y. Maintenance Firm 'Cleans Up,'" *Christian Science Monitor*, December 5, 1969).

23. Weingarten interview, September 22, 2005.

24. Michael A. Steinberg, telephone interview with the author, March 14, 2005.

25. Carole A. Krumland, telephone interview with the author, August 3, 2005.

26. James D. Steinberg, telephone interview with the author, August 19, 2005.

27. Ibid.

28. Zabel interview, September 30, 2005. According to Zabel, the trust helped fund extra security measures for the controversial 1998 production of McNally's *Corpus Christi* at Manhattan Theatre Club.

29. Robin Pogrebin, "Off Broadway Finds Ways to Keep Shows Open," *New York Times*, October 4, 2001.

30. Virginia P. Louloudes, telephone interview with the author, August 10, 2005; James D. Steinberg interview, August 19, 2005; Zabel interview, September 30, 2005; Weingarten interview, September 22, 2005.

31. Paula Vogel, telephone interview with the author, August 5, 2005

32. Vogel interview, August 5, 2005. Karolynn Lestrud is James Steinberg's wife.

33. Oskar Eustis, telephone interview with the author, September 20, 2005.

34. Eustis interview, September 20, 2005.

35. Ibid.

36. Ibid.

37. Gordon Davidson, telephone interview with the author, October 31, 2005.

38. Tony Taccone, telephone interview with the author, September 21, 2005.

39. Guidestar, "Return of Private Foundation, Form 990-PF (2003), The Harold & Mimi Steinberg Charitable Trust," November 11, 2004, http://www.guidestar.org/FinDocuments/2003/133/383/2003–133383348–1-F.pdf (accessed November 15, 2005).

40. Zabel interview, September 30, 2005.

41. Weber, "On Stage."

42. Weingarten interview, September 22, 2005.

43. Bishop interview, December 14, 2005.

44. Grove interview, September 12, 2005.

15

MODERN MEDICIS: DISNEY ON BROADWAY

Kathy L. Privatt

On May 2, 1997, after decades of disuse, the New Amsterdam Theatre reopened it doors, admitting an audience to its art nouveau interior. The production for this gala event was *King David*, a limited-run concert oratorio. The work's classical heritage, implied by the biblical subject matter treated in oratorio form, was a fitting choice to pair with the extraordinary work of the theater's restoration artisans. The surprise in the scenario was the renovator of the theater and producer of this work: the Disney Corporation. In fact, through the artistic restoration of a landmark theater and an opening production with high-art connotations, Disney positioned itself as a patron on Broadway.

The journey began April 18, 1994; Disney offered Broadway audiences their production of *Disney's Beauty and the Beast.* Well attended and apparently well received by the public, *Disney's Beauty and the Beast* set a record high the next day for single-day ticket sales, despite several critical pans. The audiences continued to attend, and *Disney's Beauty and the Beast* established Walt Disney Theatrical Productions as a popular and financially successful producing organization. Encouraged to explore other stories for future production, Disney began to entertain the possibility of its own venue on Broadway. The end result of this exploration was the renovated New Amsterdam Theatre on Forty-second Street and its opening production, *King David*, a concert oratorio. If viewed as a chess game, the Disney-on-Broadway events present a stark contrast and perhaps a careful plan: Disney placed *Beauty* on Broadway; despite the audience's embrace, critics responded with a sweeping pan and questioned Disney's presence as a producer; Disney countered with choices enlarging its role on Broadway and garnering a position for itself as a historic preservationist and patron.

The specific nature of that position as preservationist and patron is best defined by the similarity of Disney's behavior to the activities and motivations of the Renaissance patrons. After Disney's second full production, *The Lion King*, opened under the guiding hand of Julie Taymor, a couple of members of the press began to agree with this assessment. In fact, these writers equated Disney with the Medicis, the Italian Renaissance family known for its patronage of the arts. Peter Applebome, writing for

Lobby of the New Amsterdam Theatre, circa 1926.
Courtesy of the Terry Helgesen Collection, Theatre Historical Society of America.

the *New York Times*, titled his article "The Medici Behind Disney's High Art" and concluded that Michael Eisner, as Disney's chief executive officer, "has the capacity to commission culture." In his article, Applebome detailed projects like Taymor's *The Lion King* and two choral symphonies commissioned for the millennium as support for his statement.[1] Aaron Jay Kernis, the composer for one of the symphonies, labeled Eisner and Disney as "the new Medicis for our time."[2] Jack Zink, at the *Sun-Sentinel* in Fort Lauderdale, spread the Medici label with his article that cited Applebome's *New York Times* piece ("The Mouse").[3] In fact, the label was first applied by Peter Schneider, then president of Walt Disney Theatrical Productions, who referred to Eisner as a modern Medici ten months previous to Applebome's article; Schneider cited the New Amsterdam Theatre renovation as an outgrowth of Eisner's "fundamental desire to do architecture" and his long-term work on numerous buildings with world-class architects.[4] While Schneider might not be publicizing a new corporate policy, his statement certainly suggests the company's awareness of the larger role of patron accompanying the renovation. On close examination, the label of modern Medici is a good fit, in terms of both Disney's largesse and the limitations and expectations attached to it. The renovation of the New Amsterdam, and that opening oratorio, are primary examples of Renaissance-style patronage behavior.

Renovating the New Amsterdam let Disney cast itself in the role of a patron who values historic architectural preservation. The New Amsterdam, built by the infamous Syndicate, is the largest theater on Forty-second Street and now is the second-largest theater on Broadway.[5] Best known as home to the Ziegfeld's Follies, the theater housed many stars now immortalized, such as Will Rogers, George M. Cohan, and the Castles. At its opening production in 1903, critics ignored the play and lavished praise on the theater itself, especially for its use of art nouveau decoration throughout the building.[6] The *New York Times* even placed an article about the sculpture and painting in the theater on the front page of its Business and Real Estate section; the article concluded with praise for the builders' (Klaw and Erlanger, of Syndicate fame) employment of artisans "in order to perfect a theatre by the hands of American artists."[7] When Disney took on the restoration, Michael Ovitz (working for Disney at the time) reminded the press that the New Amsterdam had been "the crown jewel of Broadway."[8] By the 1990s, all of that finery had disintegrated to mushrooms growing on the floor and structural damage to the building. Both the interior and the exterior of the building had been designated historical landmarks in 1979, but all previous restoration efforts had failed.[9] When it was built, the New Amsterdam was part of a theater-building boom on Forty-second Street that, according to a 1905 *New York Times* article, raised lot values and "transformed" the block.[10] At the 1997 opening of the successfully restored theater, Mayor Giuliani credited Disney's restoration as "the beginning of a great new renaissance for this historic area of our city."[11]

Disney's faithful restoration of the New Amsterdam, far from displaying the feared "Disney aesthetic," was a legitimate restoration and renovation project. Disney further demonstrated its awareness of the importance of this work through the publication of Mary C. Henderson's *The New Amsterdam: The Biography of a Broadway Theatre*, published by Hyperion, a division of Disney, in 1997. Due to the building's status as a historic landmark, the entire project was conducted under the supervision of the New York City Landmarks Preservation Commission. Adding to the legitimacy of the preservation process, the commission had to approve all changes to the building, even those undertaken to meet safety codes.[12] Terra-cotta and plasterwork were repaired and re-created, paintings were restored and redone, original light fixtures found in a crawl space and between the walls were used as patterns to create new ones, and boxes removed for the theater's movie-house era were replaced.[13] Whenever possible, workers restored and repaired what was present. When the damage was too complete, the crews referenced old pictures and newspaper articles from the theater's prosperous past to create reproductions. Some modernization was undertaken: the colors, determined by paint analysis, were softened to create the same effect caused by lower lighting levels at the turn of the century;[14] women's restrooms were added because fashion constraints prevented women from needing such facilities in the early part of the century;[15] and the stage machinery was completely replaced to ensure safety. The completed project met Preservation Commission standards to preserve "features contributing to both the theatre's architectural significance and its layered history."[16]

The preciseness of the restoration and renovation with Landmarks Preservation Commission oversight, the reaction of critics, the continuing public demand for $10 tours on nonmatinee days, and Disney's execu-

View of interior of the New Amsterdam Theatre from the second balcony. From *New York Plaisance* (New York: H. Erkins, 1908).
Courtesy of the Theatre Historical Society of America.

tives' statements all reflect a shared acknowledgment of the value of this historic theater. When Disney had shaped a restoration funding deal with the city, Michael Eisner offered the following: "I know what 42d Street can be . . . and it is going to completely rejuvenate New York. I want to be part of that, and I want to be a part of that as an executive of the Disney Company and I want to be part of that as a former New Yorker."[17] Eisner attached himself and "his" wealth (i.e., the funding from Disney) to this project in an intentional way. Disney is the source of this valued restoration. In the language of the Renaissance patrons, Disney entered a social relationship by its involvement with this project; it served its public "clients" as patrons.

Restoring this theatrical showpiece required the vast wealth of a patron to pay numerous experts and artisans and to fund a long project time line. When it was built, the theater cost more than $1.5 million, double the norm for 1903.[18] Its lavish details, such as the encaustic painting on the medallions in the reception room, were the work of specialized artisans.

The medallions were restored with that same time- and skill-intensive process of burning colored wax into the wood surface. The same attention to detail and use of craftspeople was consistent throughout the renovation, highlighting the patron's valuation of the aesthetics and further linking its actions to the Renaissance model.

The restoration of the New Amsterdam was a project similar to some of those undertaken by Renaissance patrons. For example, the restoration of the sacristy of San Lorenzo was completed with the wealth of the Medicis (Cosimo and Lorenzo), with stucco reliefs from the life of St. John and intarsia cupboards. The New Amsterdam, originally built with the resources of the Syndicate, an organization worth several billion dollars by today's accounting, required vast resources as well for its restoration. The project, like any of this scope, also required a large payroll of workers, many on the lower end of the pay scale. In this case, a corporation rather than a Renaissance patron provides the wealth, and the collateral to obtain low-interest government loans. Disney's corporate wealth was necessary to allow it to be a patron for its less affluent clients—the public. The "inequality of power or resources" between patron and client is consistent in both eras.[19]

The model fits even more closely; patrons used both wealth and social and political influence to create and maintain their status as patrons. Corporate Disney used its vast wealth and influence to undertake such a project. After the renovation, even critics admitted Disney's role and influence as a cornerstone in the redevelopment process.[20] Frank Rich, never a Disney supporter, agreed that the rejuvenation could never have happened without Disney, "whose embrace of the New Amsterdam has helped create a gold-rush atmosphere in the entire Times Square neighborhood. The coming boon to the city's economy is incalculable."[21]

Disney's impact as a potential draw to the area was both direct and indirect. Disney executives approached and encouraged businesses that they considered consistent with the experience they wanted to create on Forty-second Street: AMC, Madame Tussaud's, and Tishman Realty & Construction (to build a hotel). In contrast, Marriott's bid failed, and Triarc Equities Corporation, Marriott's partner, credited Disney's alliance with Tishman with "assisting" Tishman's successful bid.[22] Marriott credited Disney with a network of resources and influence available only to it. This "complex of relationships," as Dale Kent notes in his book *The*

Rise of the Medici, is the foundation of patronage in Renaissance Florence, where success as a patron is proportional to the satisfaction of friends and clients.[23] The patron's power primarily lies in his or her ability to illicit actions from others, in support of friends and clients. The strength of their image or status as patrons is further amplified by the perception of their influence, even if that perception might be inaccurate or difficult to document, as is the case with Marriott. Before Disney expressed interest, New 42d Street Inc. (a nonprofit group overseeing the theater restoration in the area) only received calls about the theaters from parties interested in mud-wrestling clubs. By November of 1995 (two years after Disney signed on to renovate),[24] seven of the nine theaters had long-term leases.[25] (Two of those theaters went to Livent for the new Ford Center.)[26] Acknowledging corporate Disney's impact, New 42d Street Inc. used B.D. (before Disney) and A.D. (after Disney) to discuss its redevelopment efforts.[27] Rebecca Robertson, head of the Times Square Redevelopment Project,[28] referred to Disney as Times Square's "anchor blue chip tenant."[29]

Disney's involvement on Forty-second Street was particularly welcomed by those familiar with the area's history of failed reclamation attempts. Predating Disney's involvement, New York City first began attempts to clean up Times Square in the 1970s. During the depression of the thirties, the theaters on Forty-second Street had been converted to movie houses that eventually degenerated into porn houses. Crime escalated and buildings deteriorated. By the 1970s, the area had "almost 150 sex shops, peep shows and pornography houses."[30] New York City officials were encouraged by successful urban-renewal projects in Baltimore's Inner Harbor and Cincinnati's downtown.[31] New York State's Urban Development Corp. planned to condemn the buildings in order to eradicate the sex shops, put in a new subway station, and get private developers to redo the theaters. Forty-seven lawsuits from the sex shops opposing the condemnations cost more than $200 million, and by the end of the 1980s, the private developer footing the bill threatened to back out. At that point, the city offered tax concessions for twenty years totaling a possible $2 billion.[32] Then, in 1989, the New York real estate market dropped 20 percent and an additional 30 percent by 1994. Nothing was built or restored. The public effort, represented by the actions of the city and state governments, revealed the insufficiency of resources. These governments, then, were the clients with limited means in the Renaissance model. The old theater district on Forty-second Street needed a patron's unequal share of wealth and resources, including the intangible resource of a reliable public image, to change the perception of the blighted area and energize the transformation.

As a patron with the power of a family-friendly image, Disney required assurances of its own to protect that image.[33] Far from opposing the Renaissance model, Disney's needs mirror the "multistranded and multipurpose" nature of the patronage relationship.[34] Included in that complexity are aspects that support or increase the patron's position and status, just as the patron might bolster a client. The relationship, despite the inequity in resources, is symbiotic. Renaissance patrons might suggest the inclusion of family likenesses in a painting depicting a religious scene, such as Gentiel da Fabriano's *Adoration of the Magi*, which depicts the patron Palla Strozzi and his father behind the kings.[35] Family-friendly Disney needed a setting that supported its image before its "likeness" appeared on Forty-second Street.

The change in tone necessary to attract Disney's interest in New York City began in 1992. A group of merchants in the Times Square area formed a nonprofit improvement group, the Times Square Business Improvement District. That group hired a sanitation crew to paint over graffiti and to clean sidewalks and social workers to assist the homeless, and it financed increased security patrols. [36] Mayor Giuliani stepped in and asked police to increase patrols and crack down on panhandling and window washing by the homeless.[37] The combined result of these efforts was a 44 percent reduction in crime by 1995.[38] Fear of areas like Times Square had been the number-one reason that tourists gave for avoiding New York City;[39] now New York City had quantitative proof of a safer environment. In 1995, the New Victory, the first theater to convert to a porn movie theater, reopened as New York City's first theater devoted to productions for young people—a family destination.[40] Its restoration was a public-private partnership with state funds.[41] Hugh Hardy, the architect for the New Victory restoration, credited that project with convincing Disney that the block could be turned around and become a successful home for family entertainment.[42] (Disney later employed Hardy to restore the New Amsterdam.)

Disney's largesse was also mediated by the potential long-term benefit gained through its patronage. While a Renaissance patron might offer an artist support mostly motivated by public image and his own appreciation of the art, corporate patrons include the bottom line.[43] By the time Disney committed to renovating the New Amsterdam Theatre, the corporation had successfully mounted a Broadway production, had a library of other potential sources, and was planning to be a long-term Broadway presence. Controlling its own theater was a good business premise already proved by the theatrical traditions of the Syndicate and the Shuberts, and it was a strategy that other Disney divisions had frequently employed.[44] As Eisner knew, being the landlord rather than the renter was simply more profitable.[45] On Broadway, owning a theater guaranteed a venue where the options are limited in number and, as Eisner noted, "location is everything."[46] Disney, as patron, created the kind of long-term relationship with the public on Broadway that is characteristic of patrons. Simultaneously, the corporation was guaranteed a venue for its works—a solid business choice.

Following much critical speculation, Disney announced *King David*, a concert-version oratorio, as the limited-run production that would open the New Amsterdam Theatre on May 20, 1997. It was somewhat surprising because this production clearly deviated from a family audience but maintained high moral ground with its biblical subject matter. By its serious subject and classical form, *King David* was positioning its producers as patrons and preservers of the fine arts, an image consistent with their status as renovators of the theater housing the event. Obviously serious in tone, *King David* was more sophisticated (meaning intellectually appealing) than the family entertainment for which Disney was known. The style and the subject matter geared this production almost exclusively to adults. The oratorio style is more visually static than musicals, and this production had an almost-three-hour run time. The production told the story of David's life, as it is recorded in the Bible. Although not every event of David's life was included (no mention was made of the foreskins he was to retrieve for Saul), David's adultery and murder of Bathsheba's husband were dramatized. Clearly, Disney expected an adult audience.

King David also positioned Disney as a patron of the high arts through its extensive use of oratorio style. The work used oratorio divisions of parts or sections, not scenes or individual musical numbers like a musical or opera, although it did include arias and choral numbers. As is usual with oratorios, a combination of a large chorus, soloists, and an orchestra performed the music. Tim Rice, in a *Theater Talk* interview, referred to *King David* as a concert form that used an operatic orchestra—in other words, a full orchestra and a choir of forty.[47] True to the concert tradition, the full orchestra took a bow at the end of the production with all musicians standing. *King David*, like traditional oratorios, used a biblical subject in a lengthy work. Joab, a general and royal "assistant," functioned as the traditional narrator, shaping the individual events into a whole with recitative. Oratorios, like this one, are primarily sung, not acted and without scenery. This production used a bare playing space in the middle of the chorus and a raised platform; all musicians were in view. Frequently, oratorios are performed in concert halls, which may explain why *King David* was advertised as a concert version: those unfamiliar with the oratorio form would not expect a fully theatrical presentation as might have been suggested by the location. Reflecting a more specific oratorio element or cue, a section titled "Genius from Bethlehem" utilized both major and minor keys as Handel did. Handel, known for his oratorios, used shifts in key from major to minor for abrupt mood changes.[48] Saul's torment, reflected by his minor key, was juxtaposed with David's hopefulness, evoked by his major key. The choral number "Saul Has Slain His Thousands" used ostinato, a repeated motif, in a manner established during the Renaissance. The number began with an all-female chorus, a type of adoring fan club for David, who has slain ten thousands; and Joab, the general who served as narrator, commented on Saul's pain caused by the crowd favoring a younger successor. As the motif was repeated, the number singing in the chorus increased, matching the growing jealousy in Saul. Although the music was pop rock, the form and structure maintained the elements of the high-art oratorio experience.

Disney produced a work that was closely tied to high-art traditions, specifically opera, in an atmosphere that also implied exclusivity through the limited run and black-tie opening. Limited accessibility to a work of art and required prior knowledge are major characteristics of high art. Because these characteristics are so different from those of Disney's usual products, *King David* seemed to signal Disney Theatrical's attempt to climb the theatrical world's status ladder, positioning itself as a patron.

However, *King David* diverged from pure high-art characteristics by including pop music and anachronisms, elements that were common and popular in other Disney productions and films. Not only did some singers use a pop style, but, for example, the section "Samuel Confronts Saul" had a rock rhythm reminiscent of *Jesus Christ Superstar.* The costumes also used anachronisms to convey their messages. For example, when Saul took David under his wing, he gave David a glittery belt. When David became king, his entire shirt was made of a glittery fabric. The concept of more expensive fabric for those in power was accurate for the time period; the use of sequins and glitter was a current adaptation. All of these elements were similar to anachronisms in Disney's animated films and other stage productions, suggesting the patron's traditional influence on content, whether through input on the creation or the selection of the piece.

Disney's adaptation and development of the oratorio form enlarged the typical Disney canon, challenging its popular-art label with a high-art form. A close examination of the work revealed both strong allegiance to traditional oratorio form and incorporation of established Disney practices. Questions remain about the unification of these various attributes, but like the preservation of the New Amsterdam, the production of this work implies Disney's valuation of high culture. Also, like the preservation of the New Amsterdam, the production was a sound business decision. In his autobiography, Michael Eisner referred to the critical balance that defines Disney: "creative initiatives and the need to remain profitable."[49] In this environment, patronage and preservation activities are pursued but are limited and dictated by profitable fiscal practices.

Finally, *King David* was announced as a work in progress, not a finished product, publicly indicating that Disney would support the work of the artists through the development phase.[50] The project did not begin with Disney, but with Alan Menken and Tim Rice. The work was originally commissioned as "a commemorative spectacle to be held outside the walled city for . . . Jerusalem 3000" in 1996.[51] Jerusalem 3000 was a festival marking the date King David founded the city of Jerusalem. Disney's assumption of the project demonstrated an openness to artistic works beyond the borders of its corporation and a particular willingness to invest in the development of artists who had previously worked with Disney; both aspects are choices consistent with Renaissance patron models.

Further strengthening its standing as a Renaissance patron, corporate Disney was building a reputation as providing support to artists. As press representatives talked with actors and designers associated with *The Lion King,* they received consistent reports of the creative development funded by Disney. *The Lion King* director Julie Taymor expressed her belief that the production was "breaking ground theatrically" and credited the development time that Disney funded.[52] Samuel Wright, the original Mufasa, endorsed the patron label, discussing the necessity of "patrons to finance an artist's vision," as Disney did with Taymor's concept.[53] Disney's attitude toward development was and is consistent with current practice in the film industry, but the contracts also establish the long-term support consistent with the Renaissance patron model. Some of the development contracts are commissions, also a frequent practice of Renaissance patrons. Disney's commissioning of the two symphonies for the millennium, mentioned previously, furthers the image by expanding the type of art supported by Disney funding.

Finally, Disney funded, and is funding, the Roy and Edna Disney CalArts Theater (REDCAT), a state-of-the-art experimental theater space in the Walt Disney Concert Hall Complex in Los Angeles. REDCAT expands Disney's ongoing relationship with the California Institute of the Arts (CalArts), which began with Walt Disney's patronlike support in the school's founding. CalArts has a ninety-nine-year lease to use the Walt Disney Concert Hall Complex as a performance venue and gallery for its students and faculty. The facility also hosts a wide variety of experimental arts events for the surrounding community. The work at REDCAT will not make any direct contributions to Disney's producing lineup; the 2004–5 director's statement maps a much different role, stressing its ongoing mission to "be a home for adventurous artistic exploration and lively debate about the evolution of culture and society." REDCAT's physical space is the gift of a patron, who, with corporate compatriots, continues to fund the seasons of new and challenging works.[54] Any immediate benefit gained by Disney is through the association of its patronage with artistic work outside the Disney aesthetic.

Even granting Disney the noble intention of saving a landmark of American theater history and art nouveau design, and remaining open to the possibility of its patronlike support of individual artists and works, it is necessary to recognize the limitations of the patron's largesse; the decision to renovate the New Amsterdam was a sound business move with controlled risk factors: a typical Disney deal. Income from the theater determines Disney's payments to the city and state above and beyond the loan; debt is proportional to success. Prior to committing to the project,

Disney acquired detailed information about the theater's renovation needs and secured assurances of Times Square's change to a family-friendly entertainment district. Pre-Disney studies of the theater revealed the structural damage and had begun the negotiation process with the New York City Landmarks Preservation Commission for updates. Disney's contract with the city and state stipulated that the porn shops would be removed and that other entertainment industries had to commit to the street. This author has no reason to doubt Disney's valuation of preserving the historic theater, or its desire to play patron on Broadway with the accompanying boost to its image, but the decision to do so was based in and dependent on sound business practice.

How does the Renaissance patron label fit? Even in the limitations set by corporate Disney, the match with the Renaissance patronage model is thorough. Like the Renaissance patrons, Disney exercised its ability to commission works of art and architecture; it served their public "clients" by renovating a historic landmark valued by the society's client-members; the detailed, aesthetic approach to the renovation mirrored the Medici renovations and, along with the development of *King David*, signaled support for high-art forms; the choice of *King David* and other similar activities also established its patronlike support of artists, not just completed projects; the social and political influence of the patron (Disney), or perception of that influence, played a significant role in the project; and Disney, like its Renaissance predecessors, took steps to protect its image. Perhaps this is because Italian Renaissance patronage flourished through the business class; the Medicis in particular were bankers and merchants. Dale Kent, in his book *The Rise of the Medici*, specifically argues that banking was the foundation of the Medici power for the "fundamental reason that it made them a major financial force, not only in Florence, but throughout Italy."[55] Our romanticized view of Renaissance patrons has obscured their foundation in the business market. Current patrons acquire their wealth and extend their influence through finances using the same path: the market. Furthermore, some Renaissance scholars, such as Ronald Weissman, contend that the capitalist economy of Italy was guided by and developed from the ties of patronage, rejecting the traditional view that capitalism grew in opposition to patronage.[56] In other words, business transactions and relationships were most likely to occur between people tied by patronage; the same symbiotic relationship can still function in a capitalistic market to the advantage of the involved parties. American capitalism does function the same way. Corporations seek out mergers, acquisitions, and long-term relationships with particular entities that provide goods and services they need.

Public reaction to the activities of the patron is similarly comparable. In the Renaissance model, patronage is a "self-perpetuating system of belief and action grounded in society's value system."[57] From the public perspective, valuing an extensive restoration like that done on the New Amsterdam reveals acceptance of the hierarchical wealth structure that places such a large percentage of the financial resources under the control of a few individual entities. We may bill ourselves as centuries beyond the "restrictive" patron-artist relationship, perhaps because we inaccurately equate it with an aristocracy that disputes our capitalistic self-definition. In reality, the patronage structure remains, functioning successfully in the capitalist marketplace, and the face of the patron has, in this case, been logically assumed by a corporation.

Interesting questions remain. Is this corporation-as-patron model unique to Disney because of its movie and entertainment emphasis or the executives at the helm during this era? How necessary is a history of patronage-type activities? Perhaps most important, how do we, as theater artists, approach these potential patrons in ways that reveal the advantages beyond simple marketing exposure? How do we attain, and do we want, the symbiotic relationship of patron and client?

Notes

1. Peter Applebome, "The Medici Behind Disney's High Art," *New York Times*, October 4, 1998, late final edition, http://www.lexis-nexis.com.

2. Ibid.

3. Jack Zink, "The Mouse Lies Down on Broadway: Disney Animates the Nation's Theater Landscape," *Fort Lauderdale Sun-Sentinel*, Broward metro edition, October 11, 1998, http://www.lexis-nexis.com.

4. Laurie Winer, "On and Off the Stage," *Los Angeles Times*, January 2, 1998, home edition, http://www.lexis-nexis.com.

5. Alan Finder, "A Prince Charming? Disney and the City Find Each Other," *New York Times*, June 10, 1995, late edition, http://www.lexis-nexis.com; William Grimes, "Disney 'King' for 42d Street: No Lion Suits," *New York Times*, November 7, 1996, late final edition, http://www.lexis-nexis.com. The Syndicate managed theatrical productions and tours across the United States. By 1903, it had established a monopoly by requiring exclusive representation rights from its clients.

6. Allan Wallach, "Theme Park? What Theme Park? Disney's Restoration of Florenz Ziegfeld's New Amsterdam Theater to Its Original Splendor May Redefine the Term Disneyfication–In a Good Way," *Newsday*, May 11, 1997, C23, http://www.lexis-nexis.com. *New York Times*, "Shakespeare Treated as Musical Comedy," October 29, 1903, http://www.proquest.com. Ironically, the opening production of *A Midsummer Night's Dream* was announced with promises of "all the appurtenances of musical comedy of the Beauty and the Beast type." One hundred years later, a different *Beauty* was instrumental in convincing Disney to reopen the theater.

7. Charles De Kay, "Sculpture and Painting in a Theatrical Environment," *New York Times*, November 1, 1903, http://www.proquest.com.

8. John Istel, "Disney," *Village Voice*, September 3, 1996, http://www.lexis-nexis.com.

9. Mary C. Henderson, *The New Amsterdam: The Biography of a Broadway Theatre* (New York: Hyperion, 1997), 115–117. Henderson chronicled the various attempts concisely.

10. *New York Times*, "Forty-second Street Block Transformed by Theatres," January 1, 1905, http://www.proquest.com.

11. Douglas Feiden, "News Beat," New York *Daily News*, July 15, 1999, http://www.lexis-nexis.com.

12. Henderson, *New Amsterdam*, 115–17.

13. Wallach, "Theme Park"; Grimes "Disney King."

14. Dan Hulbert, "Disney Rescues a Faded Broadway Jewel," *Atlanta Journal and Constitution*, May 25, 1997, http://www.lexis-nexis.com.

15. Alan D. Abbey, "Disney Banking on Theater to Light Up 42nd Street," *Albany* (NY) *Times Union*, May 11, 1997, one-star edition, http://www.lexis-nexis.com.

16. Henderson, *New Amsterdam*, 132.

17. Finder, "Prince Charming."

18. Henderson, *New Amsterdam*, 15.

19. Ronald Weissman, "Taking Patronage Seriously: Mediterranean Values and Renaissance Society," in *Patronage, Art, and Society in Renaissance Italy*, ed. F. W. Kent and Patricia Simons, 25 (Oxford: Clarendon Press, 1987). Weissman offers this attribute as fundamental to the Renaissance patron-client relationship.

20. See, for example, Douglas Feiden and Michael Riedel, "Disney's Loose on Deuce Herculean Party Set for New Film and Theater," *Daily News*, April 3, 1997, http://www.lexis-nexis.com; Finder, "Prince Charming;" Thomas J. Lueck, "Returning from Decline, 42d Street Is Now a Magnet for Merchants," *New York Times*, November 15, 1995, late edition, http://www.lexis-nexis.com; and Brett Pulley, "Disney's Deal: A Special Report: A Mix of Glamour and Hardball Won Disney a Piece of 42d Street," *New York Times*, July 29, 1995, late edition, http://www.lexis-nexis.com.

21. Frank Rich "Journal: Goodbye to All That," *New York Times*, December 30, 1995, late edition, http://www.lexis-nexis.com.

22. Pulley, "Disney's Deal."

23. Dale Kent, *The Rise of the Medici: Faction in Florence 1426–1434*, (Oxford: Oxford University Press, 1978), 92.

24. William Weathersby Jr., "The New Amsterdam Theatre: Disney Revives Ziegfeld's Palace as a Home for 'The Lion King,'" *Theatre Crafts International*, July 1998, http://www.lexis-nexis.com.

25. Lueck, "Returning from Decline."

26. Karen Fricker, "New 42nd Street Org Tries to Keep Up with Changes," in "New York, Entertainment Town," suppl., *Variety*, September 18, 1995, 73, http://www.lexis-nexis.com.

27. Jonathan Weber, "Revival on Broadway: With the Help of Walt Disney Co., Times Square Is Staging a Comeback," *Los Angeles Times*, June 19, 1994, Home edition, http://www.lexis-nexis.com.

28. TSRP refers to the group assigned to the area by the state Urban Development Corp.

29. Miriam Leuchter, "Reviving Times Square: An Interview with Rebecca Robertson," *Crain's New York Business*, March 27, 1995, 76, http://www.lexis-nexis.com.

30. Malcolm Gladwell, "Bringing Back Times Square in a Big Way: Is It the Best Way?" *Washington Post*, February 21, 1995, final edition, http://www.lexis-nexis.com.

31. Ibid.

32. Ibid.

33. Disney is well aware of this expectation, as evidenced by the creation of Hyperion Theatricals as a producing wing that handles productions, like *Aida*, aimed at adult audiences.

34. Weissman, "Taking Patronage Seriously," 25.

35. Mary Hollingsworth, "Merchants and Morality," in *Patronage in Renaissance Italy: From 1400 to the Early Sixteenth Century* (London: John Murray, 1994). Hollingsworth discusses the significance of this commission; the patron's literal image is linked with the public faith imagery of the time.

36. Gladwell, "Bringing Back Times Square."

37. Joseph A. Kirby, "Mickey Goes from 'Sticks' to Big Apple: Officials See Disney Changing the 'Character' of New York," *Chicago Tribune*, August 5, 1995, north sports final edition, http://www.lexis-nexis.com.

38. Bruce Frankel, "Times Square Coming Full Circle: Family Values Return to Famous Theatrical Street," *USA Today*, October, 30, 1995, final edition, http://www.lexis-nexis.com.

39. Ibid.

40. Amy Reiter, "New York's Oldest Theatre Is Broadway's Newest Victory: Victory Theatre Renovated and Renamed New Victory," *Back Stage*, May 19, 1995, 3, http://www.lexis-nexis.com.

41. That restoration reportedly cost $11.4 million. The theater was originally built in 1900 by Oscar Hammerstein and was owned by David Belasco in the early part of the century.

42. Frederick M. Winship, "New Era Begins on 42nd Street," *United Press International*, December 8, 1995, http://www.lexis-nexis.com.

43. Peter Burke, *Culture and Society in Renaissance Italy 1420–1540*, (London: B. T. Batsford, 1972): 83–85. Burke includes a thorough discussion of the "piety, prestige, and pleasure" that motivated Renaissance patrons to support painting and sculpture, linking piety to public image.

44. Frank Rose and Erin M. Davies, "Can Disney Tame 42nd Street?" *Fortune*, June 24, 1996, 94, http://www.lexis-nexis.com. Disney acquired Buena Vista to regulate movie distribution and ABC as an outlet for television programming.

45. Finder, "A Prince Charming." Finder reports the statement rather than quoting.

46. Weathersby, "New Amsterdam." Disney signed a forty-nine-year lease in 1995. Michael Eisner with Tony Schwartz, *Work in Progress* (New York: Random House, 1998), 256.

47. Tim Rice, "King David," interview on *Theater Talk*, PBS, Theatre on Film and Tape Archive, New York Public Library. I also viewed *King David* on video at the Theatre on Film and Tape Archive.

48. Roger Kamien, *Music: An Appreciation* (New York: McGraw-Hill, 1976), 175.

49. Eisner, *Work*, 202.

50. Michael Kuchwara, "'King David' Opens Disney's New Amsterdam Theater," review of *King David*, by Alan Menken and Tim Rice, New Amsterdam Theater, New York, *Associated Press*, May 19, 1997, http://www.lexis-nexis.com; Frederick M. Winship, "Disney's 'King David' to Open Theater," *United Press International*, August 19, 1996, http://www.lexis-nexis.com.

51. Ben Brantley, "With Strobe Lights (But No Philistine Trophies), It's Disney's 'King David,'" review of *King David*, by Alen Menken and Tim Rice, *New York Times*, May 20, 1997, late edition, http://www.lexis-nexis.com.

52. Jan Breslauer, "Her Magic Kingdom: Julie Taymor's Avant-Garde Style Fits Opera, Stage . . . and Disney," *Los Angeles Times*, July 25, 1996, home edition, http://www.lexis-nexis.com.

53. Patti Hartigan, "Broadway's New 'King,'" *Boston Globe*, November 9, 1997, city edition, http://www.lexis-nexis.com.

54. REDCAT, "Director's Statement," http://redcat.org/about/directorsstatement.html (accessed July 19, 2005).

55. Kent, *Rise of Medici*, 83.

56. Weissman, "Taking Patronage Seriously," 40.

57. Jeremy Boissevain, "Patronage in Sicily," *Man* 1, no. 1 (1966): 30.

16

STATIC IN THE SIGNAL: CLEAR CHANNEL COMMUNICATIONS AND THEATER IN THE UNITED STATES

Anthony J. Vickery

> There is only one thing to be feared. That is, that the Syndicate ultimately will control most of the theatres, and will become like most other monopolies, thus making the expenses of combinations [production companies] greater and profits less.
>
> —Mr. Warner, *New York Dramatic Mirror,* 1897

> If SFX puts all the different pieces together, they are bordering on a monopoly of the Broadway road.
>
> —Chris Jones, *Variety,* 1998

The two opening quotes, separated in time by just over a century, both voice a similar concern about the threat of one large firm dominating commercial touring theater in the United States. The first quote refers to the threat posed by the partnerships that formed the Syndicate in 1896.

The anonymous rival speaking in the second quote was issuing a warning about the acquisition of numerous live entertainment assets by SFX, a corporation later acquired and renamed Clear Channel Entertainment by the media conglomerate Clear Channel Communications. Both the Syndicate and Clear Channel were aiming to rationalize business on the road by consolidating competing producers and road theaters into a single business entity to create a one-stop booking service that would allow other producers as well as their own productions to book entire coast-to-coast tours economically. While the players have changed, the driving movement of consolidating the business of the road into fewer and fewer hands was as much a part of the environment at the end of the twentieth century as at the end of the nineteenth.

Activity in the commercial theater between 1980 and 2005 mirrored activity between 1880 and 1920. Both periods saw independent producers gradually give way to large organizations consolidating activity on the road. Just as the independent producer of the 1880s and 1890s gradually went out of business or allied to the Syndicate or the Shuberts, the independent promoters of the 1960s and 1970s also gave way in the 1980s to larger theater corporations and producers. The volume of activity on the road rose in the late 1980s, peaking in the 1995–96 season (see figure). In the 1984–85 season, road companies produced 993 playing weeks on the road with 8.2 million people attending the performances. From 1984–85, attendance and playing weeks climbed to a high of 18.1 million and 1,345, respectively, in 1995–96 and gradually declined in the subsequent decade. The active years in the mid-1990s correspond to the era when corporations such as Livent, PACE, Disney, and SFX were touring shows across the country. The 1990s saw further consolidation on the road until only a few large corporations were left. Livent went bankrupt, and its assets were purchased by SFX, which earlier on had purchased all the assets of PACE and stood atop the road until the company was acquired by Clear Channel Communications. Many independent promoters began entering the market in 2005 and along with or as a member of the Independent Presenters Network compete directly with Clear Channel Entertainment.

Clear Channel Communications has grown into one of the largest media companies in the United States. The company was created in 1972, when company founder L. Lowry Mays acquired his first radio station in San Antonio, Texas. By the time the company became publicly traded on

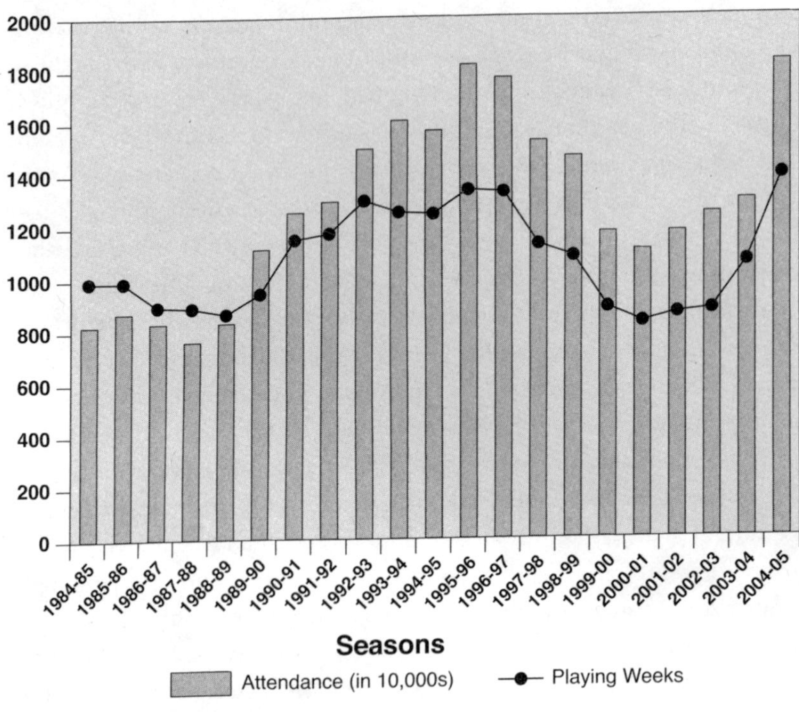

Road statistics, 1984–2005.
Adapted from "Research: Broadway Road Tours Statistics," League of American Theatres and Producers, http://www.livebroadway.com/roadstats.html (accessed August 9, 2005).

the New York Stock Exchange in 1984, it owned sixteen radio stations. The company branched into the ownership of television stations in 1988 and had acquired seven by 1992. The year 1996 marked a turning point in the history of the corporation due to the relaxing of restrictions on station ownership by the Federal Communications Commission and the lifting of regulations on nationwide station ownership. Clear Channel began to aggressively add radio stations to its portfolio after 1996 and by 1997 owned or operated 175 radio stations and 18 television stations. In addition, by 1997, Clear Channel had purchased its first outdoor advertising company.[1] Growth through acquisition was (and still is) the main method Clear Channel used, rather than organically creating business, to increase the company's holdings. There are many pitfalls to growing through mergers, with the most obvious being the difficulty in integrating different types of businesses together into one structure. However, by acquiring companies using stock or assumption of debt, Clear Channel was able to grow at an incredible rate.

Key mergers in 1999 and 2000 placed Clear Channel at the pinnacle of the radio and live entertainment business in the United States. By the time it completed these mergers, the company owned or controlled some 1,200 radio stations, 40 television stations, 800,000 outdoor advertising displays, and 125 live entertainment venues, employing 35,000 people and generating revenues of approximately $9.5 billion annually.[2] In 1999, the company purchased Jacor Communications for $4 billion, to become the second-largest owner of radio stations in the United States. The following year, Clear Channel acquired the even-larger broadcaster AMFM for $23.8 billion and became the largest owner of radio stations in the country. Also in 2000, the company purchased SFX Entertainment (which in 2001, it renamed Clear Channel Entertainment) for approximately $4 billion and became the largest promoter of live events (mainly musical concerts, sports events, and live theater) in the United States.

Much like Clear Channel, SFX Entertainment was created largely through mergers and acquisitions. The corporation was originally a part of SFX Broadcasting, a radio and television station holding company founded in 1992 by Robert F. X. Sillerman. The live entertainment division of SFX Broadcasting, SFX Entertainment, was started in 1997 and spun off from the parent corporation in 1998.

In the two years following the spin-off, SFX Entertainment acquired enough assets on the road to be considered the largest producer of live entertainment in the United States. SFX was able to go on this buying spree because its broadcasting arm sold its radio stations in July of 1997 and established a corporate war chest of $2 billion.[3] This immense amount of money allowed SFX to acquire rivals and attract top-flight talent to sign contracts to fill its venues. There really can be no comparison drawn between the financial resources of SFX and any other theater company or producer in the United States at the time. While SFX was on its acquisition binges of the 1990s, it signed a number of noncompetition agreements with many of the promoters it bought out.[4] The company's financial muscle was such that it bred many comments like the one opening this chapter that portrays SFX in a menacing light.

A part of the fear of such a large corporation is that the bottom line is the only important part of the business to it and that the actual industry in which it competes matters little. "SFX's long-term interests have nothing to do with building careers or protecting artists," rival producer Tom Ross told *Daily Variety*. "They are going to strip-mine the industry, move on in three years to airplane parts, and maybe some [of] us will still be around to put the industry back together again."[5] These comments from the head of a rival corporation that was trying to hold on to its own position in the industry point to a potential problem. SFX was a publicly traded company. Corporate strategy had to be directed at maintaining profitability to keep its share price high to allow the company to borrow money for acquisitions once it had depleted its war chest. Part of the fear generated by such a large corporation is that artists will get trampled on when the corporation seems more beholden to its shareholders than to its employees or even its audience members. For the corporation, though, revenue growth was powered through acquisition rather than operation and would require large sums of money in the future.

SFX's position as the leading promoter of road shows (such as *Chicago*, *Joseph and the Amazing Technicolor Dreamcoat*, and *Fosse*) in the United States was created by four strategic acquisitions between December of 1997 and July of 1999. SFX's first significant acquisition was the promoter PACE, for $130 million in December, 1997.[6] The theatrical arm of PACE was called the "dominant promoter of national tours" in June of 1997.[7] The entire PACE Entertainment corporation was also involved in concert promotions, motor sports, rock festivals, and venue management.

To help PACE secure booking rights for Broadway productions, the company invested directly on Broadway (a practice both SFX and Clear Channel would continue). The corporation's initial investment on Broadway was with the Shubert Organization for $750,000 for *Jerome Robbins' Broadway* in 1989.[8] In the case of *Jekyll & Hyde* in 1994, the company modified this practice by inviting producers to Houston to see an early version of the production, then touring the show around North America before opening it on Broadway with multiple partners (to be followed by further tours after a successful New York run).[9] June of 1997 saw PACE ally with Broadway theater owner and producer Jujamcyn to create a joint venture that would see the two companies create shows to be presented on Broadway (possibly in Jujamcyn theaters) and on the road in PACE theaters.[10] A number of shows were put on under this partnership, including *The Triumph of Love*, *The Civil War*, *Swing*, and a revival of *The Sound of Music*.

The PACE acquisition vaulted SFX to the forefront of Broadway touring. However, SFX continued to seek other acquisition opportunities to allow it to continue to consolidate operations, spread its marketing muscle, and enhance profits. SFX's second and third important acquisitions occurred eight months later, in December 1998. The first of these two acquisitions saw the company purchase American Artists for $25.7 million. American Artists' main assets were three theaters in Boston (the Charles and leases on the Colonial and Wilbur), which gave SFX a dominant position in the city and region. At about the same time, SFX also paid $100 million for Magicworks, another producer of touring Broadway productions, including *Lord of the Dance* and *Jekyll & Hyde* (Magicworks was a partner in the initial Broadway production and toured this show). Magicworks also controlled venues in cities where SFX did not have access, such as Salt Lake City.[11] By January of 1999, SFX owned or operated 69 venues in the United States and had sold 240,000 annual subscriptions for touring Broadway shows in 38 markets.[12]

The fourth key acquisition was the August 1999 purchase of the assets of bankrupt producer Livent, for approximately $96 million.[13] Livent, based in Canada, broke on to the Broadway scene in 1993 with a critically acclaimed production of *Kiss of the Spider Woman*. After presenting a number of Broadway productions and tours in the United States and Canada (such as *Showboat*, *Ragtime*, and *Parade*) and renovating theaters in New York, Chicago, and Toronto, the company ceased operations in 1999 under the cloud of an accounting scandal perpetrated by senior members of the corporation's management team.[14] By March of 2000, SFX owned or operated 120 live entertainment venues and promoted Broadway touring productions in 55 markets.[15] In that month, SFX was swallowed whole by an even larger entertainment industry juggernaut, Clear Channel Communications.

Clear Channel's acquisition of SFX took place in a year during which a number of large mergers took place in the media industry. In 2000, Internet service provider AOL announced that it would acquire Time Warner for $106 billion in a melding of "old" and "new" media companies.[16] CBS and Viacom merged to create a $45 billion media conglomerate in 2000 as well.[17] In comparison, Clear Channel's mergers of 1999 and 2000 only totaled approximately $32 billion (if the AMFM and Jacor deals are included), which ranked behind both of the preceding deals.

In a similar vein, the quest for synergy between related businesses, in the case of Clear Channel, chiefly radio and music promotion, drove the merger mania that saw the entire media industry (rather than just theater on the road) go through a period of consolidation. In this arena, theater is seen as just another division of an entertainment corporation without special needs. Perhaps the vision of theater as no different from radio, television, or even billboards is what rankled commentators about the SFX merger. Clear Channel founder and former chief executive officer Lowry Mays also made it very clear that the particular nuances of running the different divisions of his company meant little to him: "We're not in the business of providing news and information. We're not in the business of providing well-researched music. We're simply in the business of selling our customers products."[18]

While these comments were directed at the company's radio holdings, the same attitude pervaded its theater holdings. Clear Channel officials noted the ability that the SFX merger in particular brought to the company: "Company billboards promote radio stations, which promote the concert tours, which are managed by the in-house promotions firm and play at company-owned or operated venues, where still more billboards beckon. This lets Clear Channel flood the zone."[19] This synergy would allow the company to reach even more consumers and sell larger advertisement contracts to national or international companies.

In July of 2001, SFX was renamed Clear Channel Entertainment to allow easier identification and cross-promotion with its parent company.[20] Clear Channel Entertainment remained a wholly owned subsidiary of Clear Channel Communications. Shortly after the renaming, the company began its branding campaign for Broadway Across America, focusing on more than forty cities across the United States as a national platform for advertisers. According to a Clear Channel marketing officer, the "plan also provides sponsors with an opportunity to create national ticket promotions, in-store sweepstakes . . . as well as [to] generate brand awareness from inclusion in Broadway Across America's advertising and media programs."[21] This marketing effort recalls the advertising campaigns of old when branding a production as "direct from New York" gave the show the seal of approval no matter how directly the production actually came from New York.

The period between 2000 and 2004 was dominated by Clear Channel's tours (after it purchased SFX). In the road-statistics figure, the years 2000 to 2004 saw less activity on the road than during the 1990s, which reflected the consolidation achieved by Clear Channel. However, in the final season covered by the figure, 2004–5, attendance and playing weeks spiked to levels of the mid-1990s (18.2 million attended some 1,389 playing weeks), due to the reentry of many competitors on the road. The list of productions for the 2005 Broadway Across America season contains a number of shows that never were on Broadway (*Clifford the Big Red Dog* or *The Blue Man Group*) or have been off Broadway for some time (*Joseph and the Amazing Technicolor Dreamcoat*—last on Broadway in 1994, or *Annie*—last on Broadway in 1997).[22] The company definitely does have a number of productions that truly are direct from New York, but it must fill out its roster with other shows because of the large number of venues it must program.

While Clear Channel, for the most part, has presented Broadway musicals, it also over the years has offered other types of productions.[23] One of the most profitable types of productions were for young audiences (such as *Clifford the Big Red Dog Live!*, *Dora's Pirate Adventure*, and different incarnations of *National Geographic Live!*). However, the company also presented more challenging subject matter seemingly at odds with the commercial focus of the majority of its productions. Clear Channel presented the play *The Exonerated* in a multicity tour that included stops in Philadelphia, New Orleans, San Francisco, and Minneapolis. This play examines the lives of six individuals who were convicted of crimes and sentenced to the death penalty but later were found to be innocent after spending, in some cases, considerable time in jail. It raises questions about the legal system in the United States and is a curious choice for a mainstream corporation such as Clear Channel. Perhaps the project was rendered more palatable by its success in New York (at The Culture Project @ 45 Bleecker) and the involvement of well-known director and actor Bob Balaban and a host of celebrity guest stars (including Robin Williams, Brian Dennehy, Mia Farrow, and Stockard Channing).[24] Balaban also directed another atypical production Clear Channel presented in 2003–4, *Addicted*, written and performed by Mark Lundholm. This play, really a solo performance, discusses the author's addiction to Ritalin, alcohol, and other substances and his eventual recovery in a long comic monologue.[25] While the subject matter of this play is somewhat edgier than most Broadway productions, the economics of a one-performer show, Lundholm's performance, and the participation of Balaban caused Clear Channel to tour the production around the country, including stops in New York, Minneapolis, and Miami.

Clear Channel employs three main methods for acquiring productions for its venues. Since the company owns so many venues, the first method for acquiring productions is to book shows produced by other companies. In this case, it is merely a landlord who takes a cut of the box office or is engaged under a four-wall agreement, in which the act essentially pays rent for the space. Four-wall agreements are becoming more common on the road and are not as lucrative for the venue owner as a sharing agreement. Perhaps more common and the second manner in which Clear Channel acquires product is to directly invest in a production before its first presentation on Broadway. For a number of years, Clear Channel (and SFX before it) directly invested in productions on Broadway to secure the right to book the production when it began to tour. Since November 1996, Clear Channel or SFX has invested in thirty-two productions on Broadway (such as *Fosse*, *The Woman in White*, *Spamalot*, *The Producers*, and *Hairspray*).[26] With the exception of *Fosse*, Clear Channel produced all of these shows in association with many different Broadway producers, media companies, and other businesses. Finally, in a few cases, Clear Channel has acted as an executive producer. To facilitate the development of its own projects, the company founded Clear Channel Entertainment Productions in May 2005 to develop fixed-based attractions and touring events. Their first two projects were to begin development of a Las Vegas version of Andrew Lloyd Webber's musical *Phantom of the Opera* and to assist with the mounting of *The Blue Man Group* in Toronto.[27] *The Blue Man Group* successfully opened in Toronto in June 2005, despite initial union opposition to the nonunion company.

While analysts have admired Clear Channel's innovative business model and stunning growth,[28] the company has garnered a great deal of criticism within the theater community for its labor relations. Damone Richardson and Maria Figueroa, labor and industry researchers from Cornell University, compare the labor relations of Clear Channel to those of Wal-Mart: "Clear Channel is overwhelmingly non-union, and has shown little regard for workers—union or otherwise. Most of the fifteen unions that have or have had collective bargaining agreements with the company have described the relationship as contentious."[29]

The researchers go on to quote an interview with members of the American Federation of Musicians, Local 802, which discussed the use of "virtual orchestra" technology. This technology would allow Clear Channel to reduce or eliminate live musicians from their theater tours. While the League of American Theatres and Producers were prevented from including the use of this technology in their master agreements covering road tours by a strike by the musicians' union, Clear Channel, as well as Disney, are not signatories to the agreement.

Clear Channel has also gone head-to-head with Actors' Equity over contracts and labor practices. As early as 2002, industry members estimated that Clear Channel was using 40 percent to 50 percent non-Equity companies to fill its road theaters.[30] By February 2004, the matter had become so divisive that Actors' Equity filed an unfair labor practices charge with the National Labor Relations Board against Clear Channel Entertainment as well as the Nederlander Organization and Dodger Stage Holdings Theatricals Inc.[31] Actors' Equity filed the suit because it suspected Clear Channel was dealing with non-Equity companies when its agreement specifically required the producer not to deal with non-Equity companies. In particular, Equity accused Clear Channel of diverting work that should have been performed by Equity members to the non-Equity producer NETworks.[32] Actors' Equity and Clear Channel (as well as the League of American Theatres and Producers and other producers) came to an agreement in August 2004, but the contract included clauses for an "experimental touring program" to allow producers to tour lower-cost musical productions under a tiered system that reduces rates paid to actors until the production begins to make profits.[33] While this clause should cause producers to provide more employment for Equity members, by only allowing the actors to receive a full salary after the company makes a profit, the actors assume some of the financial risk that was formerly fully borne by the producer. However, the salaries in the experimental program are still much higher than for non-Equity shows, in which performers can be paid as little as half of a regular Equity salary.[34]

Clear Channel had to contend not only with the rising internal costs of doing business on the road but also with serious competition for acquiring touring product and audience dollars. By 2005, its biggest competitor was not a single company but a pool of presenters and promoters called the Independent Presenters Network (IPN). In 2005, IPN had fifty-five members presenting shows in seventy markets. According to members, IPN was put together late in 2000 to specifically counter Clear Channel's (and earlier SFX's) hold on touring theater in the United States.[35] Because Clear Channel was large enough to offer a production an entire year's worth of tour dates, many cities and theaters would only see a production in the second year of its tour. Members of IPN are mostly nonprofit theaters and arts centers, including Denver Center Attractions (Randy Weeks); the Orpheum Theatre, in Memphis (Pat Halloran); the Blumenthal Performing Arts Center, in Charlotte, North Carolina (Judith Allen); and Fox Theater, in St. Louis (Mike Isaacson). Members invest an amount in the original production on Broadway for every week they book the show in their venue. For *Thoroughly Modern Millie* in 2000, IPN members invested $25,000 per week the show was to play in their respective venues for a total investment of $1.1 million, or approximately 10 percent of the total budget for the production.[36] IPN is no less a commercial organization than Clear Channel; it only differs in the fact that its membership is composed of a number of companies rather than a single corporation. The types of theaters into which IPN books productions are not that different from Clear Channel, which books productions into its own commercial venues and other nonprofit venues such as the Orange County Performing Arts Center in Costa Mesa, California.[37] IPN remained the "alternate" presenter on the road until the 2005 opening of the musical *Spamalot* on Broadway. For that production, IPN invested more funds in the show and appeared above Clear Channel in the production credits. According to lead *Spamalot* producer Bob Boyett, every tour city will hold auctions to land the production, and it is expected that IPN and Clear Channel will go "head-to-head" in many markets.[38] Instead of one company knowing ahead of time that it has the right to present the production in a particular market, both Clear Channel and IPN will bid to present the production in a particular city by offering more lucrative terms to the *Spamalot* company in exchange for exclusive rights to present the show in that market.

In Clear Channel's broadcasting and outdoor-advertising divisions, the company has managed to limit cost increases and even to decrease labor costs. While the radio division maintained a profit margin of approximately 40 percent and the outdoor advertising business 30 percent, the live entertainment division of Clear Channel has only been able to average a margin of 6 percent.[39] The lower returns of the live entertainment division point out a significant difference between that sector and the radio sector: revenues in the two sectors are derived from totally different sources. The radio and outdoor-advertising divisions derive their income from advertisers. While these advertisers are influenced by consumers, they ultimately make the decisions. However, in the live entertainment field, the majority of the revenues come from audience members.

The low margins of the live entertainment division were tarnishing the overall performance of the company to such an extent that Clear Channel announced plans in April 2005 to spin off Clear Channel Entertainment into a separate corporation. Clear Channel chief executive officer Mark Mays maintains that the shift is an operational strategy rather than a financial strategy,[40] but according to an article in *Billboard* magazine, the radio and concert divisions rarely communicated with each other and ran "on separate tracks."[41] The hoped-for synergy failed to materialize just as in the other large-scale media mergers of 2000: AOL Time Warner dropped the AOL from its name in 2003, and CBS Viacom announced major restructuring in 2005.[42] Since the profit margin at Clear Channel Entertainment is so thin, the new corporation will have to run its business very carefully to survive. Another option for the new corporation is that the company is purchased once it is separated from Clear Channel Communications.[43] On August 10, 2005, Clear Channel Communications registered CCE Spinco Inc. with the Securities and Exchange Commission. This new entity housed the assets of Clear Channel Entertainment until it was renamed Live Nation in December 2005, when the spin-off was completed.[44]

One positive aspect of the spin-off is that the new company will no longer be so large that it is looked upon as a monopoly. In general, Clear Channel Communications was so large that it was accused of having the ability to shape what the public listened to, not only on radio but also in concert. In the theater, the view of the company was not wholly negative: "'It's hard to say there are good guys and bad guys here [on the road in the United States],' IPN's Halloran said. 'Clear Channel is a huge company with an enormous amount of money that goes through their bank account every year, and we're just little independent guys that have a mom-and-pop show and we bring a little bit of local color to it.'"[45] Implicit in Halloran's comments was a critique of how Clear Channel was out of touch with local situations. Since all corporate activity was directed from New York (then Houston and now Beverly Hills, California), the company was sometimes accused of presenting shows that markets did not desire. However, the theatrical division of Clear Channel Entertainment seems to have a better reputation than any other division of the corporation. The smaller Live Nation cannot be accused of wielding so much power over what people listen to and see and will have to pay more attention to consumer demands to stay alive, This is probably a positive development for both Clear Channel Communications and Live Nation, relieving both from possible regulatory trouble. While Clear Channel Communications had garnered a negative reputation for dealing with competitors,[46] Clear Channel Entertainment (at least, its theatrical division) has not: "'All of us have to have a degree of caution. You can't look at somebody who's that big a player and not think it's a matter of concern,' says Tom Viertel, an independent Broadway producer who has partnered with Clear Channel on some shows and who relies on its road venues to book others. He gives its theatrical division high marks for savvy and a 'nondisruptive, nonconfrontational' way of doing business."[47]

The reasons for Clear Channel's reorganization are twofold. First, the corporation must maintain its high level of profitability to continue to shore up its share price and to allow it to go to markets and acquire more financing. Clear Channel, in the name of synergy, tried to unite the top-down approach of broadcasting and billboards with the bottom-up approach of live entertainment and found that such different businesses did not mesh. The specialists in the live entertainment field, such as the members of IPN, know the volatility of audience-driven revenues and compensate as best they can for it. But, within a highly structured corporate environment such as Clear Channel, where steady and high returns on investment are expected, the volatility of audience- or consumer-based revenues were too risky. Therefore, the second reason for Clear Channel's reorganization is the inflexibility of the corporation in its ability to deal with volatile earnings. If the corporation was wholly dedicated to the live entertainment sector, like the Shuberts, the revenue structure would not be an issue driving corporate change (although it can cause bankruptcy as in Livent's case). Since Clear Channel Entertainment was lumped together with the seemingly similar business of broadcasting with a high and relatively steady profit, the volatile performance of the live entertainment division could only be seen as a corporate liability that could lead to declines in stock prices and questions of managerial competence from Clear Channel Communications' board of directors. Perhaps separated from the larger corporate structure, Live Nation will be able to prosper. However, since the new corporation is also publicly listed (on the New York Stock Exchange), many of the issues that challenged Clear Channel Communications will also continue to challenge Live Nation. If Live Nation does decline as a road producer, will there still be an incentive for IPN to remain united without its original reason for existence?

Live Nation is still very much a work in progress, but already the company, in the form of Clear Channel Entertainment, has had an impact on the commercial theater in North America. The company put together a large, viable circuit of theaters that allowed economical touring across the continent. Through this development, Clear Channel Entertainment demonstrated that there is a significant audience for Broadway touring productions. In fact, the audience was so expansive that, with the emergence of IPN, there seemed to be room for two large organizations on the road. The competition between Clear Channel Entertainment and IPN led to an upswing in activity on the road in 2005, just as there was an upswing in the mid-1990s when SFX, Livent, and PACE were competing, and in the first decade of the twentieth century, when the Shuberts and Syndicate were competing.[48] To assist in the creation of productions to fill its theaters, Clear Channel Entertainment became a stable source of funding for Broadway productions in New York, a role that IPN also took on. In supplying productions to many nonprofit theaters, revenues from Clear Channel Entertainment productions supported artistic activities beyond just commercial touring shows.[49] While the corporation itself supplied mostly a homogenized type of Broadway production, its financial clout allowed it to offer more experimental productions as well, such as *The Exonerated*. Clear Channel Entertainment's legacy, or at least that of its theater division, must be ultimately viewed in a positive light. While the company did not cause an aesthetic revolution in Broadway productions by any means, it did provide a great deal of employment for theater professionals. Where this legacy becomes a bit clouded is in the corporation's attitude toward unionized labor and performers, but this is an issue that plagues the relationship between all producers of touring theater and their employees, especially since the industry depends almost wholly on singularly talented individuals to make its product marketable. The labor- or talent-centric aspect of the theater business sets it apart from radio or outdoor displays, but this can lead to difficulties when all of these different businesses are lumped into one unit, as Clear Channel Communications clearly discovered and took steps to remedy.

Notes

1. Background information on Clear Channel can be found at Hoovers Company Records 2005, "Clear Channel Communications, Inc.," http://cobrands.hoovers.com/global/cobrands/proquest/factsheet.xhtml?ID=11824 (accessed August 9, 2005), and Mergent Online 2005, "Clear Channel Communications, Inc.," http://www.mergentonline.com/compdetail.asp?company_mer=38030&company=-1 (accessed August 9, 2005).

2. Hoovers; Mergent Online; Clear Channel's corporate Web site, at http://www.clearchannel.com, also gives details on its corporate history and current revenues.

3. Adam Sandler, "SFX Move Rocks Music Biz," *Variety.com*, March 9, 1998 http://www.variety.com/story.asp?1 =story&a=VR1117468544&c=16 (accessed July 7, 2005).

4. Robert Hofler, "Clear Changes Channel," *Variety.com*, May 22, 2005, http://www.variety.com/story.asp?1 =story&a=VR1117923261&c=1747 (accessed July 6, 2005).

5. Adam Sandler, "SFX Move."

6. Adam Sandler, "SFX Picks Up Promoter PACE," *Variety.com*, December 28, 1997, http://www.variety.com/story.asp?1 =story&a=VR1118173 78&c=18, (accessed July 7, 2005).

7. Rick Lyman, "2 Powerhouses of the Theater Meld Broadway and the Road," *New York Times*, June 9, 1997.

8. Eben Shapiro, "Out-of-Towners: From the Hinterlands, An Upstart Producer Barrels Up Broadway—Pace, Master of Road Shows, Aims for Original Hits; Old Guard Has Doubts—A Far Cry From Tractor Pulls," *Wall Street Journal*, April 28, 1998. http://proquest.umi.com.

9. Ibid.

10. Rick Lyman, "2 Powerhouses."

11. Markland Taylor, "Bound for Boston," *Variety.com*, August 11, 1998, http://www.variety.com/story.asp?1 =story&a=VR1117479371&c=15 (accessed July 7, 2005).

12. Richard Morgan, "SFX Lands in Chicago," *Variety.com*, January 12, 1999 http://www.variety.com/story.asp?1 =story&a=VR1117490089&c=16 (accessed July 7, 2005).

13. "Company Briefs," *New York Times*, August 28, 1999.

14. See Anthony Vickery, "Accounting Fraud at Live Entertainment Canada, Incorporated, 1993–98," *International Journal of Arts Management* 7, no. 2 (2005): 15–26.

15. Don Waller, "Loud and Clear," *Variety.com*, March 1, 2000 http://www.variety.com/story.asp?1 =story&a=VR1117778928&c=18 (accessed July 6, 2005).

16. Hoovers Company Records 2005, "Time Warner Cable, Inc.," http://cobrands.hoovers.com/global/cobrands/proquest/factsheet.xhtml?COID=102518 (accessed August 9, 2005).

17. Hoovers Company Records 2005, "Viacom, Inc.," http://cobrands.hoovers.com/global/cobrands/proquest/factsheet.xhtml?COID=12435 (accessed August 9, 2005).

18. Christine Y. Chen, "The Bad Boys of Radio," *Fortune*, March 3, 2003, 118–22, http://www.epnet.com (accessed August 10, 2005).

19. Brett Pulley, "Gee, Thanks Dad," *Forbes*, October 18, 2004, http://www.epnet.com (accessed August 10, 2005).

20. Justin Oppelaar, "SFX Restructures, Gets New Moniker," *Variety.com*, July 8, 2001, http://www.variety.com/story.asp?1 =story&a=VR1117802401&c =14 (accessed July 6, 2005).

21. Charles Isherwood, "Clear Channel Weds Legit Series in Promo," *Variety.com*, August 7, 2001, http://www.variety.com/story.asp?1 =story&a=VR1117850889&c=15 (accessed July 7, 2005).

22. Broadway Across America, "Broadway Across America," http://www.broadwayacrossamerica.com/DesktopDefault.aspx?tabindex=0&tabid=18 (accessed August 30, 2005).

23. For current touring listings, see "Broadway Across America" and http://www.cc.com.

24. See The Culture Project@45 Bleecker, "The Exonerated," http://www.45bleecker.com/exonerated.html (accessed November 9, 2005).

25. Marilyn Stasio, "Addicted," *Variety.com*, December 22, 2003, http://www.variety.com/story.asp?1 =story&r=VE1117922745&c=33 (accessed October 26, 2005).

26. League of American Theatres and Producers, "Clear Channel Entertainment: Producer, Other, Theatre Owner," http://www.ibdb.com/person.asp?ID=85474 (accessed August 30, 2005).

27. Jill Kipnis, "CCE Antes Up for Las Vegas," *Billboard*, May 14, 2005, http://www.epnet.com (accessed August 10, 2005).

28. Donald W. Mitchell and Carol Bruckner Coles, "Business Model Innovation Breakthrough Moves," *Journal of Business Strategy* 25, no. 1 (2004): 16–19.

29. Damone Richardson and Maria Figueroa, "Consolidation and Labor in Arts and Entertainment: A Peek at Clear Channel," *WorkingUSA: The Journal of Labor and Society* 8 (2004): 87.

30. Marilyn Stasio, "Solution to Equity Equation: Go 'Lite,'" *Variety.com*, September 9, 2002, http://www.variety.com/story.asp?1 =story&a=VR1117872536&c=1347 (accessed July 7, 2005).

31. "Broadway Union Files Unfair Labor Suit," *NewYorkBusiness.com*, February 5, 2004, http://www.newyorkbusiness.com/news.cms?newsId=7331&bt=actors\\\\\\\\\\\\\\\\\\\\\\'+equity (accessed August 10, 2005).

32. Robert Hofler, "Road War Leads to Equity vs. B'way 3," *Variety.com*, February 5, 2004, http://www.variety.com/story.asp?1 =story&a=VR1117899611&c=1066 (accessed July 7, 2005).

33. Robert Hofler, "Actors' Equity Ratifies Prod'n Pact," *Variety.com*, August 31, 2004, http://www.variety.com/story.asp?1 =story&a=VR1117909857&c=15 (accessed July 7, 2005). For a copy of the agreement, see http://www.actorsequity.org/Library/rulebooks/Production_Rulebook_League_04–08.pdf.

34. Stasio, "Go Lite."

35. John Fleming, "Ruth Eckerd Hall: 'Thoroughly' Pleased," *St. Petersburg Times*, April 27, 2003, http://pqasb.pqarchiver.com/sptimes/access/329795021.html?dids=329795021&FMT=FT&FMTS=ABS:FT&date=Apr+27%2C+2003&author=JOHN+FLEMING&pub=St.+Petersburg+Times&edition=&startpage=10.F&desc=%27Thoroughly%27+pleased+series%3A+SUNDAy+ARTS (accessed August 31, 2005).

36. Robert Hofler, "B'way Flapper Vs. Tough Times," *Variety.com*, April 28, 2002, http://www.variety.com/story.asp?1 =story&a=VR1117866103&c=15 (accessed July 7, 2005).

37. Mike Boehm, "Clear Channel's Cultural Plunge Brings Mixed Reviews," *Los Angeles Times*, August 24, 2004.

38. Hofler, "Clear Changes."

39. Katy Bachman, "Clear Channel Breaking Up," *Mediaweek*, May 2, 2005, http://proquest.umi.com (accessed August 15, 2005).

40. Ibid.

41. Tom Lowry, "Antenna Adjustment," *Billboard*, June 20, 2005, http://www.epnet.com (accessed August 10, 2005).

42. See "Old and New Media Part Ways," *The Economist*, June 18, 2005, http://www.epnet.com (accessed August 31, 2005).

43. Jam Productions has already announced an interest. Hofler, "Clear Changes."

44. Hoovers Company Records 2005, "Live Nation," http://cobrands.hoovers.com/global/cobrands/proquest/factsheet.xhtml?COID=55576 (accessed December 29, 2005).

45. Steven Hyden, "The Fox Cities' Newest Entertainment Center: PAC Sees Promise in Presenting Partner," *Appleton (WI) Post-Crescent*, November 17, 2002,

http://www.wisinfo.com/postcrescent/pac/archive/pac_7149717.shtml (accessed July 9, 2005).

46. In particular, see Justin Oppelaar and Michael Schneider, "Clear Cues Radio Daze," *Variety.com*, August 28, 2001, http://www.variety.com/story.asp?1 =story&a=VR1117851977&c=18 (accessed July 10, 2005), which contains allegations about exclusionary tactics used by Clear Channel's radio and concert divisions against competitors, especially from Denver-based concert promoter Nobody In Particular Productions (NIPP). NIPP took Clear Channel to court but made an undisclosed settlement at a later date (Pulley, "Gee, Thanks Dad."). For other cases, see Mary Sutter, "Clear Channel Cleared in Suit," *Variety.com*, February 5, 2003, http://www.variety.com/story.asp?1 =story&a=VR1117880065 &c=22 (accessed July 10, 2005), and Susan Crabtree, "Static for Clear Channel," *Variety.com*, April 11, 2004, http://www.variety.com/story.asp?1 =story&a=VR 1117903139&c=23 (July 12, 2005).

47. Mike Boehm, "Clear Channel's Cultural Plunge Brings Mixed Reviews," *Los Angeles Times*, August 24, 2004.

48. See Alfred L. Bernheim, *The Business of the Theatre: An Economic History of the American Theatre, 1750–1932* (New York: Benjamin Blom, 1964), 75.

49. Jerry Mandel, president of the Orange County Performing Arts Center notes that the Clear Channel productions net the center over $1 million per year and support its acclaimed ballet series. See Mike Boehm, "Clear Channel's Cultural Plunge."

RESOURCES

CONTRIBUTORS

INDEX

RESOURCES

Organizations

American Arts Alliance advocates for America's professional nonprofit arts organizations, artists, and their publics before the U.S. Congress and key policy makers. Founded in 1977. www.americanartsalliance.org

Americans for the Arts represents and serves local communities and creates opportunities for every American to participate in and appreciate all forms of the arts. Founded in 1996. www.americansforthearts.org

Association of Arts Administration Educators (AAAE) is an international organization representing college and university graduate and undergraduate programs in arts administration. Founded in 1975. www.artsadministration.org.

Business Committee for the Arts (BCA) provides businesses of all sizes with the services and resources necessary to develop and advance partnerships with the arts that benefit business, the arts, and the community. Founded in 1967. www.bcainc.org

Center on Philanthropy at Indiana University is an academic unit of the university that fosters education, research, and public service in philanthropy. The center's priority is to understand the role of philanthropy in society and to contribute to the knowledge base of the field. Founded in 1987. www.philanthropy.iupui.edu

Chronicle of Philanthropy is a newspaper for the nonprofit world, providing news and information for executives of tax-exempt organizations. Affiliated with *The Chronicle of Higher Education*, it publishes twenty-four electronic issues each year. Founded in 1988. www.philanthropy.com

Committee to Encourage Corporate Philanthropy leads the business community in raising the level and quality of corporate philanthropy. Members are chief executive officers and chairs who represent companies that account for more than 50 percent of corporate giving in the United States.

The committee publishes three newsletters each year. Founded in 1999. www.corporatephilanthropy.org

The Foundation Center supports and improves philanthropy by promoting public understanding. Founded in 1956. www.foundationcenter.org

Grantmakers in the Arts strengthens the field of private-sector arts and culture grant making. Founded in 1985. www.giarts.org

National Endowment for the Arts (NEA) supports excellence in the arts. As the largest national funder of the arts, it provides fact sheets, symposiums, annual reports, a history of the NEA, as well as the bimonthly electronic newsletter *NEARTS*. Founded in 1965. www.nea.gov

Philanthropy Roundtable puts donors in touch with peers who share similar concerns and interests. Members gain access to the full range of ideas and approaches to giving and information on what works and what does not. It includes donors who are involved in philanthropy on a professional basis, as well as individual donors for whom giving is a serious avocation. For nonmembers, the roundtable publishes an electronic journal, *Philanthropy*. Founded in the 1970s. www.philanthropyroundtable.org

Theatre Communications Group (TCG) strengthens, nurtures, and promotes the professional not-for-profit American theater with 446 theatres in 47 states. The organization publishes the monthly magazine *American Theatre* and provides an annual analysis of theater economics. Founded in 1961. www.tcg.org

Theatre Management Focus Group of the Association for Theatre in Higher Education (ATHE) serves as an advocate for representation, recognition, professional development, research, and communication for members of ATHE involved in theater management. The group publishes an electronic journal, *Theatre Management Journal*, and a biannual newsletter. E-mail: tm@athe.org, www.athe.org/getinvolved/focusgroups/tm.

Further Reading

Alexander, Jane, *Command Performance: An Actress in the Theater of Politics* (New York: Public Affairs, 2000).

Baumol, William J. and William G. Bowen, *Performing Arts, The Economic Dilemma: A Study of Problems Common to Theater, Opera, Music, and Dance* (New York: Twentieth Century Fund, 1966).

Binkiewicz, Donna M., *Federalizing the Muse: United States Arts Policy and the National Endowment for the Arts, 1965–1980* (University of North Carolina Press, 2004).

Burlingame, Dwight F., ed., *Philanthropy in America—A Comprehensive Historical Encyclopedia*, 3 vols. (Santa Barbara, CA: ABC-CLIO, ca. 2004).

Chong, Derek, *Arts Management* (New York: Routledge, 2002).

Flanagan, Hallie, *Arena: The Story of the Federal Theatre* (New York: Duell, Sloan, and Pearce, 1940).

Frohnmayer, John, *Leaving Town Alive: Confessions of an Arts Warrior* (Boston: Houghton Mifflin, 1993).

Lowry, W. M., ed., *The Arts and Public Policy in the United States* (Englewood Cliffs, NJ: Prentice Hall, 1984).

Magat, Richard, *The Ford Foundation at Work, Philanthropic Choices, Methods, and Styles* (New York: Plenum Press, ca. 1979).

Mathews, J., *The Federal Theatre: 1935–1939* (Princeton, NJ: Princeton University Press, 1967).

O'Connor, John and Lorraine Brown, eds., *Free, Adult, Uncensored: The Living History of the Federal Theatre Project* (Washington, D.C.: New Republic Books, 1978).

Patner, Andrew, ed. *Alternative Futures: Challenging Designs for Arts Philanthropy* (Washington, D.C.: Grantmakers in the Arts, 1994).

Payton, Robert L., *Philanthropy: Voluntary Action for the Public Good* (New York : American Council on Education/Macmillan; London: Collier Macmillan, 1988).

Rockefeller Brothers Fund, *The Performing Arts: Problems and Prospects; Rockefeller Panel Report on the Future of Theatre, Dance, Music in America* (New York: McGraw-Hill, 1965).

Sealander, Judith, *Private Wealth and Public Life: Foundation Philanthropy and the Reshaping of American Social Policy from the Progressive Era to the New Deal* (Baltimore: Johns Hopkins University Press, 1997).

Taylor, Fannie, *The Arts at a New Frontier: The National Endowment for the Arts* (New York: Plenum Press, 1984).

Vail, Peter B., *Managing as a Performing Art: New Ideas for a World of Chaotic Change* (San Francisco: Jossey-Bass, 1989).

Zeigler, Joseph Wesley, *Arts in Crisis: The National Endowment for the Arts Versus America* (Chicago: A Cappella Books, 1994).

CONTRIBUTORS

Robert A. Schanke is professor emeritus of theater at Central College, Iowa. His articles on theater history appear in *Theatre Survey*, *Theatre Topics*, *Southern Theatre*, and *Central States Speech Journal.* He has contributed to numerous reference books and anthologies, including *Women in American Theatre*, *Cambridge Guide to American Theatre*, and *Shakespeare Around the Globe.* He is author of *Ibsen in America: A Century of Change* (1988) and *Eva Le Gallienne: A Bio-Bibliography* (1989). His *Shattered Applause: The Lives of Eva Le Gallienne* (1992) was a finalist for both the Lambda Literary Award and the Barnard Hewitt Award for theater research. He coedited, with Kim Marra, *Passing Performances: Queer Readings of Leading Players in American Theater History* (1998) and *Staging Desire: Queer Readings of American Theater History* (2002). Their final collaboration, with Billy J. Harbin, *The Gay and Lesbian Theatrical Legacy*, was published in 2005. Schanke's *"That Furious Lesbian": The Story of Mercedes de Acosta* and his *Women in Turmoil: Six Plays by Mercedes de Acosta* (2003) were finalists for Lambda Literary Awards. *Foreword* magazine selected "*That Furious Lesbian*" as the 2004 Book of the Year in the category of gay/lesbian nonfiction. Schanke edited the international journal *Theatre History Studies* from 1993 until 2005. He is a fellow of the Mid-America Theatre Conference and was honored with alumni achievement awards by both Midland College and the University of Nebraska. In 2003, he was elected into the National Theatre Conference, and in 2004, he was elected to the College of Fellows of the American Theatre. He received the Sustained Excellence in Editing Award from the Association for Theatre in Higher Education in 2004. He edits a series titled Theater in the Americas for Southern Illinois University Press.

Stephen D. Berwind is a visiting assistant professor at the University of South Carolina. He has published in *Theatre Survey* and in *The Gay and Lesbian Theatrical Legacy: A Biographical Dictionary of Major Figures in American Stage*

History in the Pre-Stonewall Era (2005). In addition to his active participation in several academic theater associations, he has considerable experience in arts administration, serving as director of communications for the Pittsburgh Center for the Arts, associate literary manager for Pittsburgh Public Theatre, public relations associate for the Pittsburgh Symphony Society, and producing director for theater at St. Clement's in New York City.

Melanie Blood is associate professor of theater, associate director of the School of the Arts, and coordinator of women's studies at SUNY Geneseo. She has published in the *Journal of American Drama and Theatre*, *Theatre History Studies*, and *Modern Drama*. She recently served as secretary for the Association for Theatre in Higher Education. She is revising her book-length study of the Neighborhood Playhouse in the 1910s and 1920s.

Theresa M. Collins completed her Ph.D. at New York University. She studies global history and modernity. An associate research professor at Rutgers, the State University of New Jersey, she is an editor of the Thomas A. Edison Papers and the author of *Otto Kahn: Art, Money and Modern Time* (2002). Her research in theater history is currently focused on the early electric age. She is more generally developing *Designs for Global Living*, a cosmopolitan history since 1870.

David A. Crespy is an associate professor in the University of Missouri–Columbia's Department of Theatre Writing for Performance program. He is the founder and artistic director of its Missouri Playwrights Workshop and codirector of its Writing for Performance Program. His book about New York's Off-Off-Broadway theater in the 1960s, *The Off-Off Broadway Explosion*, was published in September 2003, with a foreword by Edward Albee. His plays and essays on playwriting are anthologized in *Playwriting Master Class*, edited by Michael Wright; Gary Garrison's *Perfect Ten*; and *Monologues by Men for Men*. His articles have also appeared in *New England Theatre Journal*, *Ollantay Theatre Journal*, *Theatre History Studies*, and *Slavic and East European Performance*, for which he served as an associate editor. He has served as the chair of the ATHE Playwriting Program Focus Group, cochair of the Playwriting Symposium of the Mid America Theatre Conference, and as region V chair of the National Playwriting Program of the Kennedy Center American College Theatre Festival.

Dan Friedman has been active in political and experimental theater since 1969. He is the dramaturg for the Castillo Theatre, which he helped found in 1983. He is also artistic director of Castillo's youth theater, Youth Onstage! He has written or cowritten fourteen plays. In recent years, Friedman has directed at La MaMa E.T.C., the Nuyorican Poets Cafe, and a number of New York City–area colleges, as well as at Castillo. Friedman is also a theater historian with a Ph.D. from the University of Wisconsin. His writings on Castillo and other political theater have appeared in numerous journals, most recently *Modern Drama*, *The Drama Review*, and *Back Stage*. He is the coeditor, with Bruce McConachie, of *Theatre for Working Class Audiences in the United States, 1830–1980*, and editor of *Still on the Corner and Other Postmodern Political Plays by Fred Newman*. He is the editor of *Müller in America*, a journal for the discussion of the work of the experimental political playwright Heiner Müller.

Alexis Greene is an author, theater critic, and teacher. Her books on theater include *Street of Dreams: The Theatres of 42nd Street,* with Mary C. Henderson; *Women Writing Plays: Three Decades of the Susan Smith Blackburn Prize*; the biography *Lucille Lortel: The Queen of Off Broadway*; *Women Who Write Plays*, a collection of interviews with twenty-three American dramatists; and *The Lion King: Pride Rock on Broadway*, written with Julie Taymor. She was chief critic for *TheatreWeek* magazine and *InTheater* magazine and has contributed articles to the *New York Times*, the *Village Voice*, and Yale's *Theater*, among other publications. Greene is cofounder of Literary Managers and Dramaturgs of the Americas, an international service organization, and she has taught theater at New York University, Vassar College, and Hunter College. She holds a Ph.D. in theater from the Graduate Center of the City University of New York.

Jeffrey Eric Jenkins is a member of the drama faculty at New York University, where he teaches history, theory, and criticism. Jenkins earlier taught graduate dramaturgy at SUNY Stony Brook, undergraduate directing at the University of Washington, and acting at Carnegie Mellon University. He has directed productions in theaters across the United States and has worked on the management team of Peter Brook's acclaimed productions of *The Mahabharata* and *The Cherry Orchard*. A former chair of the American Theatre Critics Association, Jenkins has published articles in major newspapers, reference books, and scholarly journals. Recent books include *Under the Copper Beech: Conversations with American Theater Critics* (2004) and his fifth volume as editor of *The Best Plays Theater Yearbook* series. Jenkins is a member of the board of directors of the American Theatre Wing and of the Theater Hall of Fame's executive committee.

Bruce Kirle heads the Music Theatre Division of the B.A. Honors Acting Course at London's Central School of Speech and Drama. He earned his Ph.D. from the City University of New York. Kirle's dissertation, "Cultural Collaborations," was awarded the Monette-Horwitz CLAGS Prize for outstanding dissertation in the humanities (2001–2). His publications include his book, *Unfinished Show Business: Broadway Musicals as Works-in-Process* (2005), as well as essays in *Theatre Journal* and *Western European Stages*. Kirle also serves as chair of the Theatre History Focus Group for the Association of Theatre in Higher Education. His work as a professional musical director and stage director includes work on Broadway, Off Broadway, and in national and regional venues, including Spoleto, U.S.A. At La MaMa, he composed the score for several musicals, including *Caution: A Love Story* (1969; book and lyrics by Tom Eyen), which was the first production to open La MaMa's current home on East Fourth Street in New York City.

Sheila McNerney Anderson is an independent scholar and production dramaturg. She has published articles in *Theatre Studies* and *Canadian Theatre Review.* Her regional theater credits include dramaturgy for American Contemporary Theatre and a season as assistant casting director for San Jose Repertory Theatre. She holds an M.A. in theater history from the University of Victoria, and a Ph.D. in drama from the University of Washington, where she was a recipient of the Michael Quinn Writing Award. Most recently, McNerney Anderson served as a visiting dramaturg for a production of Tom Stoppard's *Arcadia* at the University of Illinois, her undergraduate alma mater.

John R. Poole is an associate professor at Illinois State University and serves as associate director and codirector of the M.A./M.S. degree programs. His research interests include gay performance identity in popular culture, early-twentieth-century protest drama of the Depression era, and Southern regional/minority dramas. Currently, he serves as president of the Mid-America Theatre Conference. His work appears in *Theatre History Studies* and in *Theatre Symposium.* Several of his book reviews on nineteenth-century theatrical practice and the Negro Federal Theatre may be found in *Theatre Survey, Theatre History Studies,* and *Theatre Journal.*

Kathy L. Privatt received her Ph.D. from the University of Nebraska–Lincoln in 1999, specializing in twentieth-century American theater. Most recently, her essay "The New Theater of Chicago: Democracy 1; Aristocracy 0"was published in *Theatre History Studies,* vol. 24. Currently an associate professor of theater arts at Lawrence University in Wisconsin, she frequently presents papers at conventions of Association for Theatre in Higher Education and in the history and pedagogy symposiums of the Mid-America Theatre Conference. She is working on a book, tentatively titled "Corporate Broadway: The Mouse and the Theatre of Reassurance."

Jennifer Schlueter is a doctoral candidate in the history, literature, and criticism of the theater at Ohio State University. Her areas of study include American popular performance, modernism, contemporary devising practice, and historiography. Before returning to graduate study, she worked as a professional fund-raiser, and coedited, with E. Jane Rutter, the Corporate Funders reference series. She completed her master's thesis in 2003 on Charles Mee's body of work and has an essay on Mee's historiographical concerns published in the fall 2005 *Journal of American Drama and Theatre.*

Jeffrey Ullom received his Ph.D. from the University of Illinois. He currently teaches theater history and playwriting at Vanderbilt University and serves at the director of honors thesis study for the department. He has published articles in *Theatre History Studies, Theatre Topics,* and *Theatre Journal,* and he is currently completing a book on the history of the Humana Festival of New American Plays. Before entering academia, he served as a dramaturg for Actors Theatre of Louisville, where he worked with such playwrights and directors as Tony Kushner, David Henry Hwang, John Patrick Shanley, Anne Bogart, Craig Lucas, Doug Hughes, and Naomi Wallace. He also serves as theater history consultant for the Guthrie Theatre and sits on the advisory boards of several theaters around the country.

Anthony J. Vickery is an assistant professor of theater history at the University of Victoria in Victoria, British Columbia. His most recent publication examined accounting fraud at theatrical producer Livent and appeared in the *International Journal of Arts Management* (Winter 2005). His article on the Shubert Theatrical Corporation's activities in Canada from 1910 to 1918 is due to appear in *Theatre Research in Canada* in the near future. Currently, he is adapting and expanding his Ph.D. dissertation on touring theater in North America, circa 1896–1919, into a book covering corporate involvement in commercial touring theater in the United States and Canada from 1880 to 2000. His research interests include arts management, arts finance and funding, and theater in North America during the nineteenth and twentieth centuries.

Barry B. Witham is professor of theater and former head of the School of Drama at the University of Washington. He is author of *The Federal Theatre Project: A Case Study* (2003), *Uncle Sam Presents* (1982; with Tony Buttitta), and editor of *Theatre in the Colonies and United States* (1996). He has been active in scholarly and professional organizations and has delivered papers at meetings of the International Federation of Theatre Research in Stockholm, Dublin, Moscow, and Tel Aviv. In addition to his academic work, Barry was dramaturg for the Seattle Repertory Theatre from 1983 to 1987, where he worked with a variety of American playwrights including Herb Gardner, Richard Nelson, and Albert Innaurato. He has won outstanding teacher awards at two universities and is a member of the National Theatre Conference and the College of Fellows of the American Theatre. In August 2002, he was presented with the Betty Jean Jones Award for outstanding teaching by the American Theatre and Drama Society.

INDEX

THEATER IN THE AMERICAS

The goal of the series is to publish a wide range of scholarship on theater and performance, defining theater in its broadest terms and including subjects that encompass all of the Americas.

The series focuses on the performance and production of theater and theater artists and practitioners but welcomes studies of dramatic literature as well. Meant to be inclusive, the series invites studies of traditional, experimental, and ethnic forms of theater; celebrations, festivals, and rituals that perform culture; and acts of civil disobedience that are performative in nature. We publish studies of theater and performance activities of all cultural groups within the Americas, including biographies of individuals, histories of theater companies, studies of cultural traditions, and collections of plays.